# Economic Modelling and Computer Programming

# Economic Modelling and Computer Programming

Philip Ripley

*Senior Lecturer in Economics*
*Sunderland Polytechnic*

Hamid Seddighi

*Senior Lecturer in Economics*
*Sunderland Polytechnic*

HARVESTER · WHEATSHEAF
NEW YORK LONDON TORONTO SYDNEY TOKYO

First published 1988 by
HARVESTER · WHEATSHEAF
66 Wood Lane End, Hemel Hempstead
Hertfordshire HP2 4RG
A Division of
Simon & Schuster International Group



Printed and bound in Great Britain by
Billing & Sons Ltd, Worcester

---

British Library Cataloguing in Publication Data

---

Ripley, Philip
Economic modelling and computer programming.
1. Econometrics
I. Title II. Seddighi, Hamid
330'.0724 HB141

ISBN 0-7450-0423-7
ISBN 0-7450-0426-1 Pbk

1 2 3 4 5 92 91 90 89 88

To our parents

# Contents

# Preface

This book is written primarily for first and second year students of economics and business studies. It is designed to support and extend standard texts in theory and quantitative methods. Throughout the book there are references to empirical studies with the aim of attaching greater reality to the purely formal statements found in many texts. The computer programs are quite short and most can be typed within five to ten minutes. Much can be learned from short programs as they are relatively easy to read and adapt. The programs might also give students some ideas for project work.

This book will be found useful by non-computer users and computer users alike. However, it should be noted that computer applications are particularly beneficial in the following circumstances:

(1) where solutions to problems must be obtained by iterative methods, for example in the case of complex simultaneous equation systems which are at the heart of macroeconomic systems involving lagged variables;
(2) where optimizing strategies can only be discovered by computer simulation, for example in game theoretic situations involving continuous interaction between individuals or organizations over many time periods;
(3) where interest is focused upon a range rather than particular equilibrium or optimal solutions;
(4) where the mathematics of a problem would inhibit the development of many students' understanding and where

an alternative exposition is possible using computer analysis, for example in illustrating the principle of costs minimization and solutions to stock management problems.

Readers without access to a computer may ignore the programs listed in this book. The programs are discussed separately from the main text. Each chapter ends with a summary of the issues discussed and suggestions for further reading.

We acknowledge the useful discussion we have had with colleagues and the very considerable advice and support from Wheatsheaf Books and their reviewer's. We are grateful to Her Majesty's Stationary Office for permission to reproduce Table 7.2 and Figure 9.1, to the Open University for permission to reproduce Figure 1.1, to Basic Books for permission to reproduce Figure 5.4 and to Heinemann Books for permission to reprint an extract from Ormerod (1982). Finally, thanks to Eileen Temperley and Florence Teesdale for typing the several drafts of the manuscript and to our students for being guinea-pigs for many of the ideas introduced in this book.

The programs in this book are available on disk. Standard 40-track 5¼ inch disks, for use with BBC (Acorn) and the IBM personal computers only, are available.

They can be obtained, price £5, from:

The External Development Unit,
Sunderland Polytechnic,
Douro House,
Douro Terrace,
Sunderland, SR2 7DX.
Telephone (091) 567 6231.

Please state which disk you require. Cheques to be made payable to: 'The Borough of Sunderland'.

The External Development Unit was established in 1982 to encourage research, consultancy and external links between the staff of Sunderland and outside agencies.

# 1 Introduction

Models, in whatever form they take and no matter what the discipline, are used to ease our understanding of complex situations. In economics, models involve attempts to explain what we observe and to predict events which have not yet taken place. Sometimes a model can be expressed in terms of a number of equations. The traditional ways of analysing and solving modelling problems in economics are by means of verbal reasoning, graphical analysis and algebra. This book employs these approaches and a fourth is added: iteration by computer.

Each chapter concerns an area of study within economics. The chapters can be read individually or in sequence. Much can be learned from studying specific problems. However, the overall aim of this book is to communicate general ideas about modelling and the role which computers can play. Several sections conclude with short computer programs written in BASIC. These programs are not necessary for an understanding of the text but allow readers with a microcomputer to arrive at solutions to the mathematics of the problems studied. In this chapter we provide a description of the steps which are generally followed when models are constructed, we briefly discuss the role of econometric techniques and we explain the meaning of the terms 'iteration' and 'simulation'. We conclude with brief notes of guidance for computer users.

## 1.1 STEPS IN MODELLING

The process of modelling can be broken down into several stages. Figure 1.1 is taken from the Open University (1981a) Mathematical Modelling and Methods course. This section owes much to the approach of the Open University team. Whether a problem is within physical or social science, if a mathematical approach is adopted, the process of modelling is similar in form. In this book, we aim to show how models can be constructed to examine familiar and new problems.

Whether a problem is simple or complex, the activities in modelling are more or less the same.

(1) In step one we consider:

- (i) why we are constructing a model, what insights might follow and how the modelling approach might differ from that adopted in the past;
- (ii) what different types of models might be applied. Models come under two main headings, deterministic and stochastic. The former involve exact mathematical relations, the latter take account of uncertainty;

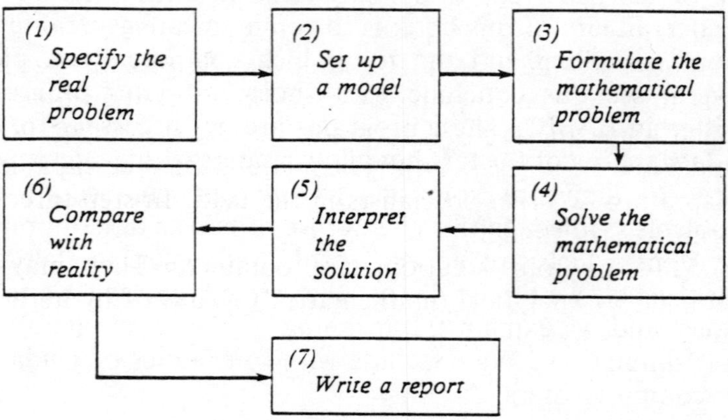


*Figure 1.1: A flow-chart analyzing the process of mathematical modelling (Source: Open University (1981): Mathematics, Science & Technology, Unit 3, Figure 2, p. 5 Open University)*

(iii) how people view a given problem from different perspectives. Two people might observe the same system, for instance a firm in the private sector; one could be a behavioural scientists, the other an economist. Each is likely to have a different model of a firm in his or her mind because their objectives for studying it, their background and the quantities they measure are not the same.

In step one we specify the problem to be studied and select an approach to study it.

(2) In step two we:

(i) draw up a list of the relevant variables;
(ii) establish the assumptions upon which the model is based;
(iii) consider which variables are under the control of decision makers and which are not;
(iv) find the relationships between the variables;
(v) recognize the limitations of the model.

At this stage we must decide what will be ignored in the model. Refinements can always be added once its underlying structure has been properly understood. In step two we set up a model.

(3) In step three we put the elements of the model together. This involves the drawing of graphs, specifying equations which relate the variables to each other and presenting the model in a structured form. The model should be capable of adaptation by other specialists in the field. In step three we formulate the model.

(4) In step four solutions are obtained. They may be obtained by analytical (mathematical) means of by iteration using a computer.

(5) Step five involves presenting the solutions in a form which is capable of being understood by the non-mathematician. It should be possible for qualitative and quantitative conclusions to be reached.

(6) Finally, we compare the solutions with reality. Here we

consider:

(i) empirical tests of the model;
(ii) to what degree the conclusions are of general validity or specific to limited situations.

## 1.2 THE ROLE OF ECONOMETRIC TECHNIQUES

The art of modelling in economics consists of identifying those variables which provide essential information about how a system behaves. The system might be a firm, a market or an economy. Once a model is developed the next stage is to confront it with data to see whether it is compatible with the facts. If the model can account for the actual behaviour of an economic system, we accept that it is valid and use it for prediction and control. The process of estimation and empirical validation of a model is the subject matter of econometrics; more specifically, econometrics is a branch of economics which deals with the measurement of economic relationships and the verification of economic theories. It integrates economic theories in the form of models, mathematics and statistics. In order to provide an introduction to the use of econometric methods, in chapter two we consider, in a step-by-step fashion, the process of economic model building, estimation and empirical validation. Simple demand functions are used to illustrate these steps. In particular, in Chapter 2, we will deal with the least squares method of estimation and show how regression techniques can be used to establish the validity of an economic model. Although the techniques are illustrated with reference to the estimation and verification of simple linear and log linear demand functions, they can easily be generalized to deal with any economic system.

## 1.3 ITERATION

Iteration is a method of obtaining a result by repeatedly

performing the same sequence of steps until a specified condition is satisfied. When a mathematical calculation is carried out the value of a variable may be obtained many different times in the search, perhaps, for an optimal solution. Calculations using a computer are typically performed within a loop such as a 'REPEAT UNTIL' or a 'FOR NEXT' loop; REPEAT operations 1,2, .., *n* UNTIL a certain condition is satisfied or FOR $X = 1$ TO ...., and so on.

Consider Program 1.1. The program concerns the rate at which the stock of goods in a retail store will run down per day if they are not replenished. It is imagined that different goods are on display and the more choice there is available the greater the daily level of demand. We can suppose the shop owner is interested in clearing old stock before new stock is introduced or, perhaps, the shop is to be closed down once the shelves are cleared. Thus, the goods disappear quite quickly to begin with but after a time it becomes difficult to dispose of the remaining items and they may be sold off cheaply or given away. How long might it take for stocks to fall to one half of their original size? Program 1.1 allows this question to be answered. Certain lines from the program are shown below. The program is explained more fully at the end of this chapter. The initial stock equals 200 units (line 30). The calculations are performed over 100 days. In day one, the reduction equals the stock divided by forty; thus REDUC = 5 units in day one. Line 60 concerns the stock at the beginning and the end of each day; it reads 'end of day stock equals beginning of day stock minus the reduction'. Line 70 reports each day's solutions; line 90 causes the program to loop back to line 40 unless 100 sets of calculations have been completed. By observing the solutions from the program over time, it is possible to find when stocks will fall to one half of their original level.

```
30  STOCK = 200
40  FOR T = 1 TO 100
50  REDUC = STOCK/40
60  STOCK = STOCK – REDUC
70  PRINT T, STOCK
90  NEXT T
```

## 1.4 SIMULATION

Simulation is applied in many disciplines wherever there is difficulty predicting what might happen in a particular situation given the large number of forces at work. Simulation models are particularly useful when the probability of different events is taken into account. Models are constructed and subjected to various tests. In physical science the model is often a scaled-down version of a ship or a bridge which is about to be built. But in all disciplines simulation can also involve non-physical experiments when a computer is used to perform controlled laboratory-like experiments. Computers can be used to carry out thousands of calculations involving a mathematical model of the problem studied. The aim may be to duplicate what could happen in the real world given the existence of random influences. Simulation models may be applied when pure analytical procedures for finding solutions to mathematical problems present too many difficulties or are impossible. 'Experience' of what might happen in a real system is obtained by considering different values of the controllable and non-controllable variables. It is possible to program a computer to review the results of a simulation exercise and to narrow down for the decision maker the range of suitable courses of action. Alternatively, a simulation exercise may be performed to discover relationships which otherwise would not be apparent. Recent discovery of the incidence of certain diseases by geographical region is an example.

But what are the limitations of this approach? The result of a simulation is an answer to a specific numerical problem without any information on why that answer was obtained or how the answer would change if different circumstances applied. In terms of understanding the forces at work, obtaining results by simulation is inferior to applying analytical means. A simulation experiment might be misleading if an insufficient number of trials have been completed or if the formulation of the model was inadequate. An inadequate model might be one which fails to identify certain important features of the real system.

To illustrate both the strengths and limitations of simulation, consider the following application which may be familiar to readers interested in war games and strategy. Admiral Nelson's fleet at Trafalgar in the year 1805 consisted of forty ships. He expected to be faced with a combined fleet of forty-six French and Spanish ships. If Nelson had not succeeded in dividing the opposition into two his numerical inferiority might have proved disastrous. It is possible to construct a simulation of the battle and how it might have been fought. See, for instance, the Open University (1984) Probability and Statistics unit on random processes or Program 1.2 of this book. In models which concern a battle, the 'kill rate' of each side is proportional to the number of units in the opposing forces at different times in the conflict and their combat effectiveness (training, weaponry, etc). It can be shown that if each force kills its opponents randomly according to a Poisson process, that is at a certain rate per hour, a force of forty-six ships will tend to defeat a force of forty ships much more often than (46/40) times. In the Open University study, after 10,000 simulations the French and Spanish fleet won almost 9,000 of the contests and usually with more than half of its number intact. This surprising result is difficult to explain without mathematics, nor is it possible to draw too many lessons on how precisely a fighting force should be employed from simulation alone. An engineer by the name of Frederick Lanchester (1916), however, provided a mathematical theory of conflict which can account for the results of simulation exercises and which also includes the combat effectiveness of the forces. In his deterministic model (i.e. the model which excludes randomness) the 'average' course of a battle is explained. By applying the rules of differential calculus (see Open University (1984) pp. 32–34 or Brown (1963)) it can be shown that

> the fighting strength of a force may be broadly defined as ... the square of its size multiplied by the kill rate of its individual units. (Lanchester's Square Law)

Thus, a force of forty-six ships has a fighting strength of $46 \times 46 = 2{,}116$ whilst a force of forty ships has a fighting strength of 40 × 40 = 1,600. Following Lanchester's Law, the combined French and Spanish fleet was 24 per cent stronger. Nelson's actual plan was to divide his fleet into thirty-two and eight ships. The eight ships were used to engage one half of the opposition fleet whilst the larger battle was being won. Remarkably, it can be shown by mathematics that Nelson's precise plan was the best which was available to him given the expected size of the opposition forces.

Our digression on conflict should serve to illustrate two points: (1) that simulation as a method for reaching solutions should only be employed if alternative mathematical means are not possible; (2) when the results of a simulation exercise have been obtained, it is important to try to explain how they were achieved even if formal proofs cannot be established. From the viewpoint of practical men, however, it is usually more important to know the recommended course of action to follow next, given the complex environment, than to fully understand the theoretical basis for decisions. If it was always possible to explain mathematically why one policy or

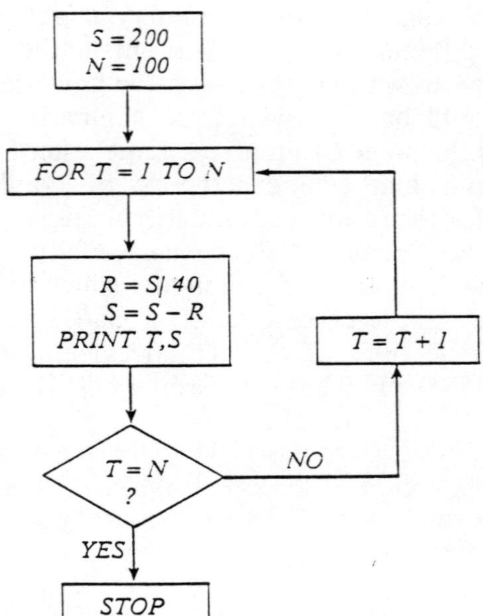


*Figure 1.2: An iterative method for obtaining solutions*

another was preferred, simulation would not have grown at the pace which it has over recent years. Its main value to academics is that it can be used to study the long-term behaviour of a system when there are many influences at work. Simulation models are, of course, widely employed in macroeconomics and they have a long history in operational research. In this book we develop a number of short (but sometimes quite complex) computer models which concern the behaviour of a system over a period of time.

## PROGRAM 1.1

The structure of Program 1.1 is illustrated in the flow diagram, Figure 1.2. The initial stock, *S*, equals 200 units. The number of iterations, *N*, that is the number of time periods over which stock is calculated, equals 100.

```
 10 REM 1.1
 20 PRINT"FIRST COLUMN TIME, SECOND COLUMN STOCK"
 30 STOCK = 200
 40 FOR T = 1 TO 100
 50 REDUC = STOCK/40
 60 STOCK = STOCK - REDUC
 70 PRINT T, INT(STOCK)
 80 A$ = INKEY$(0):IF A$=""THEN 80
 90 NEXT T
100 STOP
110 REM ***** IBM *****
120 REM LINE 80:-
130 A$ = INKEY$: IF A$=""THEN 80
```

Line 30: 'STOCK' and other variables in the program may be abbreviated.

Line 40: Calculations are to be repeated 100 times.

Line 50: The absolute reduction decreases day be day. The rate of reduction is constant over time.

Line 60: 'STOCK' on the left hand side of the expression is the end of day stock; 'STOCK' on the right hand side is the beginning of day stock.

Line 70: The comma between 'PRINT *T*' and 'INT (STOCK)' causes two columns of figures to be displayed. 'INT' denotes integer.

Line 80: This command causes the program to pause until any key is pressed.

Line 90: The program loops back to line 40.

## PROGRAM 1.2

This program involves a simulation model of a contest between two opposing forces: the red and the blue forces. The relative strengths of the forces within different time periods are reported. Chance plays a major part in determining the state of the contest within any given time period. The larger the numerical strength of a force, the greater its fire power. In a given exchange, however, numerical superiority does not guarantee success. Whether the blue or the red force gains in strength, within a given time period, depends on its size and a randomly generated number.

```
 10 REM 1.2
 20 CLS
 30 H=1
 40 R=10:B=10:PR = R/(R+B): PB = B/(R+B)
 50 PRINT"HOUR","RELATIVE STRENGTH"
 60 PRINT
 70 X = RND(1)*(PR/(PR+PB))
 80 PRINT; H;".....";
 90 FOR I = 1 TO R
100 PRINT"R";
110 NEXT I
120 PRINT;"...";
130 FOR I = 1 TO B
140 PRINT"B";
150 NEXT I
160 PRINT
170 IF X>0.25 THEN dR = 1: dB = -1
180 IF X <= 0.25 THEN dB = 1: dR=-1
190 R = R + dR
200 B = B + dB
210 PR = R/(R+B):PB = B/(R+B)
220 H = H +1
230 IF R = 0 THEN 260
240 IF B = 0 THEN 270
250 GOTO 70
260 PRINT'"BLUES WIN IN HOUR ";H:STOP
270 PRINT'"REDS WIN IN HOUR ";H:STOP
280 STOP
290 REM ***** IBM *****
300 REM LINE 70:-
310 RANDOMIZE X:X = RND(1)*(PR/(PR+PB))
```

Line 30: Time period (or hour) one.

Line 40: The initial size of the forces. The probability of a red success partly depends upon its relative fire power, measured by $R/(R + B)$.

Line 70: A random number between zero and 0.999 is generated. This is multiplied by the relative fire power of the red force to determine the probability of red success. Thus, $X$ determines whether the red or the blue force will gain in strength within a given time period. The random number has an average value of 0.5. Initially, the relative strength of the red force equals 0.5. The value of $X$ in time period one might be 0.25. If, in the first exchange, $X$ exceeds 0.25 the random number must have exceeded 0.5. This would be to red's advantage (see line 170).

Lines 90 to 110: The actual strength of the red force is displayed; values of $R$ from 1 to $R$ are reported. If the red force grows in strength over time the number of red units increases.

Lines 120 to 150: The blue force is printed alongside the red.

Line 170: If $X >= 0.25$ the red force increases by one unit, the blue force decreases by one unit.

Lines 190 and 200: The relative sizes of the forces change over time.

Line 210: The probabilities of red and blue successes are revised in line with the outcome of the most recent contest.

Lines 230 and 240: If either force is reduced to zero the engagement ends.

## PROGRAM 1.3

Program 1.2 does not involve a true Poisson Process. A Poisson process concerns the average rate per period of time that an event takes place or the average number of observations of an event. In terms of a naval battle, it would be the number of successes which could be expected per period of time. If each ship has a certain strike rate, the strike rate of the fleet is a simple multiple of the individual rate. Program 1.3 can be used to illustrate the irregularity of an event which might be expected to occur at a given average rate. A 'kill' is achieved if a random number between one and three is generated. The number of successes in each of twenty four hours are reported.

```
 10 REM 1.3
 20 CLS
 30 PRINT
 40 PRINT"HOUR","NUMBER OF SUCCESSES"
 50 FOR HOUR = 1 TO 24
 60 PRINT;´HOUR;"...........";
 70 FOR SHOT = 1 TO 1000
 80 X = INT (1000*RND(1))
 90 IF X = 1 OR X = 2 OR X = 3 THEN PRINT;"K";
100 NEXT SHOT
110 NEXT HOUR
120 STOP
130 REM **** IBM ****
140 REM LINE 80:-
150 RANDOMIZE X:X = INT (1000*RND(1))
```

Lines 70 to 100: These lines are 'nested' within the loop formed by lines 50 and 110. Thus, within hour one, one thousand shots are completed. When the one thousandth shot has been completed, shots within hour two begin.

Line 80: An integer between one and 1000 is generated.

## 1.5 NOTES FOR COMPUTER USERS

The programs in this book are written in BBC and IBM Basic. These dialects of BASIC are very close to Microsoft Basic, the generally accepted standard. In many instances, the programs will run on either machine without any difficulty. Whenever a difference applies a note at the end of the listed program indicates a particular command for IBM users, the BBC command being used in the body of the program. Users of machines which are not entirely compatible with BBC or IBM Basic should have no difficulty adapting the listings as tab and graphics commands, which do vary considerably between machines, have not been used.

When typing in programs, note that 'REM' statements are included simply to guide the reader around the listing; they play no part in the running of a program and should be omitted to save time. Be careful of the difference between the letter 'O' and the number '0' and the letter 'I' and the number '1'. Distinguish between semi colons, colons and commas. When a series of full stops are listed their intention is to recommend that a space, a given number of characters long, should be allowed for between columns of figures. IBM users should omit apostrophes after print statements (apostrophes are used in BBC and most Basics to create a space between lines) and should ensure that integer statements are in brackets; thus, 'PRINT INT T' should be typed as 'PRINT INT (T)'. Users of the BBC computers will find that the display will be improved if the formatting command '@% = &20209' is included as line five at the commencement of each program. IBM users should insert 'RANDOMIZE TIMER' whenever random numbers are to be generated.

# 2 Demand Estimation

Manufacturers of consumer goods are forever seeking to vary their existing product range with the aim of developing new markets. They try to assess consumer preferences by reference to market research data of various kinds, by their own 'double blind tests' (where consumers are asked to compare products, the identity of which is not disclosed), by group discussions in the homes of potential and representative consumers, etc. The British Market Research Bureau is a particularly rich source of information (see Robinson (1986) for an account of its work and for a fascinating discussion of marketing issues). This bureau surveys, in enormous detail, 24,000 people each year. Every aspect of their purchasing behaviour, lifestyle and recreational habits is enquired into. Research takes much of the guesswork out of developing new products, allows data from numerous different sources to be assembled, provides information on where to advertise, which consumers to aim for and so on. But research only enables information to be collected rather than decisions to be made. Using data creatively is the job of the marketing consultant and professional economist.

Once a manufacturer has decided to launch a new product, questions on pricing strategy and on whether to sell nationally or to try test markets first are asked. Of particular interest is knowledge of the consumers' response to changes in the price of the product. For example, a manufacturer would like to know how many more units he could sell if he lowered price by 5 per cent. To determine an appropriate pricing strategy, it is useful to obtain an estimate of the price elasticity of demand for the product. Knowledge of this enables the manufacturer to forecast sales, plan investment and formulate an appropriate marketing strategy. To this end manufacturers can use test market experiments whereby the product is sold at different prices in several different locations around the country. From this analysis, the cross-section data on quantities and prices can be used to estimate demand elasticity.

In order to estimate the price elasticity of demand for a product, an analyst needs three basic ingredients: (1) a model of the relationship between the quantities demanded and the factors influencing market sales; (2) information in the form of cross-section or time series data on the variables in the model; (3) econometric procedures to determine the relationships.

## 2.1 SPECIFICATION OF THE MODEL

The first and perhaps most important component of the analysis is a model relating quantities demanded to the factors determining sales. The development of the model is guided by economic theory which, based on logical reasoning and real world observations, stresses the influence of prices, advertising expenditure and incomes on demand. A general model may be stated as follows:

$$Q_1 = f(P_1, P_2, \ldots, P_n, A, Y) \tag{2.1}$$

where:

$Q_1$ = quantity demanded of a product, say product one, per period
$P_1$ = price of product one per period
$P_2, \ldots, P_n$ = prices of closely related products per period
$A$ = advertising expenditure per period
$Y$ = a measure of consumers' income per period

For the purpose of estimation, the functional form of the general relationship must be specified. In empirical work, the most commonly used functions are linear and log-linear demand functions. A linear demand function relates quantities demanded to prices, advertising expenditure, and income as follows:

$$Q_1 = a_0 + a_1 P_1 + a_2 P_2 + \cdots + a_n P_n + b_1 A + b_2 Y \quad (2.2)$$

where $a_0$, $a_1$, ..., $a_n$ and $b_1$ and $b_2$ are unknown parameters to be estimated on the basis of a set of observations on the dependent variable, $Q_1$, and explanatory variables $P_1$, $P_2$ ..., $A$ and $Y$.

A more widely used functional form is the constant elasticity or log-linear demand function:

$$Q_1 = cP_1^{a_1} P_2^{a_2} \ldots P_n^{a_n} A^{b_1} Y^{b_2} \quad (2.3)$$

where $c$ is a scaling constant. Taking natural logs of both sides yields the log-linear form of the model:

$$\ln Q_1 = a_0 + a_1 \ln P_1 + a_2 \ln P_2 + \cdots + a_n \ln P_n + b_1 \ln A + b_2 \ln Y \quad (2.4)$$

where $a_0 = \ln c$ and $\ln$ = natural log. In this model it can be shown that the parameters $a_1$, $a_2$ ..., $a_n$, $b_1$ and $b_2$ are constant elasticities (see for example Lawler and Seddighi (1987). In other words, the demand elasticities with respect to product price, $a_1$, prices of other products, $a_2$, ..., $a_n$, advertising expenditure, $b_1$, and income, $b_2$, are taken as constant over time. Therefore, the estimated values of the parameters directly reveal the estimated elasticities. This is the main reason for the popularity of this particular demand function in empirical work.

The functions (2.2) and (2.4) indicate the amount demanded given alternative combinations of prices, advertising expenditure and income. The special case of demand functions where $P_2$, $P_3$, ..., $P_n$, $A$ and $Y$ are held constant is discussed widely in the literature; the *ceteris paribus* demand function is known as the demand curve. The demand curves corresponding to the above linear and log-linear demand functions may be written as follows:

$$Q_1 = a_0 + a_1 P_1 \qquad \text{(linear demand curve)} \quad (2.5)$$

$$\ln Q_1 = a_0 + a_1 \ln P_1 \qquad \text{(log-linear demand curve)} \quad (2.6)$$

Demand curves show the effect of a change in price on the

quantity demanded, holding other prices, advertising expenditure and income constant. If other price(s), advertising expenditure, and income change, the result is a shift in the demand curve. Before the problem is discussed further, it is worth considering the orthodox text book approach to demand using simple diagrams. Let us begin with linear demand curves. Consider Figure 2.1. We know that, for all demand curves, the measure of demand elasticity equals the proportionate change in demand/proportionate change in price, that is:

$$E_p = \frac{\text{\% change in quantity demanded}}{\text{\% change in price}}$$

$$= \left(\frac{\Delta Q}{Q}\right) \Big/ \left(\frac{\Delta P}{P}\right) = \left(\frac{\Delta Q}{\Delta P}\right) \left(\frac{P}{Q}\right)$$

where $E_p$ denotes price elasticity of demand. When the change is small conventionally, we use d in place of $\Delta$. That is,

$$E_p = \left(\frac{dQ}{dP}\right) \left(\frac{P}{Q}\right)$$

Now, $\mathrm{d}Q/\mathrm{d}P$ is the gradient or slope of the demand curve indicating the degree that demand falls for each one unit increase in price. In the normal case, demand falls as price increases hence $\mathrm{d}Q/\mathrm{d}P$ has a negative value. Notice that in the linear equation (2.5), $a_1$ is the slope of the line. Therefore, $a_1 = \mathrm{d}Q_1/\mathrm{d}P_1$ and we expect that $a_1$ will take on a negative value. For curve one in Figure 2.1, the gradient of the demand curve equals $-4/4 = -1$. If the price is set equal to two then two units are demanded. Hence demand elasticity at point $C_1$ equals $(-4/4)\ (2/2) = -1$. For curve two the gradient equals $-4/2$. When the price is set at two, the quantity demanded is two. Hence, the demand elasticity equals $(-4/2)\ (\frac{1}{2})$ which again equals $-1$. Of course, for each curve the measure of demand electricity varies along its length; the gradient of each curve remains the same but price/quantity values differ. In the case of linear demand curves, we would estimate elasticity (1) by reference to the gradient of the curve; (2) by reference to a price/quantity combination.

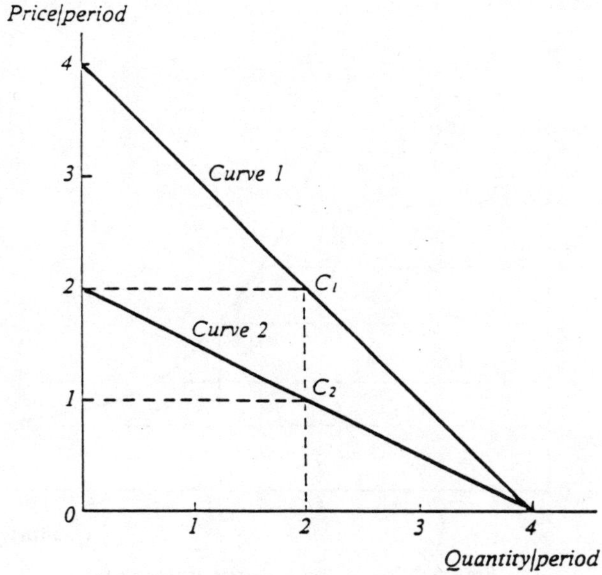


*Figure 2.1: Linear demand curves*

Let us now consider the equation of the log-linear demand curve (2.6) to derive the corresponding price elasticity of demand. In order to find this elasticity we need to evaluate $(\mathrm{d}Q_1/\mathrm{d}P_1)\ (P_1/Q_1)$. To derive $\mathrm{d}Q_1/\mathrm{d}P_1$, it is easier to work with the non-linear specification of the model: $Q_1 = cP_1^{a_1}$. Now, differentiate $Q_1$ with respect to $P_1$ to yield:

$$\frac{\mathrm{d}Q_1}{\mathrm{d}P_1} = \mathrm{ca}_1 P_1^{a_1 - 1}$$

Substitution for $\mathrm{d}Q_1/\mathrm{d}P_1$ from the above into the elasticity expression yields:

$$E_p = (ca_1 P_1^{a_1 - 1})\ (P_1/Q_1)$$

Now, substitute for $Q_1$ to obtain:

$$E_p = (ca_1 P_1^{a_1 - 1}) \left(\frac{P_1}{cP_1^{a_1}}\right)$$

which upon simplification yields $E_p = a_1$. Thus, under the log-linear specification, the price elasticity of demand is $a_1$, the power of the price variable.

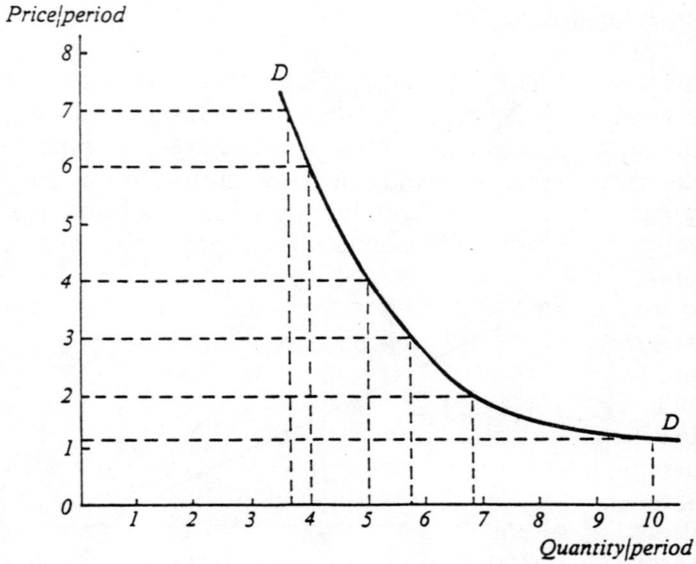


*Figure 2.2: A log-linear demand curve*

Figure 2.2 presents a log-linear demand curve. For the purpose of illustration, the price elasticity is set at – 0.5 and the scaling constant at 10. That is, $Q_1 = cP_1^{a_1}$ where $c = 10$ and $a_1 = -0.5$. We substitute for the parameter values and take the natural logs of both sides to generate the equation of the demand curve as follows:

$$\ln Q_1 = \ln 10 - 0.5 \ln P_1$$

$$\ln Q_1 = 2.3 - 0.5 \ln P_1$$

At any point on *DD* in Figure 2.2, the price elasticity of demand is – 0.5. That is, for a one per cent increase in price, the quantity demanded falls by half a percentage point. One of the attractive properties of the logarithmic demand curve is that the measure of demand elasticity is constant for all values of price. In the following sections we show the price elasticity of demand can be estimated using regression techniques.

## 2.2 NATURE OF THE DATA

Having specified the model, the next step is to obtain data on the variables included in the model. There are basically two types of data available: cross-section data and time series data. Cross-section data provide information on the aggregate purchases of a product by a group of households at a moment in time, for example, in a particular week or a month. The study described in Section 2.1 is an example of the cross section approach to demand analysis. Time series data provide information on quantity sold of a product over time, usually on a quarterly or annual basis. A particular problem associated with time series studies is called the 'identification problem'. Identification problems arise when pairs of observations on quantity demanded of a product and prices are used for estimation. Observations on quantities reflect the amounts bought and sold over time, providing information on the levels of demand as well as supply. Moreover, the observed market prices are the result of the interaction of demand and supply and hence must lie on both the demand and supply curves. Given the nature of the data, the problem is whether it is possible to identify a demand curve from pairs of observations on quantities and prices. More specifically, given the data, how do we know whether a demand or a supply curve is being estimated? Generally, if demand is stable over the period of estimation whilst supply has been subject to shifts, the data identifies the demand curve. The shifts in demand result from changes in consumers' income, taste, advertising expenditure and prices of closely related products. If these determinants of demand have remained fairly constant over the period of investigation, whilst the supply curve has shifted, then the curve is identified. This situation is frequently experienced in the case of agricultural produce whose supply is subject to fluctuation due to climatic changes, with demand remaining constant over time. Figure 2.3 illustrates this case.

The identification problem is a significant issue in empirical analysis. This problem has been discussed widely in the literature particularly with respect to demand estimation (see for example Baumol (1977)).

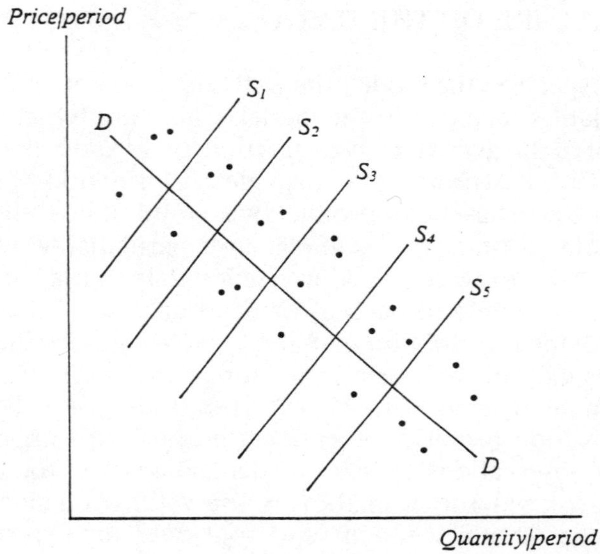


*Figure 2.3: Data identify a demand curve; supply curve is unidentified*

## 2.3 ESTIMATION TECHNIQUES

The final step in the empirical analysis of demand is the use of statistical techniques in the form of econometric methods of estimation. In this section we explain the techniques with reference to a simple linear model of demand. We then illustrate the method by estimating a log linear model using a hypothetical set of observations on quantities and prices.

Let us begin by considering the estimation of the following model of demand:

$$Q = a_0 + a_1 P; \qquad a_0 > 0, \quad a_1 < 0 \tag{2.7}$$

The above specification implies that the relationship between quantity and price is exact, that is all variation in the quantity demanded is caused by changes in price; all the price–quantity pairs of observations fall on a straight line when plotted on a two-dimensional diagram. Such a simple specification is clearly unrealistic. It should be noted that estimation is based on real observations and these seldom suggests a one-to-one relationship between quantities and prices. Even if other variables are constant, it is seldom the case that the quantity demanded, at a given price, remains unchanged in different markets over time. For example, suppose a product is sold in four different markets at a specific price. Most probably, contrary to what equation 2.7 implies, we would observe four different levels of sales: one for each market over a specific period of time. Many factors other than price influence sales. Some of these non-price factors have a systematic impact on the quantity demanded, such as advertising. Others are purely random reflecting the random behaviour of consumers, changes in weather conditions and the like. These factors influence sales generating a range of quantities demanded at each possible price level. In other words, in reality, there is likely to exist a probability distribution of quantities demanded at a given price.

The observed data capture the influence of all variables, including random factors, on the quantity demanded. Their influence, however, is completely ignored in (2.7) leading to discrepancies between actual data and the model. It follows that, for the purpose of estimation, the model must be modified to take account of the imprecise nature of the data. A simple way of formulating a model which reflects real observations is to assume that for each possible price there exists a probability distribution of quantities demanded. Having made this fundamental assumption, all that is needed is a statement of the characteristics of each distribution. It is reasonable to assume that the quantities demanded are distributed normally and independently at each possible price level. This assumption implies that the distribution of quantities demanded, for a given price, can be approximated by a bell-shaped symmetrical normal curve. Moreover, each distribution is generated independently of other distributions. As a first approximation, we may also assume each distribution has the following characteristics: first, the mean of each distribution of quantities demanded is a linear function of price; and second, the variance of quantities demanded for each price is constant and equal to $\sigma^2$ ($\sigma^2$ is a notation conventionally used to represent the variance of random variable). In order to state these assumptions symbolically, let $E\,(Q \mid P)$ represent the expected or the average level of demand for a given price and Var($Q$) represent the variance of $Q$ for each $P$. Thus:

$$E\,(Q_i \mid P_i) = a_0 + a_1 P_i \qquad \text{(for all observations)} \quad (2.8)$$

and

$$\text{Var}(Q_i) = \sigma^2 \qquad \text{(for all observations)} \qquad (2.9)$$

where $P_i$ is the $i$th observation on price. For each level of price there now exists a probability distribution of quantities demanded. Expression (2.8) represents the mean of each distribution and (2.9) specifies the variance. The relationship (2.8) is called the population regression line and the parameters $a_0$ and $a_1$ are the population regression parameters. The parameter $a_0$ is the intercept of the line on the vertical axis; it represents the expected level of sales when price is set equal to zero. The parameter $a_1$ is the slope of the population regression line; it measures the change in the expected sales for a one unit change in a given price. Expression (2.9) implies that there is a uniform scatter of quantities demanded about the population regression line.

Figure 2.4 is a graphical statement of the above assump-

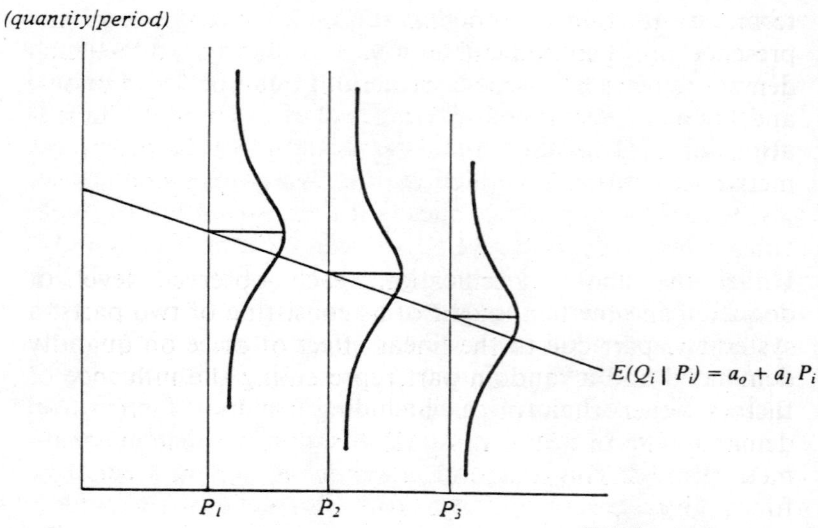


*Figure 2.4: Distributions of quantities demanded at various price levels*

tions. Following convention in regression analysis, the dependent variable, $Q$, is now measured on the vertical axis and the explanatory variable, $P$, on the horizontal axis. According to the first assumptions, there exists a probability distribution of quantities demanded, for each possible price level. In Figure 2.4 a number of these distributions are shown as the bell-shaped normal curves. The second assumption implies that the expected value (mean value) of each distribution lies on the straight line; $E(Q_i \mid P_i) = a_0 + a_1 P_i$. Finally, the assumption of constant variance implies that the dispersion of the quantities demanded about their respective mean values is constant for each given price, as shown in Figure 2.4.

To proceed further, suppose that $Q_i$ and $P_i$ represent any pair of observations. By the nature of the above assumptions we cannot expect $Q_i$ to coincide with the expected level of sales at this price. Let $u_i$ represent the difference between the observed level of sales, $Q_i$, and the expected level of sales, $E(Q_i \mid P_i)$, when price is set at $P_i$. That is:

$$u_i = Q_i - E(Q_i \mid P_i) \qquad (2.10)$$

In regression analysis, $u_i$ is called the random disturbance term. In the context of demand analysis, it arises from the presence of unpredictable chance factors influencing demand, errors in the measurement of quantities and prices, and from an incomplete specification of the model. Substitution for $E(Q_i \mid P_i)$ from (2.8) into (2.10) and the rearrangement of the expression yields the following regression model:

$$Q_i = a_0 + a_1 P_i + u_i \qquad \text{for all } i \qquad (2.11)$$

Under the above specification, each observed level of demand can now be thought of as consisting of two parts: a systematic part due to the linear effect of price on quantity demanded and a random part representing the influence of factors other than price, including random factors, on demand. The relationship (2.11) constitutes a simple econometric model. This relationship is *stochastic* in the sense that, for a given price level, quantity demanded may assume various values depending on the particular value that $u$ happens to assume.

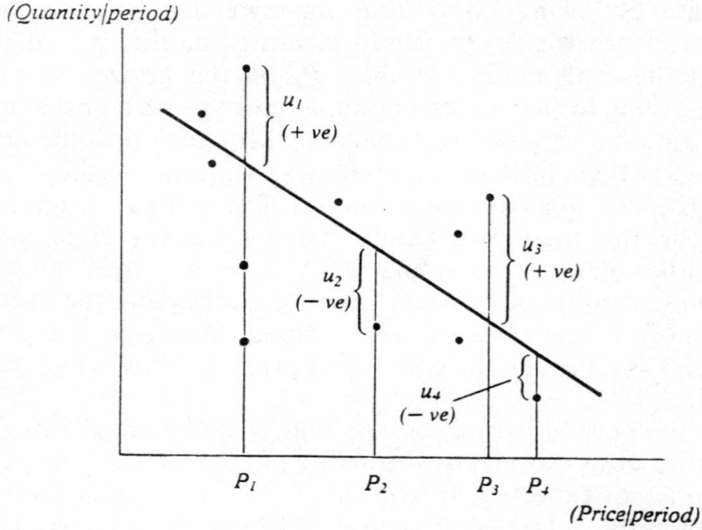


*Figure 2.5: Deviations of observations from the 'true' regression line*

The relationship (2.11) is presented graphically in Figure 2.5. The scatter of observations represent the actual relationship between quantities and prices. The line shows the deterministic or exact part of the relationship and the deviations of the observations from the line represent the stochastic component of the relationship. For example, suppose a product is sold in three different markets at the price $P_1$. As is shown in Figure (2.5) we are likely to observe three different levels of sales: one for each market. The average or the expected level of sales, at the price $P_1$, lies on the straight line which represents the regression line. The deviation of each quantity sold from the line represents the influence of factors other than price on sales in each market. As is shown in Figure 2.5, the deviations from the line might be positive or negative depending on the influence of random factors on sales in each market.

Before proceeding it will be useful to restate the assumptions of the model in terms of the disturbance term $u_i$ instead of variable $Q_i$. Since $u_i = Q_i - E(Q_i \mid P_i)$ and the $Q_i$'s are normally and independently distributed variables, it follows that $u_i$'s are also normally and independently distributed random variables. The implication of this assumption is two-fold: first, the values of $u$, for each level of price, have a bell-shaped symmetrical distribution; and second the disturbance terms corresponding to one observation is independent of the disturbance term corresponding to another observation. The mean of each distribution of disturbance terms is zero for a given price level. That is $E(u_i) = 0$; since $E(u_i) = E(Q_i \mid P_i) - E(Q_i \mid P_i) = 0$. Finally, the variance of each distribution of the disturbance term is constant and equal to $\sigma^2$. It must be emphasized that these assumptions by no means hold in every practical situation. For example, in estimating demand functions, particularly when time series data is used, the assumptions of independence of successive observations is likely to be violated, and needs to be tested against the available data. The consequences arising from the non-fulfilment of this assumption will be briefly discussed in section 2.3.1. below. Having specified the regression model (2.11) and its assumptions we are now in a position to estimate the parameters $a_0$ and $a_1$. In order to compute the numerical values of these parameters we should have all conceivable values of quantities demanded at all conceivable prices. Given that such a data set is impossible to obtain, in practice we get a sample of observed values of quantitites and prices and attempt to obtain satisfactory estimates of the parameters on the basis of sample data. The starting point is, therefore, a scatter diagram showing pairs of observations on quantities and prices in a sample. Figure 2.6 shows one such scatter diagram containing twelve hypothetical pairs of observations. Any line drawn through this scatter of points may be regarded as an estimate of the true regression line. In Figure 2.6, one such line is shown as the line:

$$\hat{Q}_i = \hat{a}_0 + \hat{a}_1 P_i \tag{2.12}$$

where:

$\hat{a}_0$ = estimated value of parameter $a_0$
$\hat{a}_1$ = estimated value of parameter $a_1$
$\hat{Q}_i$ = estimated average level of demand at the $i$th price

As it is shown in Figure 2.6, some data points lie above the

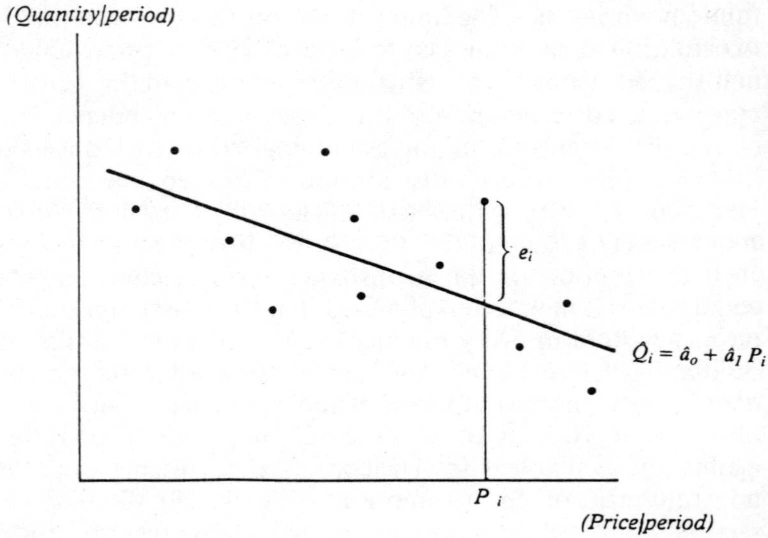


*Figure 2.6: A line fitted to a setter of observations on quantities and prices*

fitted line and some below the line. Let us define the deviation of the $i$th observation from the fitted line by $e_i$, that is:

$$e_i = Q_i - \hat{Q}_i \qquad \text{for all } i \tag{2.13}$$

The residual, $e_i$, shows the difference between the observed quantity demanded and the estimated average level of demand, at the $i$th price. It is intuitively obvious that the smaller the residuals from the line, the better is the fit of the line to the scatter of points. From all possible lines, we may therefore choose the one for which the sum of residuals, ($\sum e_i$) is the smallest possible. The problem with this procedure is that positive residuals tend to cancel out negative residuals resulting in a small value for $\sum e_i$. To avoid this problem, the convention is to square each residual and then fix the line so that the sum of squared residuals is made as small as possible. This method of fitting a line to a scatter of points is called the Ordinary Least Squares (OLS) method (so called since the method involves attempts to minimize the sum of the squares of the deviations of the actual observations from the fitted line). To determine the values of $a_0$ and $a_1$ that satisfy the requirements of the OLS method consider first the sum of the squared residuals, where we have:

$$\sum e_i^2 = \sum_{i=1}^{n} (Q_i - \hat{a}_0 - \hat{a}_1 P_i)^2 \tag{2.14}$$

The method operates by selecting $\hat{a}_0$ and $\hat{a}_1$ such that the above sum is a minimum. The solution to this minimization problem is obtained by differentiating $\sum e_i^2$ partially with respect to $a_0$ and $a_1$ and equating the resulting derivatives to zero (for details of solutions, see for example Gujarati (1978)). This procedure yields the following two equations, where $n$ = the number of observations:

$$\sum_{i=1}^{n} Q_i = n\hat{a}_0 + \hat{a}_1 \sum_{i=1}^{n} P_i$$

$$\sum_{i=1}^{n} Q_i P_i = \hat{a}_0 \sum_{i=1}^{n} P_i + \hat{a}_1 \sum_{i=1}^{n} P_i^2 \tag{2.15}$$

These equations are known as the normal equations for determining $\hat{a}_0$ and $\hat{a}_1$. Solving the equations for $\hat{a}_0$ and $\hat{a}_1$ we have from the first equation.

$$\hat{a}_0 = \bar{Q} - \hat{a}_1 \bar{P} \tag{2.16}$$

Where $\bar{Q}$ is the sample mean of quantities sold and $\bar{P}$ the sample mean of prices. From the second, we have:

$$\hat{a}_1 = \frac{\sum Q_i P_i - n\bar{Q}\bar{P}}{\sum P_i^2 - n\bar{P}^2} \tag{2.17}$$

with:

$$\bar{Q} = \frac{1}{n} \sum Q_i$$

and:

$$\bar{P} = \frac{1}{n} \sum P_i$$

The expression for $\hat{a}_1$ can be further simplified by putting $q_i = Q_i - \bar{Q}$ and $p_i = P_i - \bar{P}$, where $q_i$ and $p_i$ are the deviations of $Q_i$ and $P_i$ from their respective sample means. This procedure yields

$$\hat{a}_1 = \frac{\sum p_i q_i}{\sum p_i^2} \tag{2.18}$$

The formulae (2.16) and (2.18) are, respectively, the OLS estimates of $a_0$ and $a_1$. They provide a mechanism for converting a sample of observations on quantities and prices into numerical (estimated) values for the parameters. The estimated relationship may now be written as follows:

$$\hat{Q}_i = \hat{a}_0 + \hat{a}_1 P_i \qquad \text{for all } i \tag{2.19}$$

where $\hat{a}_0$ and $\hat{a}_1$ are the OLS estimates of the parameters given by the expressions (2.16) and (2.18). Equation (2.19) provides a measure of the *average* relationship between $Q$ and $P$, such that for the price, $P_i$, $\hat{Q}_i$ is the value of quantity demanded which we would expect to be associated with $P_i$.

An advantage of the OLS method is that while being computationally simple, it also yields estimators with certain desirable statistical properties. To clarify this point, consider our example of a new product in test markets. Suppose we consider sales over several consecutive weeks in a number of markets. Within each market a given fixed price applies and sales may be recorded day by day. This process is known as repeated sampling. In each market variable levels of sales are likely to be found, day by day. The aim of the analysis is to determine how sales vary as *between* test markets after taking account of variability *within* each market. If the number of test markets, $n$, equals ten, we take repeated samples of ten observations on quantities demanded at the given price. With prices fixed in each test market, the only source of variation in the quantities demanded, from sample to sample, is due to the disturbance term. Therefore, although the prices are fixed, because of the influence of factors other than price, each sample generates different values for quantities demanded. If we repeat this process a large number of times, say 1,000 times, we obtain 1,000 samples of $n$ observations on quantities and prices. Each sample will contain the same values for prices but different values for quantities demanded at those prices. The application of OLS method to each sample would thus yield 1,000 pairs of values for $\hat{a}_0$ and $\hat{a}_1$.

By arranging these values in frequency distribution tables we can obtain the sampling distributions of the estimators. The characteristics of the sampling distribution, obtained in this fashion, provide a criterion upon which the desirability of the estimators are assessed. There are, essentially, two features of a sampling distribution—its mean and its variance—that are important to the assessment of an estimator. Firstly, it is considered desirable for the mean of the sampling distribution to coincide with the true parameter. This means that for a very large number of samples, the estimator on average generates the true value of the parameter. An estimator which possesses this property is called an 'unbiased estimator'. The second desirable property concerns the variance of the sampling distribution of an estimator. The variance measures the spread of distribution about its mean and the smaller the variance the greater is the accuracy of the estimator. It is, therefore, considered desirable for an unbiased estimator to have the smallest variance possible. Such an estimator is called a 'best unbiased estimator' or an 'efficient estimator'. The efficiency property provides a criterion under which the choice between different methods of estimation is made. In particular, in empirical work, among all available methods of estimation, we choose the method which generates efficient estimators. This is precisely the reason why we estimated the demand function by OLS. Under the assumptions of the model, it can be shown that the OLS estimators $\hat{a}_0$ and $\hat{a}_1$ are both unbiased and have minimum variances (see for example Gujarati (1979)). The OLS method is, therefore, the best available method of estimation, given the assumptions of the model.

Having fitted the regression line by the OLS method, the next step is to establish how 'good' is the fit of the line to the sample data. Clearly, the closer the observations to the line the better is the explanation of the variations in the quantity demanded. A measure of the goodness of the fit, based on the dispersion of observations around the regression line, is provided by the coefficient of determination, $R^2$. The coefficient of determination shows the percentage of the total variations of the dependent variable (quantity demanded) which can be explained by the variations in the explanatory variables (price) over the sample period. This coefficient is given by the following expression:

$$R^2 = \frac{\sum (\hat{Q}_i - \bar{Q})^2}{\sum (Q_i - \bar{Q})^2} = 1 - \frac{\sum e_i^2}{\sum (Q_i - \bar{Q})^2}$$

where:

$\bar{Q} = \frac{1}{n} \sum Q_i$ = the sample mean of observations on quantities

$\sum (Q_i - \bar{Q})^2$ = total variations of quantities demanded around the sample mean

$\sum (\hat{Q}_i - \bar{Q})^2$ = explained variation, that is the variation in the quantities demanded which can be explained by variations in the price, over the sample period

$\sum e_i^2$ = unexplained (residual) variation, that is the variation in quantities demanded which is due to changes in factors other than price, over the sample period.

The coefficient of determination, $R^2$, provides a measure of goodness of the fit of the estimated line to the data. The closer $R^2$ is to unity (or 100 per cent) the better is the fit of the regression line to the scatter of observations on quantities and prices.

### 2.3.1 Inference about Population Parameters

The regression method outlined above provides a simple mechanism for generating parameter estimates. All we have to do is to apply the OLS formulae to a sample of observations on quantities and prices. The estimated values are, however, likely to differ from the population parameters. This is because they are generated from sample information rather than from all the observations on quantities and prices. It is, however, possible to make inferences about the population parameters on the basis of the sample information. In particular, the sampling distributions of the OLS estimators provide a mechanism for testing a number of simple hypotheses concerning the population parameters.

These tests shed some light on the nature of the relationship between the quantity demanded of a product and its price, providing valuable information on the 'true' price elasticity of demand. In this section we show how the regression model can be used for testing hypotheses about population parameters. The discussion which follows presupposes that the reader has some knowledge of basic statistics, including hypothesis testing, confidence intervals and the t-distribution.

Before proceeding, let us state the properties of the sampling distributions of the OLS estimators. Firstly, under the assumption of normality, the distributions of the OLS estimators will be normal, as presented in Figure 2.7. Secondly, the OLS estimators are unbiased; this implies that the centre of the distribution in each case (i.e. the mean of distribution) coincides with the 'true' parameter values as shown in Figure 2.7. Thirdly, the variances of the sampling distributions of the OLS estimators are smaller than those of any other unbiased estimators. These variances are given by:

$$Var(\hat{a}_0) = \frac{\sigma^2 \sum P_i^2}{n \sum p_i^2} \tag{2.20}$$

and,

$$Var(\hat{a}_1) = \frac{\sigma^2}{\sum p_i^2} \tag{2.21}$$

where $\sigma^2$ = variance of the disturbance term; $P_i$ = $i$th observation on price; $p_i = P_i - \bar{P}$, deviation of the $i$th price from the sample mean; and $n$ = number of observations. The variance of the disturbance term, $\sigma^2$, is seldom known and must be estimated. An unbiased estimator for $\sigma^2$, is given by:

$$\hat{\sigma}^2 = \frac{\sum e_i^2}{n-2} \tag{2.22}$$

where $\sum e_i^2$ is the sum of the squares of the OLS residuals.

The above provide the necessary tools for testing a number of simple hypotheses concerning demand functions. To illustrate these tests with direct reference to the price elasticity of demand, it would be easier to work with a log-linear

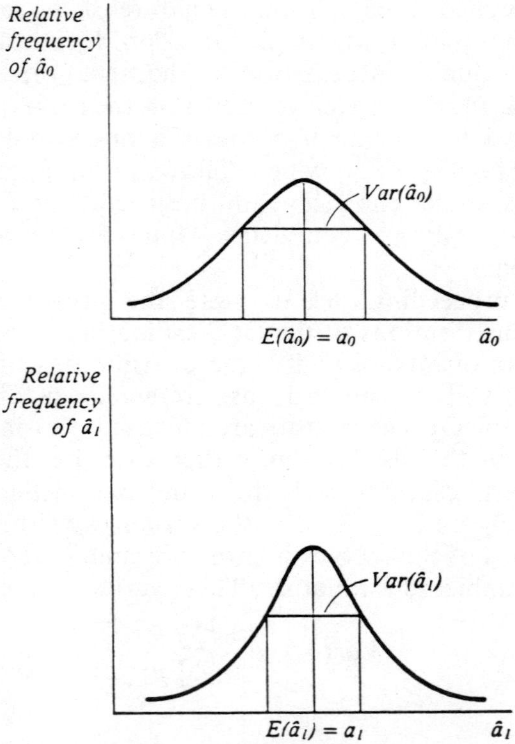


*Figure 2.7: Sampling distributions of $\hat{a}_0$ and $\hat{a}_1$*

regression model such as the one below:

$$\ln Q_i = a_0 + a_1 \ln P_i + u_i \qquad \text{for all } i = 1, \ldots, n \quad (2.23)$$

Under this specification, the parameter $a_1$ represents the price elasticity of demand for the product. Let us first test to see whether or not a relationship exists between quantity demanded of the product and its price. Clearly, if no relationship exists between these two variables, the price elasticity of demand, the parameter $a_1$, would be close to zero. The null and alternative hypothesis of this test, may, therefore, be stated as follows:

Null hypothesis $\quad H_0: a_1 = 0 \quad$ (No relationship between quantity demanded and price—price elasticity is zero)

Alternative hypothesis $H_1 : a_1 < 0$ (A negative relationship between quantity demanded and price Negative Price elasticity)

The statistic corresponding to this test is derived from the sampling distribution of the OLS estimator $\hat{a}_1$. In particular, it can be shown that the following test statistic has a student's $t$ distribution with $v$ degrees of freedom on repeated sampling:

$$t = \frac{\hat{a}_1 - a_1}{\hat{S}\hat{a}_1} \sim t_v \tag{2.24}$$

where:

$$\hat{S}\hat{a}_1 = \sqrt{\frac{\hat{\sigma}^2}{\Sigma p_i^2}}$$

is the estimated standard error of $\hat{a}_1$, derived from the expression (2.22) and (2.21).

The student's t distribution is similar to the standard normal distribution. It is also bell-shaped, symmetrical, and centred at zero. However, a $t$ distribution is shorter and flatter and its variance is larger than that of the standard normal. The degrees of freedom of a $t$ distribution show the difference between the number of observations and the number of estimated parameters. In the above illustration, $v = n - 2$, since the number of observations is $n$ and two parameters ($a_0$ and $a_1$) have been estimated. Figure 2.8 shows a $t$ distribution with $v$ degrees of freedom ($v$ is set equal to four in this illustration). With reference to this figure, let $t_{v,\alpha}$ denote that value of $t$ which cuts off $\alpha$ per cent of the area under the right hand tail of distribution. We have, by definition $P(t > t_{v,\alpha}) = \alpha$, where $P$ denotes probability. Given that the $t$ distribution is symmetric around zero, we may also write: $P(t < -t_v, \alpha) = \alpha$.

The values of the $t$ distribution are tabulated for different degrees of freedom and different levels of $\alpha$ in the tables of the $t$ distribution. These tables can be found in any statistics test. Across the top row of these tables are levels of $\alpha$, and down the outside column are listed the degrees of freedom.

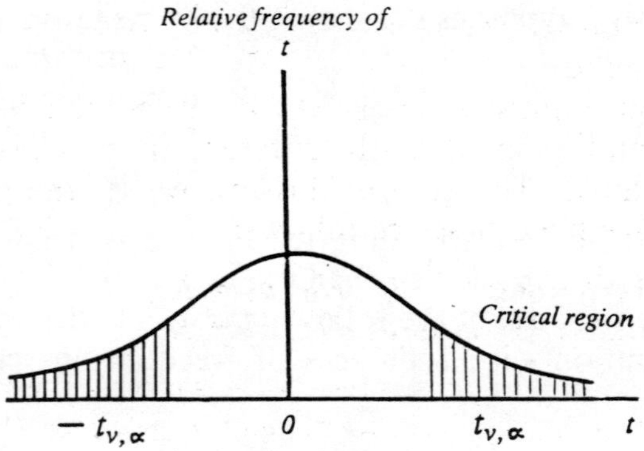


*Figure 2.8:* *Critical region of* $t_{v,\alpha}$

By using these tables the value of $t$ for any level of $\alpha$ and $v$ can easily be found.

Let us now return to the problem in hand to show how the $t$ distribution can be used to test the null hypothesis. To perform the test, we first calculate the value of the test statistic (2.24) under the null hypothesis. That is under $H_0; a_1 = 0$, we have:

$$t^* = \frac{\hat{a}_1}{\hat{S}_{\hat{a}_1}}$$

The calculated values of the $t$ statistic, $t^*$, is then compared with the value of the $t$ distribution with $v$ degrees of freedom at a predetermined level of significance, $\alpha$. If $t^*$ falls in the critical region of the distribution, the null hypothesis is rejected at $\alpha$ percent level of significance. This implies that the price elasticity of demand, $a_1$, can be considered to be significantly different from zero. The decision rule of the test may be summarized with reference to Figure 2.8 as follows:

$$\text{Reject } H_0 \text{ if } t^* < -t_{v,\alpha}$$

In Figure 2.8, the shaded area under the left hand tail of the distribution represents the critical region of the test. For example, if the number of observations, $n$, is 16 and $\alpha = 0.05$, then the critical region of the test is:

$$\text{Reject } H_0 \text{ if } t^* < -t_{14,0.05} = -1.761$$

where $-t_{14,0.05} = -1.761$ is obtained from the table of the $t$

distribution by considering the value of $t$ corresponding to $\alpha = 0.05$ and $v = 14$.

We may now wish to test whether or not the price elasticity of demand is significantly different from a predetermined value, say $K$. To perform this test we set the null and the alternative hypotheses as follows:

Null Hypothesis $H_0 : a_1 = K$
Alternative Hypothesis $H_1 : a_1 \neq K$

The test statistic for this test is the same as the previous test and is given by (2.24). Under the null hypothesis, the value of the test statistic is:

$$t^* = \frac{\hat{a}_1 - K}{\hat{S}_{\hat{a}_1}}$$

Once again, if $t^*$ falls into the critical region of the $t_{v,\alpha}$ distribution the null hypothesis is rejected at $\alpha$ per cent level of significance. Figure 2.9 shows the critical region of this test for $\alpha = 5\%$ and $v = 15$.

We reject $H_0$ if $t^* > t_{15,0.025} = 2.131$ or if $t^* < -t_{15,0.025} = -2.131$, concluding that the price elasticity of demand is significantly different from the preguessed value, $K$.

As was pointed out above, the OLS estimate of price elasticity is likely to differ from the true population parameter. We can, however, find the range of values within which the true price elasticity lies with a high level of

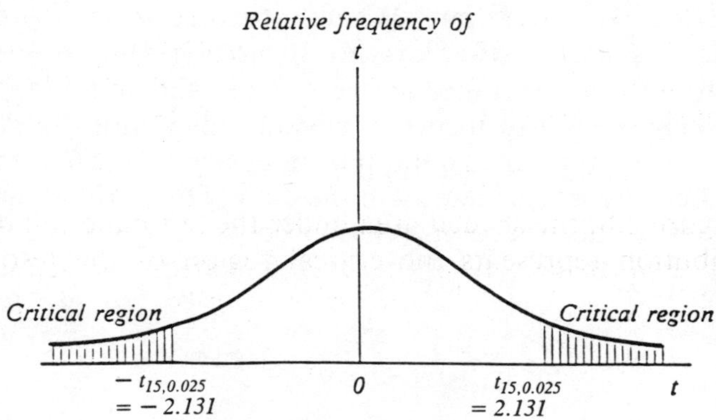


*Figure 2.9: Critical region of a two tailed test for $v = 15$ and $\alpha = 0.05$*

probability, on the basis of the OLS estimate and its sampling distribution. This range of values is called a confidence interval. For example, a 95 per cent confidence interval for the parameter $a_1$ is given by:

$$\hat{a}_1 \pm (t_{v,0.025})(\hat{S}_{\hat{a}_1}) \tag{2.25}$$

where $v = n - 2$, the degrees of freedom of the $t$ distribution. Expression (2.25) provides us with the range of values within which the true price elasticity of demand lies with a 95 per cent probability.

Before we illustrate the above procedures by way of numerical example, it is important to point out that the use of the OLS method, and its associated statistics, provide us with meaningful results only if all the assumptions concerning the model and the disturbance term are valid. In some practical situations, these assumptions can be expected to hold. In other cases their validity needs to be tested against available data. In particular, in fitting demand functions to *time series* data, it is almost always the case that, the data exhibits some degree of serial dependence. In this situation, the assumption that observations are independently generated is not justified and needs to be tested. The breakdown of this assumption is called autocorrelation. Autocorrelation occurs when the disturbance term in one time period is related to the disturbance term in the next due to the influence of variables omitted from the model, and the influence of random factors on quantity demanded which tend to persist over time. When autocorrelation is present, the least squares estimators are no longer efficient. In addition, the $t$ tests outlined above are not valid and, if applied, are likely to lead to incorrect conclusions about the model. When using time series data, it is necessary to test first for the presence of autocorrelation in the data. The most commonly used test to determine correlation between successive values of the disturbance term is the Durbin-Watson test defined as:

$$\text{D-W} = \frac{\sum_{t=2}^{n} (e_t - e_{t-1})^2}{\sum_{t=1}^{n} e_t^2} \tag{2.26}$$

where $e_t$ is the OLS residual, and $n$ is the number of observations. If there is no autocorrelation in the data the value of the test statistic will be approximately two. Alternatively, if the disturbance terms are positively correlated the value of the D-W will be less than two, and if there is negative correlation the value of D-W exceeds two. The D-W statistic lies in the rage (0, 4). It should be emphasized that the Durbin-Watson statistic is a test statistic having a distribution and the above rules are essentially 'rules of thumb' for the interpretation of a given value of the D-W statistic. (For more details on this test and form of its distribution see, for example, Pindyck and Rubinfeld (1981).)

## 2.4 THE ESTIMATION OF A SIMPLE LOG-LINEAR MODEL OF DEMAND

Let us now illustrate the above techniques by way of a numerical example. For the purpose of illustration we use ten hypothetical pairs of observations on quantities and prices to estimate the parameters of the following log-linear demand function:

$$\ln Q_i = a_0 + a_1 \ln P_i + u_i; \qquad i = 1, 2, 3, \ldots, 10 \quad (2.27)$$

where: $Q_i$ = quantity demanded (sold) at the $i$th price
$P_i$ = $i$th price
$a_0$ = unknown parameter representing the intercept term
$a_1$ = unknown parameter representing the price elasticity of demand.

Table 2.1 presents the hypothetical data set. The figures are the anticipated annual sales for a product following pilot tests in regional markets of the kind referred to in Section 2.1.

Programs 2.1 and 2.2 are used to generate the OLS estimates of the parameters and some associated statistical values.

*Table 2.1: Hypothetical data on the results of regional test trails*

| Price (P) | ln Price | Sales (thousands) | ln Sales |
|---|---|---|---|
| 85 | 4.4426 | 9 | 2.1972 |
| 80 | 4.3820 | 11 | 2.3979 |
| 75 | 4.3175 | 11 | 2.3979 |
| 70 | 4.2484 | 12 | 2.4849 |
| 65 | 4.1744 | 13 | 2.5699 |
| 60 | 4.094 | 13 | 2.5649 |
| 60 | 4.094 | 15 | 2.7081 |
| 55 | 4.007 | 17 | 2.8332 |
| 55 | 4.007 | 20 | 2.9957 |
| 50 | 3.9120 | 20 | 2.9957 |

The regression results may be summarized as follows:

$$\ln \hat{Q}_i = \underset{(0.672)}{8.628} - \underset{(0.161)}{1.443} \ln P_i \tag{2.28}$$

The figures in brackets are the estimated standard errors.

Coefficient of determination : $R^2 = 0.91$
Durbin-Watson statistic : D-W = 1.755
Number of observations : $n = 10$

According to the results, the OLS estimate of the price elasticity, $\hat{a}_1$, is $-1.443$ implying that for a one per cent rise in the price the quantity demanded is likely to fall by 1.4 per cent. Notice that this value represents the estimated value of the slope of the log-linear demand function. The OLS estimate of the intercept term, $\hat{a}_0$, is 8.628 indicating that the estimated log-linear demand function has a positive vertical intercept term, as is expected. According to the value of $R^2$, the log-linear model fits the data quite well. This value suggests that 91 per cent of total variations in the quantity sold, over the sample period, can be explained by the variations in the price of the product, and only 9 per cent of the total variations can be attributed to the non-price factors, whose influence in the model is captured by the disturbance term.

Let us now carry out a number of simple tests concerning

the 'true' price elasticity of demand. We start with the test of significance for the parameter $a_1$. The null and alternative hypotheses of this test may be stated as follows:

| | | |
|---|---|---|
| Null hypothesis | $H_0: a_1 = 0$ | (Price elasticity of demand is zero: no relationship between quantity sold and price) |
| Alternative hypothesis | $H_1: a_1 < 0$ | (Negative Price elasticity: a negative relationship between quantity sold and price) |

The test statistic is $t = (\hat{a}_1 - a_1)/\hat{S}_{\hat{a}_1}$ which has a '$t$' distribution with eight degrees of freedom on repeated sampling. Under the null hypothesis the calculated value of $t$ is:

$$t^* = \frac{\hat{a}_1}{\hat{S}_{\hat{a}_1}} = \frac{-1.443}{0.161} = -8.926$$

From the $t$ distribution table, the value of $-t_{8,0.05}$ is found to be $-1.860$. Since $t^* < -t_{8,0.05} = -1.860$ we reject the null hypothesis at the five per cent level of significance, concluding that the price elasticity of demand is significantly different from zero. This result suggests that the model is compatible with the actual observations.

Next, we calculate at a 95 per cent confidence interval for $a_1$ to find the range of values within which the 'true' price elasticity of demand lies with a 95 per cent probability. This range of values can be calculated as follows:

$$\hat{a}_1 \pm (t_{8,0.05})(\hat{S}_{\hat{a}_1})$$

where:

$$\hat{a}_1 = -1.443; \; t_{8,0.025} = 2.306; \; S_{a_1} = 0.161$$

Substitution for these values into the expression for the confidence interval yields the following range of values: $(-1.814, -1.071)$. Thus, there is a probability of 0.95 that the true price elasticity of demand lies between $-1.814$ and

−1.071. Notice that the OLS estimate of the price elasticity lies within this range.

We may also test whether the 'true' price elasticity is significantly different from a pre-guessed value, say minus one. The null and alternative hypotheses of this test may be stated as follows:

$$H_0 : a_1 = -1$$
$$H_1 : a_1 \neq -1$$

Under the null hypothesis, the calculated value of $t$ is:

$$t^* = \frac{-1.4443 + 1}{0.161} = -2.751$$

From the table of $t$ distribution we have $t_{8,0.025} = \pm 2.306$. Since $t^* < -t_{8,0.025} = -2.306$ we reject the null hypothesis and conclude that the price elasticity of demand is significantly different from unity at the five per cent level. The null hypothesis is, however, accepted at the one per cent level of significance as $t^*$ falls in the critical region of the test in this case. That is: $t^* > -t_{8,0.005} = -3.55$. We therefore conclude that the price elasticity is not significantly different from unity if the level of the test is set to one per cent.

Finally notice that the value of the Durbin-Watson test is close to two, indicating the lack of serial correlation in the data.

Given that the estimated model fits the data well, it may be used to predict the average quantity sold at a price outside the range of the sample data. For example, suppose we set the price at ten. By substituting for this level of price into the estimated model a point prediction for the average quantity sold may be obtained as follows:

$$\begin{aligned} \ln \mathring{Q}_{10} &= 8.628 - 1.443 \ln 10 \\ &= 8.628 - (1.443)(2.3025) \\ &= 5.30537 \end{aligned}$$

Taking the antilog of the above value yields a point prediction for the average quantity sold at the price ten:

$$\mathring{Q}_{10} = 201.4$$

The average quantity sold at the price ten is therefore expected to be 201.4 units.

# PROGRAMS 2.1 AND 2.2

These programs may be used for calculating regression and correlation coefficients and the associated standard errors in a simple two variable model. Quantity demanded is taken as the dependent variable and price as the independent variable. Of course, data for any pair of variables could be adopted by program users. Two programs are listed so as to show more clearly how the calculations are performed. The programs will be of interest only to readers who wish to see how a computer program can be written to sum values in statistical calculations.

## PROGRAM 2.1

```
 10 REM 2.1
 20 CLS
 30 PRINT
 40 PRINT "ENTER THE NUMBER OF OBSERVATIONS": INPUT n
 50 DIM P(n):DIM Q(n):DIM A(n):DIM B(n)
 60 PRINT
 70 FOR i=1 TO n
 80 PRINT "OBSERVATIONS FOR (P,Q) SET NUMBER ";i
 90 INPUT "PRICE ";P(i)
100 INPUT "QUANTITY ";Q(i)
110 A(i) = P(i)*P(i)+A(i-1)
120 B(i) = P(i)*Q(i)+B(i-1)
130 P(i) = P(i) + P(i-1)
140 Q(i) = Q(i) + Q(i-1)
150 PRINT
160 NEXT
170 i=n
180 a1 = (n*B(i) - P(i)*Q(i))/(n*A(i) -P(i)*P(i))
190 a0 = (1/n)*Q(i) - (1/n)*a1*P(i)
200 PRINT "SALES = ";a0;"    ";a1;"*PRICE"
210 STOP
```

Line 40: $n = 10$ in the hypothetical example of Section 2.4 and in Table 2.1.

Line 50: $n$ dimensional arrays for $P_i$, $Q_i$, $\Sigma P^2$, and $\Sigma P_iQ_i$ are set up.

Line 110: $A(i) = \Sigma P_i^2$. $A_i$ increases as $i$ increases. This line reads: '$A(i)$ equals the square of $P(i)$ plus the value of $A(i-1)$'.

Line 120: $B(i) = \Sigma P_iQ_i$.

Line 130: $\Sigma P_i$ is calculated.

Line 180: The formula:

$$a1 = \frac{n \Sigma P_iQ_i - \Sigma P_i \Sigma Q_i}{n \Sigma P_i^2 - (\Sigma P_i)^2}$$

is used to calculate the gradient, that is, the parameter $\hat{a}_1$.

Line 190: The formula: $a0 = \Sigma\, Q_i/n - a1\ \Sigma\, P_i/n$ is used to calculate the intercept, that is, the parameter $\hat{a}_0$.

## PROGRAM 2.2

```
 10 REM 2.2
 20 CLS
 30 PRINT "ENTER THE NUMBER OF OBSERVATIONS": INPUT n
 40 DIM P(n):DIM Q(n)
 50 DIM A(n):DIM B(n):DIM C(n):DIM F(n)
 55 DIM G(n):DIM H(n):DIM J(n)
 60 PRINT
 70 FOR i=1 TO n
 80 PRINT "OBSERVATION FOR (P,Q) SET NUMBER ";i
 90 INPUT "PRICE ";P(i)
100 INPUT "QUANTITY ";Q(i)
110 A(i) = P(i)*P(i) + A(i-1)
120 B(i) = Q(i)*Q(i) + B(i-1)
130 C(i) = P(i)*Q(i) + C(i-1)
140 P(i) = P(i) + P(i-1)
150   Q(i) = Q(i) + Q(i-1)
160 PRINT
170 NEXT
180 i=n
190 F(n) = A(i) - (1/n)*(P(i)*P(i))
200 G(n) = B(i) - (1/n)*(Q(i)*Q(i))
210 H(n) = C(i) - (1/n)*(P(i)*Q(i))
220 J(n) = ((F(n)*G(n)) - H(n)^2)/F(n)
230 RR = 1 - (J(n)/G(n))
240 sa0 = SQR((J(n)*A(i)/(n-2))/(n*F(n)))
250 sa1 = SQR((J(n)/(n-2))/F(n))
260 s = SQR(J(n)/(n-2))
270 PRINT'"COEFFICIENT OF DETERMINATION= ";RR
280 PRINT'"ST. ERROR OF INTERCEPT= ";sa0
290 PRINT'"ST. ERROR OF GRADIENT= ";sa1
300 PRINT'"ST. ERROR OF REGRESSION= ";s
310 STOP
```

Lines 110 to 150: See the notes for Program 2.1

Line 190: $\Sigma\,(P_i - \bar{P})^2 = \Sigma\, P_i^2 - (1/n)(\Sigma\, P_i)^2$ is calculated.

Lines 200 and 210: $\Sigma(Q_i - \bar{Q})^2$ and $\Sigma(P_i - \bar{P})(Q_i - \bar{Q})$ are similarly calculated.

Lines 220: The value of the key expression:

$$\frac{\Sigma(P_i - \bar{P})^2\ \Sigma(Q_i - \bar{Q})^2 - (\Sigma(P_i - \bar{P})(Q_i - \bar{Q}))^2}{\Sigma(P_i - \bar{P})^2}$$

is calculated. The value of this expression correspondents to $\Sigma\, e_i^2$, that is, the 'unexplained variation' (see equations 2.10 to 2.14).

## 2.5 MULTIPLE REGRESSION

So far, we have considered the estimation of demand functions with only one explanatory variable, the price of the product. Although the quantity demanded of a product is significantly influenced by variations in its price, there are several other potentially important variables, such as prices of closely related products, advertising expenditures and consumers' income, influencing demand. In order to capture the influence of these factors, we can include them explicitly in the model as explanatory variables. The resulting model is called a multiple linear regression model. Equation 2.29 presents a multiple linear regression model with four explanatory variables:

$$Q_t = a_0 + a_1 P_t + a_2 A_t + a_3 \bar{P}_t + a_4 Y_t + u_t \qquad (2.29)$$

where $Q_t$ = quantity demanded (sold) in period $t$
$P_t$ = Price of the product
$\bar{P}_t$ = an index of closely related products
$Y_t$ = a measure of consumers' income
$a_0, \ldots, a_4$ = unknown parameters

The use of the OLS method in multiple linear regression models is just an extension of the one variable case. The estimation of these models, however, involves a number of key econometric problems which emerge as a result of the break-down of the assumptions concerning the regression model and the disturbance term. In particular, when using time series data, in addition to the problems of identification and autocorrelation we are likely to be faced with the problem of multicollinearity. Multicollinearity refers to the existence of a high degree of correlation between the explanatory variables of the model. In the context of demand estimation, this problem arises because time series data on income/expenditure and prices tend to be highly correlated making it difficult to estimate their separate effects on quantity demanded. In the face of these problems, the estimation of multivariate models of demand is a formidable task requiring advanced knowledge of econometric methods whose coverage is beyond the scope of this chapter. (For a discussion of the estimation of multivariate models, see Lawler and Seddighi, (1987).)

## SUMMARY

1. In this chapter we introduced the processes of economic model building, estimation, and empirical validation, using simple models of demand for illustration. Models were developed on the basis of economic theory which stresses the influence of prices, incomes, etc. on demand. Two simple specifications were considered: linear and log-linear models of demand.
2. In order to see how well the model conforms with reality, it must be confronted with actual observations. For this purpose, the model must be modified to take account of the imprecise nature of the data. This was carried out by adding a random term, called the disturbance term, to the model. The disturbance term captures the influence of omitted variables and chance factors on the dependent variable, demand.
3. The modified model and its assumptions constitute a simple econometric model. The assumptions of the model need to be tested against available data, as they may not always hold.
4. In order to estimate the parameters of the model we introduced the least squares approach to regression analysis. Under this approach the estimated parameters are obtained so as to minimize the sum of the squares of the residuals from the estimated regression line. This shows the average relationship between the dependent variable (quantity demanded) and the explanatory variable (price).
5. An important advantage of the method of least squares is that it is computationally simple and it yields estimators with certain desirable statistical properties. In particular, under the assumptions of the model, this method produces estimators which are linear, unbiased, and have minimum variances.
6. To find out how 'good' is the fit of the regression line to the sample observations, we introduced the coefficient of determination, $R^2$. This shows the strength of the relationship between the dependent and independent variables. It indicates the proportion of the variations in the dependent

variable which can be accounted for by variations in the explanatory variable(s), over the sample period.

7. The sampling distributions of the OLS estimators provide a mechanism for testing hypotheses concerning population parameters. The appropriate test statistic usually follows a well-defined distribution such as the normal and *t*. To perform the test, the value of the test statistic obtained from the sample is compared against its critical value(s) obtained from the tables of the relevant distribution. If the calculated value of the test statistic falls in the critical region, the null hypothesis may be rejected at a predetermined level of significance.

8. When fitting demand functions to time series data it is necessary to test for the presence of autocorrelation. A simple test statistic is the Durbin-Watson (D-W) statistic. If there is no autocorrelation in the data the value of the test statistic will be approximately equal to two.

## FURTHER READING

For a general account of process of economic model building see, for example, Intriligator (1978), Chapter 2. The regression methods and hypotheses testing procedures can be found in any econometric text—see, for example, Gujarati (1978), and Younger (1985). For an interesting discussion on the empirical analysis of demand and the identification problem, see Baumol (1977), Chapter 10. For further details on demand estimation and some numerical examples, see Lawler and Seddighi (1987), Chapter 3 and Thomas (1985), Chapter 6. For an interesting example of demand estimation, see Allan (1981).

# 3 Cost Analysis: Stock Control

A distinction is drawn in economics between costs of production in the short and long run. In this chapter, the relation between costs and time is examined but the example chosen is from operations research. The subject, optimization and stock control, is useful because of its widespread application and because the principles which apply are central to economic theory. Economics is sometimes defined as the discipline which is concerned with man's competing wants and the limited resources available for satisfying them. To obtain maximum benefit, waste must be avoided. This principle applies in a vivid form in the case of stock control. A U-shaped total cost curve is derived by addition of various cost functions. Cost minimization involves search for the minimum point on this curve.

Every firm and office has a stock management problem of one kind or another. A clerk in an educational establishment has to decide upon the stock of notepads, pens, etc. which should be kept on hand. A car sales company has to decide how many cars should be on display in their showrooms. The producer of manufactured goods has to decide what stock of raw materials should be held. There are costs and benefits attached to small and large stocks. These considerations apply whether or not materials are perishable or subject to deterioration with time. A shopkeeper finds it costly to maintain large stocks in terms of the funds which are tied up. On the other hand, if only small stocks are maintained, customers are likely to find the range of goods unsatisfactory. A car sales company would like to have a wide range of models available but it knows if they are not sold by the end of the year model changes will bring capital losses.

All organizations have two problems in common:

(1) stocks are costly in terms of funds and space tied up;
(2) there are costs involved in repeating orders.

How should a balance be struck between these costs? Is it necessarily damaging to be out of stock? Might it be sound policy to accept 'stock-outs' from time to time even if customers have to join a waiting list, sales are lost or production is held up?

Sections 3.1 to 3.4 concern stock models when demand is known with certainty. The exact mathematical relationship between the variables is assumed to be known hence the models are *deterministic*. Except in the case of the basic model the solutions can be quite difficult. Computer programs are used to help to find these solutions. Section 3.5 concerns a model where demand is randomly determined. A simulation model involving many of the concepts used in the earlier sections is applied. Computer users are invited to search for the minimum costs solution.

## 3.1 THE BASIC MODEL

Let us begin by describing the stock management costs of a motor manufacturing company. Consider the assembly of the components of a vehicle. Every vehicle has thousands of different components. What is the optimal quantity of each component at the assembly plant? Clearly, this will vary item by item. Some components are expensive to hold because of their high value or bulkiness, others are not. Suppose the annual demand for transmission units for a particular vehicle is known with confidence to be 10,000 units. Suppose the company has a long-established policy of having 2,500 units delivered to the assembly plant on four occasions each year. This policy would involve planning for a run-down of stocks as shown in the solid lines of the four triangles of Figure 3.1. Supplies arrive at the beginning of January, April, July and October. Stocks are planned to run down from 2,500 units to zero, hence the planned *average* size of stocks is 1,250 units. (This figure is simply the average of the highest and lowest values recorded. It is calculated in the same way as any average.) It is likely that the assembly of transmission units at any given time does not correspond exactly with the planned rate and actual stocks might be as shown in the broken line. 'Stock-outs' would cause delays in production. The gap between the solid and the broken line measures the difference between planned and actual use. However, assume that variations in the rate of use even themselves out and that stock-outs do not take place.

The aim of the basic model is to allow a comparison between existing and alternative ways of doing things. Stock management costs are considered as a function of the number of reorders per annum and the quantity of units ordered. The quantity of units ordered determines the required number of orders and the height of the stockpile at any moment of time. If deliveries take place often, average stocks are low. If they are infrequent, average stocks are high. Small stocks involve a small amount of tied up capital, little space in storage and smaller vehicles used in transshipment. At the limit, stock costs are zero if deliveries take place, say, two or three times per day. Large stocks allow a reduction in the number of duplicate orders, a smaller

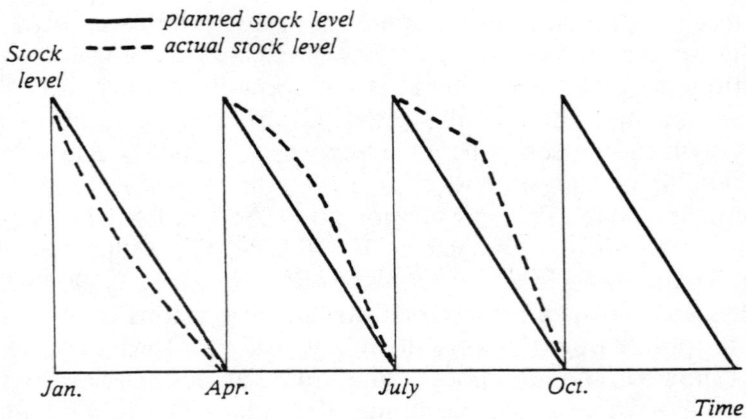


*Figure 3.1: Stock over time (basic model)*

number of clerical staff, economies of transportation and, in the case of components or machines purchased, quantity discounts. If the problem of balancing these costs is not tackled systematically, costs might be unnecessarily high. Failure to appreciate the concept of optimality results in repeated 'losses' even though they do not show up in accounting records.

To determine the optimal solution it is necessary to add 'holding costs' (sometimes known as 'carrying costs') to 'reordering costs'. The expression reordering costs is preferred to ordering costs. Total costs are to be calculated with respect to variations in the quantity of units in each order. This quantity is known as the *order quantity*. The aim is to discover the order quantity which minimizes total stock management costs.

In the model, the following notation is used:

$D$ = annual demand
$Q$ = order quantity
$N$ = number of reorders
$hc$ = holding cost per unit of stock per annum
$rc$ = reorder cost per reorder
$R$ = total reorder cost per annum
$H$ = total holding cost per annum
$T$ = total cost per annum

The cost of holding stocks varies with the quantity in stock. In our example, the consignment, $Q$, equals 2,500 units and the average size of stocks is $(Q+0)/2$. Total holding costs equal the average size of stocks throughout the year multiplied by the holding cost per unit held in stock. Thus:

$$H=\left(\frac{Q}{2}\right)hc \qquad (3.1)$$

The cost of reordering stocks, $R$, varies with the number of reorders. In the example $N=4$. Since annual demand, $D$, equals 10,000 units, the order quantity, $Q$, equals 2,500 units. The number of reorders equals the annual demand divided by the order quantity: $N=\mathrm{D}/\mathrm{Q}$. Total reordering costs equal the number of reorders multiplied by the paper work and delivery costs associated with each reorder. Thus:

$$R = Nrc \tag{3.2}$$

Since $N = D/Q$, $R = (D/Q)rc$. Summarizing the argument:

$$T = H + R$$

$$T = \frac{Q}{2}hc + \frac{D}{Q}rc \tag{3.3}$$

$D$, $hc$ and $rc$ are constants. If $T$ is to be minimized a value of $Q$ must be chosen which sets the derivative $\partial T/\partial Q$ equal to zero. The cost curves are shown in Figure 3.2. The total cost curve is obtained by addition of the cost functions for $H$ and $R$. Differentiating $T$ with respect to $Q$:

$$\frac{\partial T}{\partial Q} = \frac{hc}{2} - \frac{D\,rc}{Q^2}$$

$$0 = \frac{hc}{2} - \frac{D\,rc}{Q^2}$$

$$Q = \sqrt{\frac{2\,D\,rc}{hc}} \tag{3.4}$$

The value of $Q$ when $\partial T/\partial Q = 0$ is determined by $D$, $rc$ and $hc$. It is to be noted that the second derivative of equation 3.3 is positive hence the solution for (3.4) is a minimum point on the total cost curve.

Suppose each reorder costs £1,000 and holding cost equals £200 per unit. Expressing values in £1,000 units, $rc = 1$ and $hc = 0.2$. Denoting the optimal solutions by asterisks, it is found that $Q^* \approx 316$, $N^* \approx 32$ and $T^* \approx 63$. Comparing $T^*$ with the cost which applies when $Q = 2{,}500$, in the latter case, $T \approx 254$. Consider a doubling of the demand for transmission units. Does the optimal order quantity double? As can be seen from equation 3.4, clearly it does not. If demand doubles, $Q^*$ increases from 316 to 447 units; $Q^*$ is proportional to the square root of demand multiplied by the reorder cost: holding cost ratio.

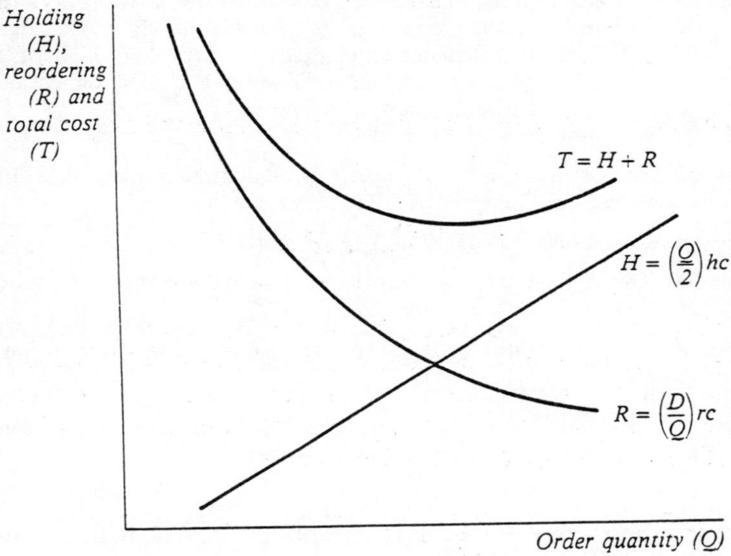


*Figure 3.2: Holding, reordering and total costs*

## PROGRAM 3.1

The above results may be confirmed using Program 3.1 It is based on equations 3.1, 3.2 and 3.3. *H*, *R* and *T* may be calculated for different parameters set in line 30. Program 3.1 could be used in considering the optimal order quantities for the different items assembled in a motor car plant. Everything from nuts and bolts to engines has to be brought in from outside in many UK car plants.

```
 10 REM3.1
 20 DIM H(600):DIM R(600):DIM T(600)
 30 D = 10000:hc = .2:rc = 1
 40 PRINT"Q....H.....R........T"
 50 FOR Q = 1 TO 600 STEP 10
 60 R(Q) = rc*(D/Q)
 70 H(Q) = hc*(Q/2)
 80 T(Q) = H(Q) + R(Q)
 90 PRINT;Q;"....";INT (H(Q));"....";INT (R(Q));"....";INT (T(Q))
100 A$ = INKEY$(0):IF A$ = "" THEN 100
110 NEXT Q
120 STOP
130 REM *** IBM ***
140 REM LINE 100:-
150 A$ = INKEY$: IF A$ = "" THEN LINE 100
```

Line 20: Arrays are set up which enable data to be stored as memory for later use, for instance when graphics are to be displayed. Up to 600 values of $H$, $R$ and $T$ may be calculated and stored. The arrays are *numeric* as opposed to *string*. Before setting up an array, we enter a DIM (dimension) statement to reserve a given amount of memory.
Line 30: The parameters of the model.

Line 50: The calculations commence. Calculations take place in STEP intervals of ten; i.e. For $Q = 1, 11, 21, \ldots$, etc.

Line 80: Corresponds to equations 3.1, 3.2 and 3.3.

Line 100: This command brings the program to a halt until the user presses any key.

Line 110: The program loops back to line 50 unless 600 iterations have been completed.

## 3.2 LEAD TIME

Considering Figure 3.1, it is the policy of the firm to run down stocks to zero units on four occasions each year. Stocks would have to be renewed instantly if delays to production are to be avoided. Suppose it was decided to place advance orders. Would this make any difference to the cost function? Allowing for this factor is known as allowing for 'lead time'.

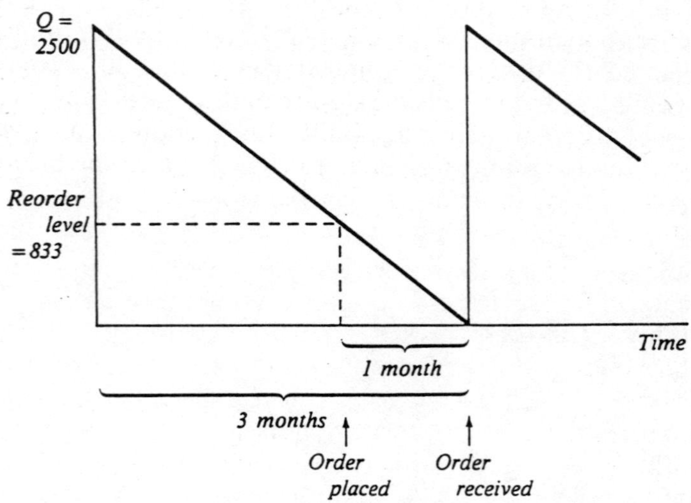


*Figure 3.3: Effect of allowing for lead time*

For instance, if the lead time is one month then orders are placed one month in advance. This is illustrated in Figure 3.3 where we assume, for convenience, that $N = 4$. Given the plan is to run down stocks at an even rate, stocks fall to 833 units two months after the last delivery and then an order is 'triggered'. If it takes approximately one month for deliveries to arrive, stock management costs are not affected by the lead time. When stocks are used up at a predictable rate because demand is known with certainty, the *reorder level*, that is, the level that stocks must fall to before an order is triggered, is simply read from the diagram. If demand is uncertain, however, the reorder level involves an important decision. Further discussion of this issue is delayed until Section 3.5.

## 3.3 BACKORDERS AND STOCK-OUT COSTS

Are there any circumstances when it might be sensible to allow stocks to run out? Many firms accept 'negative stocks' routinely. In such cases it must be supposed that 'stock-out' costs are not prohibitive. In the case of a retail car sales company, for instance, it would be enormously expensive always to have on display all the makes they normally supply and in the quantities demanded by the public. Figure 3.1 illustrated a difference between planned and actual stock levels. Values below the horizontal axis, if they occurred, could be said to refer to negative stocks or to 'back orders' which accumulate because orders have not been met. When stocks are replenished a part of the new delivery would be needed to meet past orders; the remaining stocks would be available to meet new demand.

Suppose a retail motor company expects an annual demand for 1,200 cars. Suppose it obtains its supplies monthly. It expects to sell 100 cars per month. It plans to have unfulfilled orders of twenty cars at certain times each month. Deliveries to the showrooms take place once a month. Figure 3.4 illustrates the intended position in one month. Stocks are positive above the horizontal axis and negative below it. When new deliveries arrive, most are required for forward orders but some are required for back

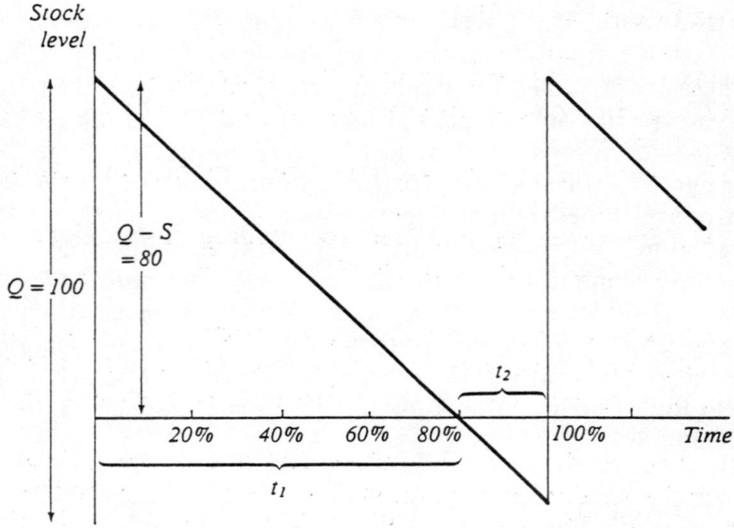


*Figure 3.4: Percentage of time in and out of stock*

orders. In the figure, the size of back orders when a new delivery arrives equals twenty units. Of the 100 units in the delivery, eighty are available to meet new demand. The cycle is repeated each month. Hence, in calculating the average level of stocks and stock-outs for each month, we are also calculating the average for the whole year.

Two questions need to be asked:

(1) Is the company sensible in planning stock-outs?
(2) If so, what is the optimal stock level?

In considering these questions, the following additional notation will be used:

$S$ = planned stock-out level each month in numbers of cars
$Dp$ = total demand which management plans to meet each month
$sc$ = stock-out costs per unit of stock per month
$B$ = total back-order or stock-out cost per month
t = time interval
$t_1$ = time positive stocks are planned as a percentage
$t_2$ = time negative stocks are planned as a percentage

In particular, we need to know:

(1) what is the cost per unit of negative stock;
(2) is the equation for reorder costs affected by stock-outs;
(3) what percentage of time each month are stocks positive;
(4) how does the equation for holding costs change if stock-outs are introduced?

(1) Stock-out costs per unit, *sc*, are calculated in terms of goodwill and customers lost through orders being fulfilled late, plus the cost of meeting orders late. A monetary value can be set for set for *sc*.
(2) The reorder cost equation is not affected by stock-outs since the fundamental relationship between $D$, $Q$ and $N$ is unchanged. The equation $R = (D/Q)rc$ applies, as in the basic model.
(3) For how long each month will stocks be positive? Given time, $t$, equals one month, what is the fraction of time that back-orders *do not* exist? This fraction, $t_1$, is positively related to $Q$ and negatively related to $S$ and $Dp$. In each month the expression: $t_1 = (Q - S)/Dp$ applies. But what is the value of $Dp$? $Dp$ is total planned demand, that is demand which has not been met because of unfulfilled orders plus the current demand which management intends to meet. It would be pointless having cars in stock unless it was intended to meet demand and $Dp$ cannot exceed $Q$. Hence, the value of $Dp$ is the same as the value of $Q$; planned demand equals the stocks available for sale at the beginning of each cycle. Substituting $Q$ for $Dp$: $t_1 = (Q - S)/Q$. In the numerical example, $Q = 100$, $S = 20$ and $Dp = 100$, hence $t_1 = 80$ per cent. It follows that time stocks are negative $= S/Q$. This follows since $(Q - S)/Q + S/Q = 1$.
(4) To calculate the costs each month of holding stocks it is necessary to multiply the costs of holding stocks by the percentage of time that stocks are positive. From the numerical example, it is clear that *whilst* stocks are positive, average stocks equal $(100 - 20)/2$ units. Over the whole month, then, the average size of stock is $[(100 - 20)/2]\ 0.8$.

The general form of the expression for the average stock level is:

$[(Q-S)/2](Q-S)/Q$, which simplifies to: $(Q-S)^2/2Q$.

Considering the cost of this stock:

$$H = \frac{(Q-S)^2 hc}{2Q}$$

Of course, if $S = 0$, $H = (Q/2)hc$.

To calculate stock-out costs, it is necessary to multiply the costs of being out of stock by the percentage of time stocks are negative. For example, we can see that *whilst* stocks are negative the average stock-out level equals (20/2) units. Over the whole month, the average of this sum equals $(20/2)t_2 = (20/2)0.2$. The general form of the expression for the average stock-out level is: $(S/2)\ (S/Q) = S^2/2Q$. Considering the costs of 'back-orders': $B = (S^2/2Q)\ sc$.

When the elements of the total cost equation are brought together it is clear that:

$$T = R + H + B$$

$$T = \frac{Drc}{Q} + \frac{(Q-S)^2 hc}{2Q} + \frac{S^2 sc}{2Q} \qquad (3.5)$$

In words, equation 3.5 reads: total costs equal (i) reordering costs plus (ii) average stocks held, adjusted for the time they are positive, multiplied by holding costs, plus (iii) average negative stocks, adjusted for the time they are negative, multiplied by stock-out costs. Denoting the optimal order quantity by $Q^*$ and stock-out level by $S^*$, it can be shown by calculus that:

$$Q^* = \sqrt{\left(\frac{2Drc}{hc}\right)\left(\frac{hc+sc}{sc}\right)} \qquad (3.6)$$

$$S^* = \left(\frac{hc}{hc+sc}\right)Q^* \qquad (3.7)$$

PROGRAMS 3.2A and 3.2B

Programs 3.2A and 3.2B use the assumed values: $D = 1200$,

*hc* = 10, *rc* = 100 and *sc* = 50. $Q^*$ and $S^*$ are equal to 169 and 28 respectively. These solutions confirm the results obtained using equations 3.6 and 3.7. Compare the cost figures which are obtained when $S = 0$. When stock-outs are allowed, cost equals 1,414, given $Q^* = 169$, $S = 28$. If stocks are not allowed to run out, cost equals 1,549, given $Q^* = 155$ (applying the equations for the basic model). Program 3.2A is based on equation 3.5. Line 60 is used in the calculations. In order to determine *T* with respect to *Q*, it is necessary to assume an initial value for *S*. If a value for *S* is not included (see line 30) an error is reported when the program is run. Hence, Program 3.2A depends on equations 3.6 and 3.7 for its solutions! In order to obtain solutions using an iterative procedure two loops are needed. Program 3.2B is based on this programming procedure.

```
 10 REM3.2A
 20 D = 1200:rc = 100:hc = 10:sc = 50
 30 S=28
 40 PRINT'"ORDER QUANTITY......TOTAL COST"
 50 FOR Q=1 TO 1200 STEP 10
 60 T=(D/Q)*rc + (((Q-S)^2)/(2*Q))*hc + ((S^2)/(2*Q))*sc
 70 PRINT Q;".........";T
 80 A$ = INKEY$(0): IF A$="" THEN 80
 90 NEXT Q
100 STOP
110 REM *** IBM ***
120 REM LINE 80:-
130 A$ = INKEY$: IF A$="" THEN 80

140 REM3.2B
150 D = 1200:rc = 100:hc = 10:sc = 50
160 PRINT'"ORDER QUANT.   STOCK OUT    TOTAL COST"
170 FOR S = 25 TO 30
180 FOR Q=140 TO 170
190 T=(D/Q)*rc + (((Q-S)^2)/(2*Q))*hc + ((S^2)/(2*Q))*sc
200 PRINT;Q;"...........";S;"...........";T
210 A$ = INKEY$(0): IF A$="" THEN 210
220 NEXT Q
230 NEXT S
240 STOP
250 REM *** IBM ***
260 REM LINE 210:-
270 A$ = INKEY$: IF A$="" THEN 210
```

Lines 130 and 220: These lines lie *within* the loop formed by lines 170 and 230. Calculations are performed for values of *Q* and *S*.

Line 170 sets the initial value of *S* ( = 25) and *T* is calculated for all values of *Q* in the range 140 to 170. The initial value of *S* is quite arbitrary. Too low a value would involve many more iterations. When all the solutions for *T* as a function of *Q* have been completed, with $S = 25$, a second round of calculations for $S = 26$ takes place.

## 3.4 GRADUAL RECEIPT OF STOCK

Supplies need not be delivered all at once. An order might be placed and materials received over a period of time if an arrangement has been made with the supplier or if it is the normal practice to operate this way. Figure 3.1 applied to the delivery and use of transmission units in a car assembly plant. Clearly, it would be in the manufacturer's interests if stocks could be lowered without at the same time increasing reorder costs. To examine the issues involved refer to Figure 3.5. An order is placed for ten units of stock. It is delivered over two days and one unit of stock is used up per day. For two days the receipt rate exceeds the use rate and stocks build up; thereafter they decline. Let $U$ equal the use rate, $I$ equal the items received per day and $L$ equal the number of days over which an order is delivered. As before, let $rc$ denote the reorder cost per delivery and $R$ equal total reorder costs. In order to apply this model it must be assumed that $rc$ is independent of $L$. This would be the case, for instance, when a fixed order charge is imposed for meeting an order for supplies irrespective of the number of deliveries and when the costs of a manufacturer are not increased when $L$ is extended. Suppliers might prefer to deliver over a period of time since peaks and troughs in their workload might be reduced. Similarly, manufacturers, from the viewpoint of

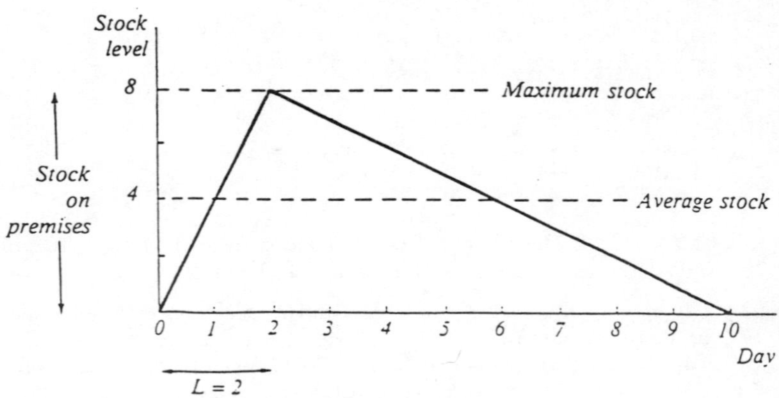


*Figure 3.5: Gradual receipt of stock*

their warehouse staffing requirements, might wish to avoid having to deal with very large deliveries at particular times.

Adopting the same mathematical procedure as in the earlier sections, we need to calculate the maximum stock which is ever on the premises and the average size of stocks. In our example this is straightforward. The maximum stock equals eight units. In the general case we first determine $L$. $L$ equals the order quantity divided by the receipt rate; $L = Q/I$. Now, components are used up over the period of time a delivery takes place. The number of units used up equals $L$ multiplied by the daily use rate, $U$. Thus, the total use during the delivery period equals $(Q/I)U$. In our numerical example, $U = 1$, $Q = 10$ and $I = 5$.

The maximum stock is the stock which is on the premises just after the last delivery (in the example, after day two). Prior to this time $U(Q/I)$ units have been used up. Thus, the maximum stock is equal to the amount delivered throughout the delivery period minus the total use during the delivery period.

$$\text{Maximum stock} = Q - \left(\frac{UQ}{I}\right) = Q\left(1 - \frac{U}{I}\right)$$

Since the average stock is half the maximum stock:

$$\text{Average stock} = \frac{Q}{2}\left(1 - \frac{U}{I}\right)$$

Considering holding, reorder and total costs:

$$H = \frac{Q}{2}\left(1 - \frac{U}{I}\right)hc$$

$$R = \left(\frac{D}{Q}\right)rc$$

$$T = \frac{Q}{2}\left(1 - \frac{U}{I}\right)hc + \left(\frac{D}{Q}\right)rc \qquad (3.8)$$

The optimal order quantity, $Q^*$, is given by:

$$Q^* = \sqrt{\frac{2Drc}{hc(1 - U/I)}} \qquad (3.9)$$

Applying the data from section 3.1, where the annual demand is for 10,000 units, the use rate over 365 days is approximately twenty seven units per day. At least twenty seven units must be delivered per day for production to take place. By reference to equation 3.8 it will be seen that as $I$ increases (from a minimum value of twenty seven units) the ratio $U/I$ decreases and hence the possibility of lowering holding costs is reduced.

## 3.5 A SIMULATION MODEL

Stock control often cannot be analysed exactly. As real situations are complex and variables like demand and lead time are subject to random disturbances, it is often necessary to use a simulation model to predict what might happen. Provided a sufficient number of trials or iterations are completed, it is possible to arrive at policy recomendations as the optimal solutions converge upon certain long run values. In our model we apply the *Monte Carlo* method. This is a procedure for generating random samples in such a way that they conform to a designated probability distribution. Our model will involve a small number of possible events and a simplified probability distribution.

Consider the stock control problem of the storage depots of British Coal. Storage depots all round the UK are used to maintain supplies of equipment to the mines. Consider one item—the bits used in drilling equipment in mining. The storage depots can obtain their supplies at short notice, usually within one day. The lead time, then, is one day. The demand for bits is highly variable. Suppose from past experience the levels of demand are distributed as in Table 3.1. This data is to be used in estimating future demand. Our problem is to determine when the storage depots should

*Table 3.1: Data on past levels of daily demand*

| | | | |
|---|---|---|---|
| Level of demand | 40 to 60 | 60 to 80 | 80 to 100 |
| Percentage of days | 40% | 40% | 20% |

renew their order for supplies. The average levels of demand, within each range, are fifty, seventy and ninety units. On the basis of these figures the expected *daily* demand equals sixty-six units; the expected *annual* demand is for 24,090 units. Suppose the holding cost, *hc*, is £0.2 per bit *per day* and the cost of each reorder, *rc*, is £40. Applying the basic model, the optimal order quantity is 162 units. Recall from equation 3.4 that the optimal order quantity is obtained when

$$Q^* = \sqrt{(2Drc)/hc}$$

hence

$$Q^* = \sqrt{(2 \times 24{,}090 \times 40)/(365 \times 0.2)}$$

= 162 units. It follows that 24,090/162 orders per year are needed to meet demand, that is $N = 149$. An order needs to be placed once every 2.4 days when the basic model is applied.

The question which is raised by uncertain demand is *when* precisely a reorder should take place. Suppose the cost of being out of stock (backorders) is £10 per day for each unit of

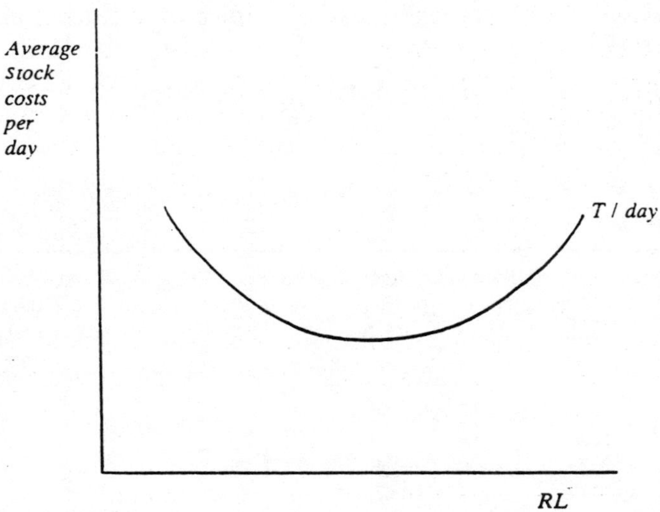


*Figure 3.6: Relationship between reorder level and average daily stock cost*

negative stocks (this could be the cost of lost production which the depots 'internalize') and that supplies arrive in batches of 162 units. In order to know when replacements need to take place we need to find the appropriate stock level to 'trigger' replacements. This stock level is known as the *reorder level*. If the reorder level is set too low stock-outs would be frequent. If it is set too high holding costs would be excessive. The higher the reorder level, the higher is the average level of stocks. Figure 3.6 concerns the relationship between reorder levels, *RL*, and average stock management costs per day. A computer program is helpful in determining the minimum point on the curve.

## PROGRAM 3.3

Different reorder levels are set by the user and costs are calculated over 365 iterations. Several values of *RL* must be entered before the least cost solution can be found. Table 3.2 presents the results of a simulation over just six iterations for $RL = 66$. The fluctuation in average daily costs to date continues until a very large number of iterations have been completed. In order to obtain a time plot of the data, insert as line 175:

```
PRINT; N; '...'; Q; '...'; D; '...'; INT (H);
'...'; R; '...'; B;'...'; INT (T/N)
```

*Table 3.2: Simulation of stock management cost data for RL = 66 (time plot)*

| Day (N) | Quantity of bits at the beginning of the day | Demand for bits, day N | Holding costs, day N | Reordering costs, day N | Stock out costs, day N | Average daily cost to date |
|---|---|---|---|---|---|---|
| 1 | 200 | 70 | 40 | 0 | 0 | 40 |
| 2 | 130 | 90 | 26 | 40 | 0 | 53 |
| 3 | 202 | 70 | 40 | 0 | 0 | 48 |
| 4 | 132 | 50 | 26 | 0 | 0 | 43 |
| 5 | 82 | 90 | 16 | 40 | 80 | 62 |
| 6 | 162 | 70 | 32 | 0 | 0 | 50 |

Figure 3.7 may be referred to in support of Program 3.3.

```
 10 REM 3.3
 20 CLS
 30 T=0:Q=200:R=0:H=0:B=0
 40 INPUT "ENTER THE VALUIE OF RL ";RL
 50 CLS
 60 FOR N = 1 TO 365
 70 X = 100*RND(1)
 80 IF X<40 THEN D = 50
 90 IF X>=40 AND X<80 THEN D = 70
100 IF X>=80 THEN D = 90
110 H = .2*Q: STOCK = Q - D
120 IF STOCK <= 0 THEN STOCK = 0: B=10*(D-Q):GOTO 150
130 B=0
140 IF STOCK > RL THEN R = 0: GOTO 170
150 STOCK = STOCK + 162
160 R=40
170 T=T+H+R+B
180 Q=STOCK
195 NEXT
200 PRINT
220 AV = T/(N-1)
225 PRINT "AVERAGE DAILY STOCK COST"
230 PRINT "GIVEN RL = ";RL;" IS ";AV
240 STOP
250 REM *** IBM ***
260 REM LINE 70:-
270 RANDOMIZE X:X = 100*RND(1)
```

Line 30: Initializes the data.

Line 40: The program user determines the reorder level.

Lines 45 to 54: To save time typing, these lines can be omitted.

Line 60: Calculations over 365 days begin

Line 70: A random number between 0 and 99.99 is selected

LInes 80 to 100: Demand is determined by the random number.

Line 110: Holding costs for day $N$ and end of day stocks are determined.

Lines 120 and 140: Alternative routes through the program and their associated costs are determined.

Line 150: Stock is increased unless stock $> RL$.

Line 170: Total costs to date are calculated.

Line 180: The quantity of units for the next day depends on the end of day stock.

Line 195: The program loops back unless $N = 365$

Line 220: Average costs over 365 days are calculated.

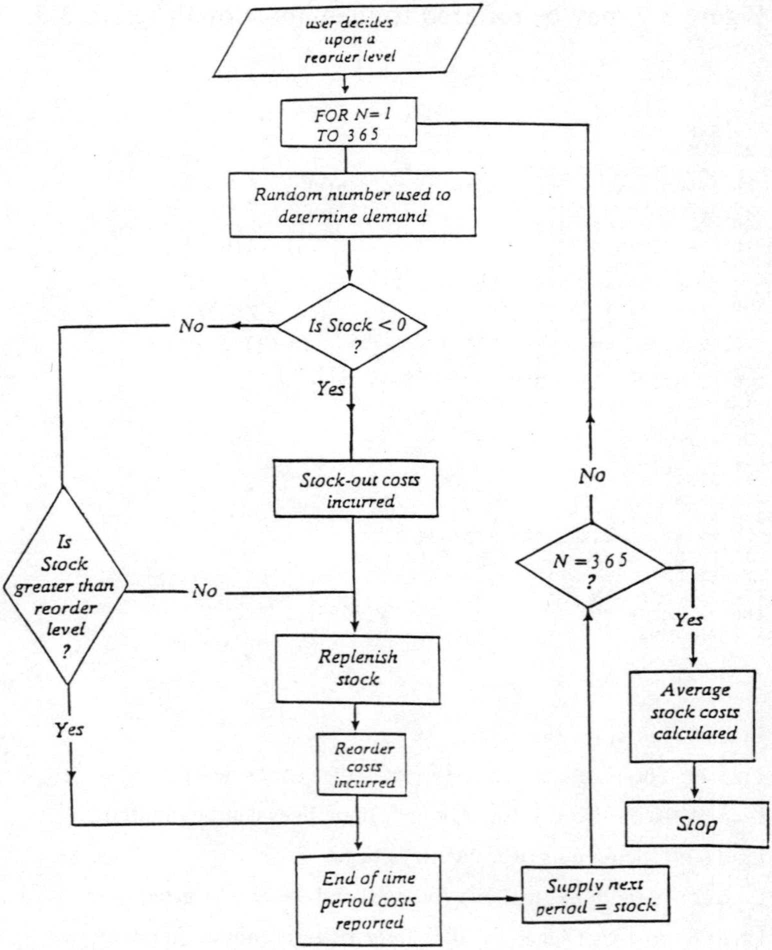


*Figure 3.7: Flow diagram illustrating the determination of average stock costs using a simulation model*

## SUMMARY

1. Stock control models are widely applicable and focus upon an issue which has long been the concern of economists—the efficient use of resources.
2. The most important elements in stock control models are:

(i) the demand, $D$, for items per unit of time
(ii) the holding costs, $hc$, per unit per period of time
(iii) the reordering cost, $rc$, per reorder.

The aim of the basic model is to determine the optimum size, $Q^*$, of the order quantity:

$$Q^* = \sqrt{\frac{2Drc}{hc}}$$

3. When problems become complex it is useful to apply computers to reach solutions. In nearly all cases the more complex models involve an extension of the basic model.
4. There are many instances when firms accept that stock-outs must occur because holding costs are so high. 'Negative stocks' can be incorporated into the model with little difficulty but a decision must be taken on the percentage of time a particular item will be out of stock.
5. Simulation models are an effective means of costing alternative policies when variables like demand are randomly determined. Within a computer program various routes may be followed. Simulation models are very useful in gathering information which otherwise could only be obtained through costly experience.

## FURTHER READING

Baumol (1977) explains how the disciplines of management science and economics can usefully exchange ideas. Dorfman (1968) illustrates how a training in economics is of value in operations analysis. Cohen (1985) provides a text in operations analysis for readers with little mathematics background. Dennis and Dennis (1986) have written an excellent low price book plus accompanying software for use with the IBM personal computer and compatibles such as the Amstrad 1512. Lewis (1981) is useful specifically on inventory models. McLaughlin and Pickhardt (1979) is recommended as a general text.

# 4 Production Functions

In this chapter, empirical studies of production are applied. They should help to provide a greater understanding of the physical form of production relationships and the nature of many production decisions within firms. Section 4.1 concerns additive functions, Section 4.2 neoclassical or 'continuous substitution' functions and Sections 4.3 to 4.8 linear functions. Finally in Section 4.9 a comparison is made between neoclassical and linear production functions.

## 4.1 ADDITIVE FUNCTIONS

Functions of the form:

$$Y = aX_1^{\alpha} + bX_2^{\beta} \tag{4.1}$$

are described as 'additive'; $Y$ = output, $X_1$, $X_2$ = inputs, $\alpha$ and $\beta$ are production coefficients, $a$ and $b$ are positive constants. Output is a function of the cumulative total of the inputs used. The inputs are simple substitutes for each other rather than complements since there is no 'interaction' reflecting the multiplication of inputs (by contrast, see the functions 4.3 and 4.4). Given the form of equation 4.1, the relationship $dY/dX_1$, for instance, is not affected by the value of $X_2$.

Often in manufacture joint products are produced. For example, consider the manufacture of animal feedstuffs. Animal feedstuffs are mixtures of raw materials containing various nutrients: protein, carbohydrate, fibre, etc. Protein is one of the most important value enhancing inputs and it may be provided by a variety of raw materials: soya, wheat, barley and so on. Total protein input is measured by addition of the amounts of each input fed. Soya is rich in protein (48.5 per cent by weight), wheat feed is less so (15.5 per cent by weight). Thus, protein input is counted in the same way as humans count their total calorie intake. (The data used in this section are drawn from the Open University (1981b).) As relative raw material prices change the optimum mix changes. Animal feedstuffs manufacturers, such as BOCM Silcock the market leader, are anxious to increase the growth-enhancing qualities of their products whilst holding down costs and meeting a number of production constraints. BOCM select from eighty possible raw materials and sell approximately 110 different products. BOCM as a consumer of raw materials may be modelled using an approach developed by Lancaster (1966, 1979). Following Lancaster, products are purchased not because they offer a single well-defined service but because they provide a complex bundle of characteristics or attributes; a joint production function applies. Goods may be regarded as intermediate inputs in the production of the basic attributes individuals and manufacturers want. Figure 4.1 involves just two attributes: carbohydrate and protein, which are supplied by three raw materials. Barley is high in carbohydrate whilst soya is high in protein; *b*, *w* and *s* denote the quantities of carbohydrate and protein obtained from one tonne of barley, wheat feed and soya. In the Open University study, the price of soya is £150 per tonne, wheat feed is £95 per tonne and barley is £100 per tonne. Considering just one of the objectives of a foodstuffs manufacturer: to increase the protect content, soya is preferred to wheat feed since protein is supplied in the ratio 48.5/15.5 whilst its cost is in the ratio 150/95. When several objectives are considered in the practical solution of problems of this kind, linear programming is used.

Considering the general form of the Lancaster model, there are *n* product characteristics and *m* different inputs. For each product characteristic, an additive function of the

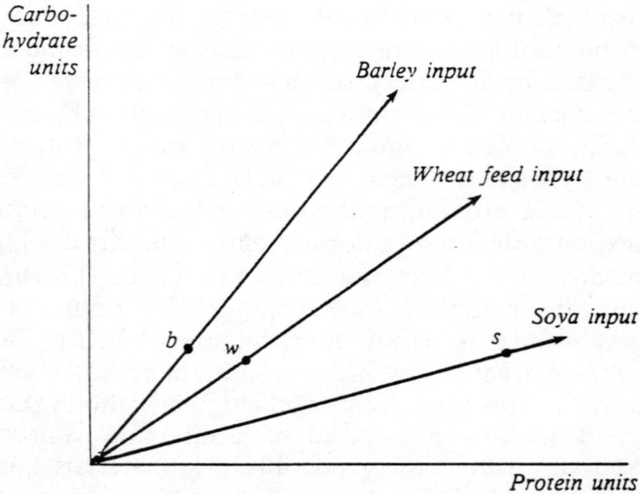


*Figure 4.1: Characteristics of food inputs*

form:

$$Y_i = \sum_{j=1}^{m} a_{ij} X_j \qquad (4.2)$$

applies, where $Y_i$ = $i$th product characteristic, $i = 1, 2, \ldots, n$ and $X_j$ = $j$th input, where $j = 1, 2, \ldots, m$. The $a_{ij}$ coefficients are known as input-output coefficients since they refer to the quantity of a particular characteristic obtained from a given input, for example the quantity of protein per unit of soya.

For various reasons, food inputs are unlikely to serve as such simple substitutes for each other as might be suggested by the food characteristics data. In particular, one input is likely to become progressively less satisfactory when it is combined in larger quantities with other inputs because of diminishing returns to the variable input. The model applies to the choice between alternative inputs in the search for the best means of satisfying the various nutritional requirements, rather than to the food input/livestock growth relationship.

## 4.2 COBB-DOUGLAS AND CES FUNCTIONS

Earl O. Heady, an agricultural economist, conducted control

experiments on pigs belonging to three size intervals to determine the optimum diet. Farmers typically changed diets for sound nutritional reasons about three times in each animal's lifetime. A diet high in protein was needed and was fed to young pigs when they were in their growing stage, whilst a high carbohydrate diet was fed close to marketing. Despite this biological constraint, considerable scope for substitution between inputs was found possible in all three age groups. Given the aim to feed a low cost diet, how could solutions to the problem be found?

Heady's study (1957) was carried out on 302 pigs in weight intervals 34–75 pounds, 75–150 pounds and 150–250 pounds. Observations on weight gain were used to estimate market value as a function of soya and corn. The results obtained are given below, where WG denotes weight gain or *absolute growth* from some initial value, $S$ is soya bean input and $C$ is corn input, measured in pounds per pig. The figures in brackets below the relevant coefficients refer to the $t$ values.

$$\text{34–75 lb weight interval } WG = 1.605S^{0.30}C^{0.53} \quad (4.3)$$
$$(14.3) \quad (19)$$
$$\text{75–150 lb weight interval } WG = 0.714S^{0.14}C^{0.77} \quad (4.4)$$
$$(8.7) \quad (31)$$

The exponents of $S$ and $C$ indicate the relative importance for weight gain of protein input in young pigs, whilst older pigs grow more by weight when fed carbohydrate. Whatever the precise diet fed, the general relationship between food input and weight is as shown in Figure 4.2. Diminishing returns to *scale* apply as well as to the variable factor input.

The first problem we set ourselves is how the least cost diet can be found for animals of a particular size interval. The common textbook approach is to apply Lagrange's method. This involves a procedure where a function is maximized (using calculus) subject to a resource constraint. The general form of functions (4.3) and (4.4), which are commonly known as Cobb-Douglas functions, is:

$$WG = AS^{\alpha}C^{\beta} \quad (4.5)$$

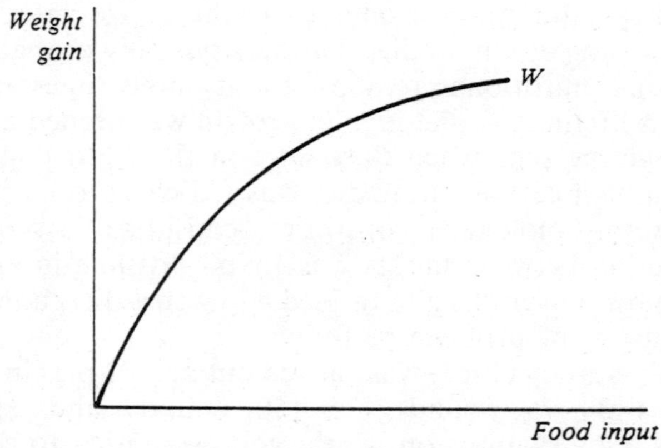


*Figure 4.2: Relationship between food inputs and weight gain*

where $\alpha$ and $\beta$ are the production coefficients, $WG$, $S$ and $C$ are variables and $A$ is a positive constant. Equation 4.5 specifies the objective function. Suppose the *budget constraint*, that is the limit on the resources available, is:

$$B = pcC + psS \tag{4.6}$$

$B$ is the constraint, $pc$ and $ps$ are the prices of corn and soya respectively. Maximizing (4.5) subject to (4.6) involves fairly sophisticated calculus but the principle involved can be illustrated using Figure 4.3. The figure concerns the problem under discussion. Maximizing $WG$ given the budget constraint involves maximizing the difference between $TR$ and $TC$ for a given food input. Since market value is closely related to pig weight, the total revenue function has the same shape as the weight gain: food input relationship. The total cost function shows cost increases at a constant rate for each increase in food input. The function is based on the assumption that a fixed combination of corn to soya is fed to pigs belonging to a particular weight interval irrespective of the total amount fed. It will be shown that, for a particular weight interval, the optimal combination of inputs is the same whether a small or a large amount is fed. Maximising weight gain given the budget constraint involves finding the ratio of $C$ to $S$ which enables the manufacturer to obtain the largest value for the objective function. Inefficient diets involve higher costs for a given value of the objective function. For pigs in the smallest size interval, if we set $ps = 2$ and $pc = 1$, the optimal ratio of soya to corn is $0.27S:1C$. Setting the budget arbitrarily at twenty units, $C = 12.9$, $S = 3.6$. These results can be shown to apply using Program 4.1.

Consider next the problem of determining the optimal budget. In terms of Figure 4.3 this corresponds to the diet where the gap between the revenue and cost functions is greatest and the gradients have the same slope. Relaxing the budget constraint, a gain in growth may be possible at a cost which is less than the gain in revenue. The function (4.5) exhibits non-constant returns to scale since, whichever weight interval is considered, $(\alpha + \beta) < 1$. Nevertheless, the original situation is non-optimal. To determine the optimal budget, the market value of weight gain must be known. Assume that each unit of weight gain has a market value of four pounds sterling. By Lagrange's method, or by using Program 4.1, it can be shown that the optimal budget applies when $C = 27.8$, $S = 7.7$. Let us now pause for a moment to try to assess the method which has been employed. The budget constraint is expressed in terms of monetary units, the objective function is in terms of physical units. Is there a problem of different

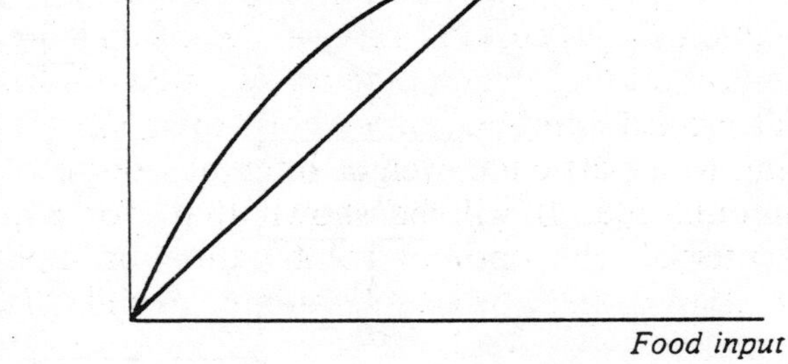


*Figure 4.3: Relationship between TR and TC assuming inputs are fed in a constant combination*

dimensions here? There is not. The budget constraint simply sets a limit on the resources which can be used, thereafter, all calculations are in physical units. If the budget constraint is relaxed, a monetary value is placed on both the product and the inputs used and the maximum profit solution is found.

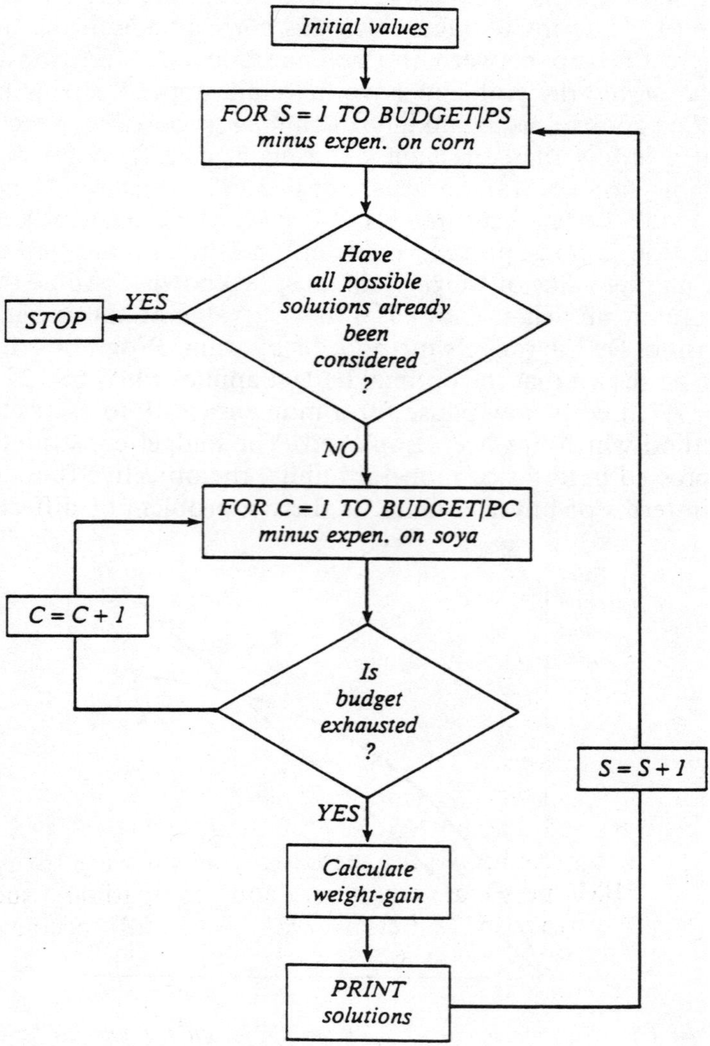


*Figure 4.4: Flow diagram for use with Program 4.1*

## PROGRAM 4.1

Figure 4.4. shows how Program 4.1 works. The program is based on the 'nested loop' principle. It is useful when a large number of inputs are involved. Nested loops involve the following programming procedure:

FOR $X = 1$ TO . . . .<br>
FOR $Y = 1$ TO . . .<br>
FOR $Z = 1$ TO .<br>
VALUE OF FUNCTION ($F$)<br>
NEXT $Z$ . .<br>
NEXT $Y$ . . .<br>
NEXT $X$ . . . .

The value of the function is determined for all values of $X, Y$ and $Z$ subject to the limit set by the budget constraint. To begin with, $X$ and $Y$ are set equal to one and all values of the function corresponding to the feasible values of $Z$ are determined. The program operates within the innermost loop. Next, with $X$ set equal to one, $Y$ is increased to two and all the feasible solutions with $F$ dependent on $Z$ are determined. In terms of the animal foodstuffs problem, as one input becomes larger the degree to which other inputs can be increased from their minimal values is reduced.

```
 10 REM4.1
 20 REM WEIGHT GAIN = REVENUE
 30 REM EACH UNIT OF WEIGHTGAIN ADDS `4 REVENUE
 40 REM THUS, PROFIT=4*WEIGHTGAIN-BUDGET
 60 CLS
 80 PRINT"IT....SOYA....CORN...WEIGHTG. ..PROFIT"
 90 ps=2:pc=1:M=1.605:a=.297:b=.533
 95 REM M = A in equation 4.5, a = alpha, b = beta
100 ITERATION = 0
110 BUDGET = 20
120 FOR S=1 TO (BUDGET/ps)-pc*1 STEP .2
130 FOR C=1 TO (BUDGET/pc) -S*ps STEP .2
140 IF (C*pc+S*ps) < BUDGET THEN NEXT C
150 ITERATION = ITERATION + 1
160 WEIGHTG = M*S^a*C^b
170 PRINT;ITERATION;"......"INT(100*S)/100;".....";
180 PRINT;INT(100*C)/100;"....";INT(100*WEIGHTG)/100;
190 PRINT;"...."; INT(100*4*WEIGHTG)/100 - BUDGET
200 A$ = INKEY$(0): IF A$="" THEN 200
210 NEXT S
220 STOP
230 REM *** IBM ***
240 REM LINE 200:-
250 A$ = INKEY$: IF A$="" THEN 200
```

Line 90: Initializes the data.

Line 110: The initial budget size. This is to be increased by the user subsequently in the search for the optimal budget.

Line 120: The limit to the value of $S$ depends on the budget, $ps$ and the expenditure on other inputs. STEP sizes of 0.2 are used in reaching solutions.

Line 140: If the budget is not exhausted for given values of $S$ and $C$ the next value of $C$ is selected.

Lines 170 to 190: Solutions to two decimal places are displayed. The computer reads mathematical expressions from left to right but firstly it calculates the value of all terms in brackets. In line 170, 100 * $S$ is calculated, then the integer value of 100 * $S$ is obtained and finally division by 100 takes place to return a solution to two decimal places.

N.B. (1) The *exact* ratio of $S/C$ for $ps = 1$ can be found by using much smaller STEP intervals.
(2) Whatever the budget, the optimum ratio of inputs remains the same. (Within each weight interval, the function applied in line 160 is homogeneous).

## PROGRAM 4.2

This program focuses upon the degree to which inputs may be substituted for each other following a price change. A given weight gain, $WG$, is assumed and the alternative combinations of inputs are costed. It is imagined that manufacturers have decided upon the weight gain to aim for and that they wish to consider the alternative combinations of inputs which will achieve this target. The objective is to *minimize* cost. Consider the following rearrangement of equation 4.5:

$$C^{\beta} = \frac{WG}{AS^{\alpha}}$$

$$C = \left(\frac{WG}{AS^{\alpha}}\right)^{1/\beta} \qquad (4.7)$$

In Program 4.2 equation 4.7 is stated as:

$$C = (WG/(A * S\uparrow.297))\uparrow 1.876$$

In using such complicated expressions within computer programs, considerable care must be taken over the placing of brackets. The program provides solutions for $WG = 9.29$, $A = 1.605$, $pc = 1.0$ and $ps = 2$. The least-cost combination of inputs is found when $C = 12.9$ and $S = 3.6$:—a ratio of 0.27 units of soya to corn. This ratio is the same as when we considered the *maximization* of an objective function. The solution corresponds to $\phi$ in Figure 4.5. If input prices are changed so that $pc = 2$ and $ps = 2$, it will be found that the optimal quantity of corn to soya is 10.15 to 5.6: a ratio of $0.55S/C$. Thus, if the relative price of soya is halved, the ratio of soya used to corn is exactly doubled. The *elasticity of substitution* of corn for soya (defined simply as the percentage change in the ratio of inputs used in production divided by the percentage change in their prices), denoted by $e_s$, is equal to one. It should be noted that the property $e_s = 1$ applies to all functions of the form given by equation 4.5.

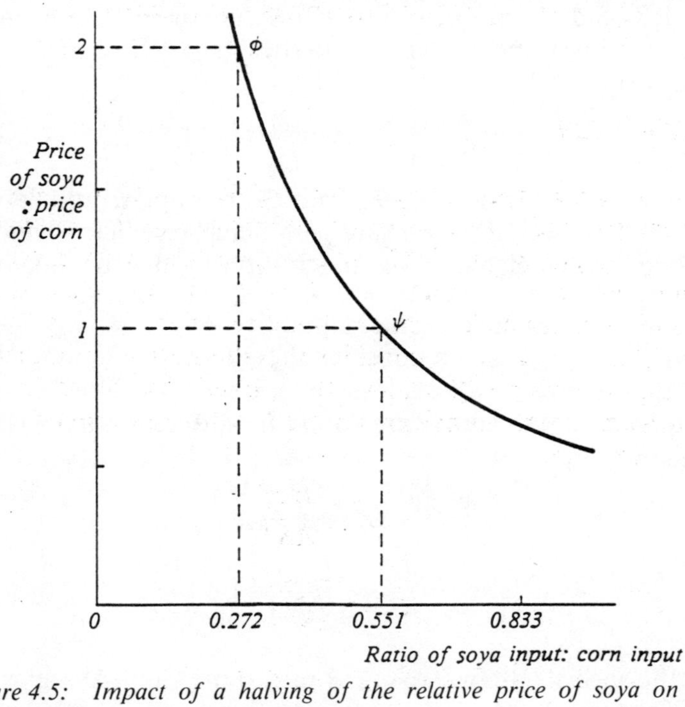


*Figure 4.5: Impact of a halving of the relative price of soya on the soya:corn ratio*

```
 10 REM4.2
 20 CLS
 40 WG=9.29:A=1.605:ps=2:pc=1
 50 PRINT"SOYA   CORN   COST:- ps=";ps;" pc=";pc
 55 PRINT
 60 FOR S = 1 TO 20 STEP.2
 70 C = (WG/(A*S^.297))^1.876
 80 PRINT;S;"......";INT(100*C)/100;
 90 PRINT;".....";INT(100*(S*ps+C*pc))/100
100 A$ = INKEY$(0):IF A$="" THEN 100
110 NEXT S
120 STOP
130 REM *** IBM ***
140 REM LINE:- 100
150 A$ = INKEY$: IF A$="" THEN 100
```

## PROGRAM 4.3

Program 4.3 is used to calculate different values of a constant elasticity of substitution (generally known as CES) function for various inputs of $L$ and $K$, the 'factor' inputs. A single loop is employed. The program may be used in helping to understand the properties of CES functions. We begin by considering some of these properties. The CES function has the form:

$$Q = A(DK^{-\rho} + (1 - D)L^{-\rho})^{-(1/\rho)} \tag{4.8}$$

where $A$ is a constant, $K$ and $L$ are capital and labour, $\rho > -1$, $D < 1$, $D$ is a 'share parameter' (see below) and $\rho$ is related to the elasticity of substitution by the formula:

$$e_s = \frac{1}{(1 + \rho)} \tag{4.9}$$

The marginal products are found by differentiation. Thus:

$$\text{capital: } \frac{\partial Q}{\partial K} = \frac{D}{A^{\rho}} \left(\frac{Q}{K}\right)^{(1+\rho)} \tag{4.10}$$

$$\text{labour: } \frac{\partial Q}{\partial L} = \frac{(1 - D)}{A^{\rho}} \left(\frac{Q}{L}\right)^{(1+\rho)} \tag{4.11}$$

In the special case where $e_s = 1$, $\rho \approx 0$ the Cobb Douglas and CES functions yield the same solutions and equations 4.10

and 4.11 simplify to:

$$\frac{\partial Q}{\partial K} = D\left(\frac{Q}{K}\right) \tag{4.12}$$

$$\frac{\partial Q}{\partial L} = (1 - D)\left(\frac{Q}{L}\right) \tag{4.13}$$

which means that the marginal products are a constant fraction of the average products. Four of the properties of CES functions are:

(1) that the marginal products of capital (MPK) and labour (MPL) are as given by equations 4.10 and 4.11;
(2) $K(\text{MPK}) + L(\text{MPL}) = Q$, and hence the sum of the 'factor payments' when marginal productivity theory is applied, is equal to the value of $Q$;
(3) the 'relative shares', defined by $K(\text{MPK})/Q$ and $L(\text{MPL})/Q$, are equal to the share parameters $D$ and $(1 - D)$;
(4) the function exhibits constant returns to scale.

Proposition (1) applies to the input of labour, for instance, since we can see from the print-out of columns 3 and 4 that equation 4.11 holds true (note in the program how the solutions for column 4 are obtained and that the difference between two solutions in column 3 measures the increment in output). By comparison of columns 3 and 5 proposition (2) is confirmed. Proposition (3) can be shown to apply by simple arithmetic. For instance, if $L = 2$, $\mathrm{d}Q/\mathrm{d}L = 3.53$ and $(3.53 \times 2)/14.11 = (1 - D) =$ labour's share parameter when $D = 0.5$. Finally, constant returns to scale can be shown by simply doubling or trebling input values and noting the effect upon output.

Lines 130–150: When solutions are displayed an exact correspondence between $\mathrm{d}Q/\mathrm{d}L$, using the expression here for MPL, and $(Q(L) - Q(L - 1))$, the third column of figures reported, will not be found. The discrepancy is explained by the fact that *discrete* values of $L$ are used. If, however, an average of two of the differences in $Q$ is taken this will approximate the reported value of $\mathrm{d}Q/\mathrm{d}L$. For instance, if $L = 3$, $\mathrm{d}Q/\mathrm{d}L = 2.88$. Considering $L = 2$, $L = 3$ and $L = 4$, $Q(2) = 14.11$, $Q(3) = 17.29$, $Q(4) = 19.97$, the average increase is $(3.18 + 2.68)/2 = 2.93$.

```
 10 REM4.3
 20 REM IF p = .001 CES = COBB DOUGLAS
 30 REM IF p = 0 DIVISION BY ZERO
 40 REM p > -1
 60 D=.5:A=1:K=100:p=.001
 70 PRINT"L.....K....Q......dQ/dL....(MPL*L+MPL*K)"
 80 PRINT
 90 FOR L = 1 TO 20
100 Q = A*(D*K^-p +(1-D)*L^-p)^(-1/p)
110 MPL = ((1-D)/A^p)*(Q/L)^(1+p)
120 MPK = (D/A^p)*(Q/K)^(1+p)
130 PRINT;L;"....";K;"....";INT(100*Q)/100;".....";
140 PRINT;INT(100*MPL)/100;"....";
150 PRINT;INT(100*(K*MPK+L*MPL))/100
160 NEXT L
170 STOP
```

## 4.3 LINEAR PRODUCTION FUNCTIONS

In Sections 4.3 to 4.8 we examine the choice between several inputs in the production of two or more commodities. Linear programming (LP) is applied. Linear programming concerns the maximization or minimization of a function when there are constraints upon the resources available for production and upon the degrees of substitution between inputs. In the following sections the focus is upon maximization of a function but the arguments apply equally to the case of minimization. In Section 4.4 graphical methods and the 'primal problem' are considered. This provides a useful basis for understanding the general form of solutions to LP problems. We then consider the nature of the 'dual' in LP. The issues will be discussed mainly by reference to coffee production.

## 4.4 THE GRAPHICAL METHOD

Several major coffee manufacturers either own coffee plantations or purchase coffee beans on the forward exchange markets in order to minimize uncertainty over future prices. They resort to spot purchase on the open market only in exceptional circumstances. Coffee is typically a blend of beans from different species and sources. Three of the important beans are the arabica, the robusta and the liberica. Suppose to begin with only two kinds of coffee are manufactured: premium and standard, and we consider a single manufacturer. Further, let us suppose consumers are conservative and will not accept any variation in the blend of beans used in the production of each product. If our manufacturer wishes to blend beans in different proportions to those which are customarily adopted, a new product must be introduced. If premium coffee is manufactured, beans in the ratio 3 : 2 : 1 (that is, three arabica to two robusta to one liberica) must be used. Standard coffee requires beans in the ratio 1 : 5 : 1. In terms of weight, a smaller amount of coffee is extracted for use from the robusta beans than the arabica and liberica beans hence the sum of the numbers 3, 2, 1 and 1, 5, 1 is not the same. Let the stocks currently available for production consist of 6 million tons of arabica, $a$, 10 million tons of robusta, $r$, and 8 million tons of liberica, $l$. The manufacturer can sell each unit of premium coffee, $p$, at a net profit of £4 and each unit of standard coffee, $s$, at a net profit of £3. The figures are net since plantation, purchasing, manufacturing and distribution costs have been taken into account in arriving at the figures for profit.

Let us denote net profits by $\pi$. Profits depend on the amounts of $p$ and $s$ produced. All units produced can be sold. The aim is to maximize:

$$\pi = 4p + 3s \qquad (4.14)$$

subject to the constraints:

$$3p + s \leqslant 6 \qquad \text{(arabica)} \qquad (4.15)$$

$$2p + 5s \leqslant 10 \qquad \text{(robusta)} \qquad (4.16)$$

$$p + s \leqslant 8 \qquad \text{(liberica)} \qquad (4.17)$$

$$p \geqslant 0, \; s \geqslant 0$$

Equation 4.14 is the objective; equations 4.15 to 4.17 are the constraints. The trivial constraints $p \geqslant 0$, $s \geqslant 0$ are set to ensure that negative values are not included in the solutions.

The problem is illustrated in Figures 4.6, 4.7 and 4.8. Each linear inequality restricts the possible pair of values $(p, s)$ to one side of a line. For instance, the inequality $3p + s \leqslant 6$ restricts us to the region given by the triangle in Figure 4.6. Thus, equation 4.15 permits equality and inequality solutions

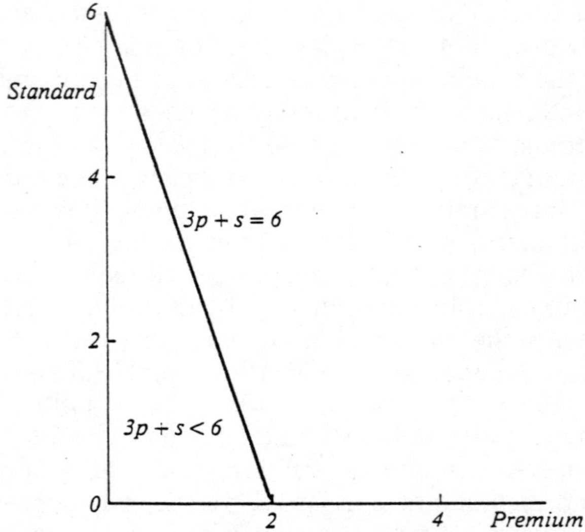


*Figure 4.6:* *Production limits: the arabica constraint*

but the total demand for arabica ($3p + s$) must not exceed the supply available. Hence, the left-hand side of equations 4.15, 4.16 and 4.17 refer to the demand for inputs, the right-hand side to supplies.

When all three constraints are taken into account it can be seen that production is limited to the area bounded by the three constraints. The area defined by ABC in Figure 4.8 is known as the *feasible region*. It contains all the values of ($s$, $p$) which are potential solutions to the linear-programming problem.

The first thing to note is that the liberica line is not an *effective* constraint. No matter what combinations of ($s$, $p$) are produced, there are spare liberica beans. Next, we consider the net profit levels associated with producing along the line $3p + 4s = 12$. This line is known as an 'isoprofit line' or contour. Any point along it corresponds to twelve units of profit: if three units of premium or four units of standard coffee or combinations along the line could be produced, twelve units of profit would obtained. But all points along this line lie outside the feasible region. If we construct a line parallel to this contour which just touches the boundary of

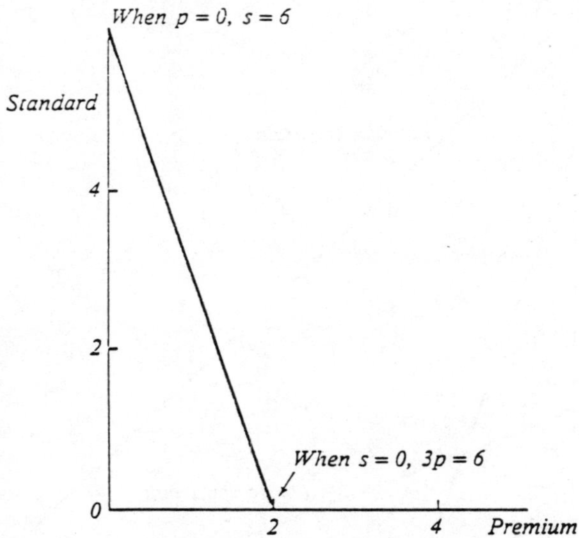


Figure 4.7: The arabica constraint

the feasible region, we will have constructed a line which defines the maximum profits obtainable. This line is shown as $\pi = 10.31$. The corner or vertex at B is known as the optimum solution. A feature of all linear-programming problems is that the optimum lies on the edge of the feasible region and usually at a vertex. This point helps us considerably when larger problems are tackled.

It is unnecessary to try to read off the coordinates of the optimal vertex from the graph. It is only necessary to know which lines are intersecting at the optimal vertex since we then find which constraints are effective. When constraints are effective, demands for inputs equal the supplies available and the inequality relationships are converted into equalities. Thus: $3p + s = 6$; $2p + 5s = 10$, and we find the optimal value of $p$ is 1.539 whilst the optimal value of $s$ is 1.385. The corresponding profit is $(1.539 \times 4 + 1.385 \times 3) = 10.31$. We may compare profit at B with profit at the vertexes A and C; at A, $\pi = 6$, at C, $\pi = 8$.

We know that spare units of liberica are available. Would it be worthwhile marketing a third product even if it is thought of as a low grade, low value product? If such a

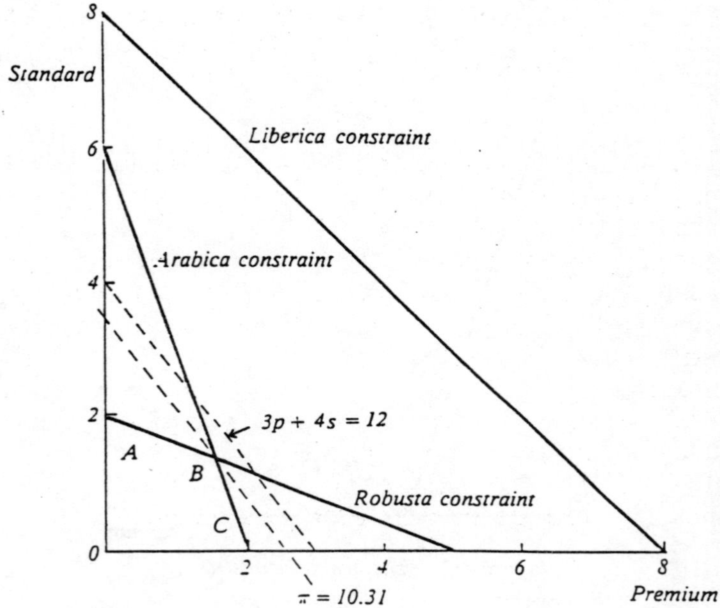


Figure 4.8: Revenue maximization—the primal solution

product was marketed, it might require inputs of the higher grade arabica and robusta beans. Given our assumption that beans are not purchased on the open market, this would require a reduction in the production of premium and standard coffee.

## 4.5 THREE VARIABLE MODELS

Let us call the proposed third product basic or $b$ and let its net profit = 2. Suppose this product requires the input of arabica, robusta and liberica in the ratio 1 : 1 : 2. If the third product is introduced, we would have a linear-programming problem with three variables where the aim is to mazimize:

$$\pi = 4p + 3s + 2b \qquad (4.18)$$

subject to:

$$3p + s + b \leqslant 6 \qquad \text{(arabica)} \qquad (4.19)$$

$$2p + 5s + b \leqslant 10 \quad \text{(robusta)} \tag{4.20}$$

$$p + s + 2b \leqslant 8 \quad \text{(liberica)} \tag{4.21}$$

$$p \geqslant 0,\ s \geqslant 0,\ b \geqslant 0$$

Figure 4.9 illustrates the constraints involved. Each of the constraints restricts the set of solutions $(p, s, b)$ to a region which is bounded by six planes. There are eight vertexes. For instance, at A we consider the constraint imposed by the availability of liberica beans: at the limit, four units of $b$ may be produced. At the vertex B we have the intersection of two planes: two constraints are effective. At B, $s$ equals $1\,^1/3$ hence, considering the liberica constraint, $b$ must be reduced to $3\,^1/3$. We can see this by noticing that $p = 0$ at $B$, hence the demand for liberica beans is for the production of $s$ and $b$; $[1(0) + 1(1\,^1/3) + 2(3\,^1/3)] = 8$. But what of the constraint imposed by robusta beans? At B the demand for robusta

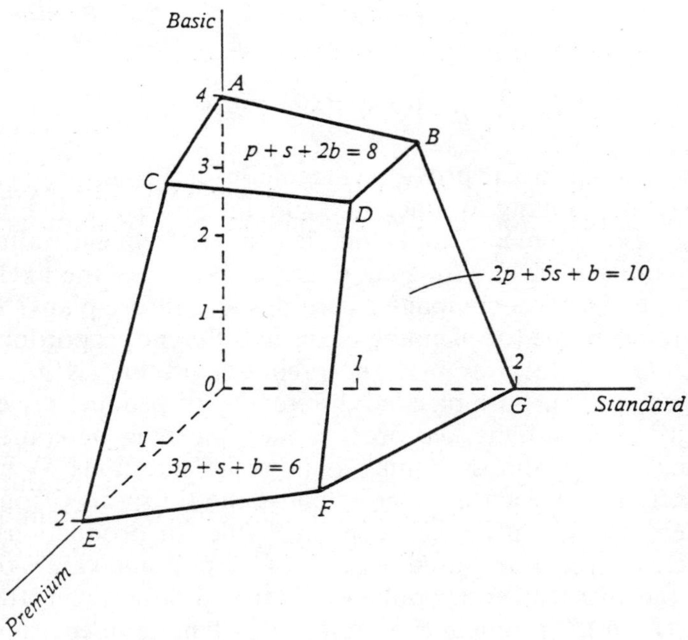


*Figure 4.9: The feasible area of production: three products, three constraints*

beans = [2(0) + 5(1 $^1/3$) + 1(3 $^1/3$)] = 10; hence the robusta constraint is effective. The equations corresponding to the vertex at B are: $2p + 5s + b = 10$; $p + s + 2b = 8$. Since $p = 0$, the coordinates at B are easily found and the solutions above are confirmed: $(p, s, b) = (0, 1\,^1/3, 3\,^1/3)$. The profit corresponding to these production levels is $\pi_\beta = 10.666$. As in the two-product model, profit is most likely to be maximized at one of the vertexes of the feasible region. When the simplex method is applied within computer programs to LP problems, a search takes place for an optimum by a comparison between all the feasible solutions. In the three-product, three-constraint model, with the exception of one vertex, all the feasible solutions involve two products. The exception is at D. It so happens that D is the most profitable solution, $\pi_D = 12.0$; $(p, s, b) = (0.571, 1.143, 3.143)$, but there is no reason why this is generally the case. Often, solutions in the several-product, several-constraint model involve 'slack variables' and zero values for certain products.

## 4.6 CONTINGENCY PLANNING

The data used in LP provide valuable information to management in planning for uncertain and unforeseeable circumstances. Environmental and climatic changes frequently alter the quantity of beans for manufacture. What are the likely consequences for a company's earnings and future plans? Is there much scope for blending beans in different proportions in *certain* products even if the premium product is never changed. If beans are blended differently, or product prices change in line with market forces, what is the likely outcome? LP enables an almost infinite number of questions to be considered. For each new set of constants (in terms of our problem, the quantities of beans available for production), coefficients (the inputs used per unit of output) and values of the objective function (values of the products on the market), an LP problem can be solved. Changes in environmental or market conditions need not *dictate* future plans. Given the anticipated market conditions and forecasts of coffee bean production, feasibility studies can be conducted before a decision is taken which will commit a manufacturer to a particular course of action. Alternative options can be evaluated simply be using different parameters in the solution of the LP problem.

Consider the following scenario. News comes in that the coffee crop is badly affected by frost. Supplies of robusta beans will be significantly lower than was expected. Imagine that management in the short term cannot alter the blend of beans used. Contracts with retailers have been entered into on quality, price, etc. The quantities to be supplied, however, have not been included in the contract since it was recognised that climatic factors are beyond human control. Before the supplies are known for certain, a simulation of the various possibilities could be performed. Suppose the question is asked 'how large a reduction in the supply of robusta beans will be needed to cause the production of any product to fall to zero?' The linear programming package available from University Software (1985), was used to answer this question. Equations 4.22 to 4.25 and the associated solutions form part of the output from the package. The objective function, coefficients of production and constants are the same as before except that the robusta constraint has been reduced from ten to 5.2 units. For all values of the robusta constant greater than 5.2 units it would be worth continuing production of all three products. When robusta equals 5.2 units, the standard product drops out of the optimal solution. Given the circumstances described, net profit would fall from twelve to 10.4 units.

$$\text{Max } \pi = 4p + 3s + 2b \tag{4.22}$$

Subject to:

$$3p + s + b \leqslant 6 \tag{4.23}$$

$$2p + 5s + b \leqslant 5.2 \tag{4.24}$$

$$p + s + 2b \leqslant 8 \tag{4.25}$$

Optimal solution: $(p, s, b) = (0.8, 0, 3.6)$

$$\pi = 10.4$$

## 4.7 COST MINIMISATION

In Section 4.1 BOCM as a manufacturer of animal foodstuffs was referred to in connection with Lancaster's theory of consumer behaviour (1966, 1979). His theory emphasises the importance of the characteristics of products in consumer choice. BOCM as a consumer of inputs aims to minimise its costs of production. The Open University study referred to (1981b) is useful for the great detail it provides on BOCM's production problem. Input prices change frequently. Several constraints must be satisfied in meeting production and nutritional demands. An LP package is used in the search for least cost solutions but what information other than on the feasible solutions is obtained? (We restrict ourselves for the time being to information in connection with the *primal* solutions).

First, let us begin by looking at the form of the problem to be solved. In the Open University study the objective function in the production of one of the products is:
Minimize 150 Soya + 100 Barley + , ..., + 75 Molasses
(The cost of soya is £150 per tonne, barley is £100 per tone, etc.) subject to the conditions:

| | |
|---|---|
| (Weight) | Soya + Barley + , ..., Molasses = 1 tonne |
| (Protein) | 48.5 Soya + 10.5 Barley + , ..., 3 Molasses $\geqslant$ 14% |
| (Fibre) | 5.0 Soya + 5.0 Barley + , ..., 0 Molasses $\geqslant$ 5% |
| (Max. Fat) | . . . $\leqslant$ 3% |

(The product must weigh one tonne in total, contain at least 14 per cent protein, by weight, five per cent fibre, etc.) The solution to this problem has much in common with the coffee example except that many more inputs and constraints are involved. Readers should also note the different types of constraints which apply. BOCM use a LP package to answer several questions which arise in day to day production. For instance, if particular inputs increase in price at which point is it no longer worth using them? What are the detailed nutritional implications of such decisions? When is it worth discontinuing the production of certain products altogether? BOCM's 'multi-mix' package enables questions to be asked involving comparisons *between* products. If a particular constraint is relaxed or becomes more stringent, for example an increase in the protein requirement from fourteen to fifteen per cent, what are the cost implications? The most interesting general conclusion which follows from these enquiries is that it is often necessary to reformulate an entire LP problem if parameter changes beyond a certain limit take place.

## 4.8 THE DUAL AND LINEAR PROGRAMMING

From the point of view of economics, solution for the dual is one of the most interesting features of linear programming. To illustrate the principles involved, let us return to the original two-product model of Section 4.4. It will be recalled that we began by assuming the resources available for production were constant. But what if one or more inputs could be increased? What would happen to the value of the objective function? Increased input of arabica or robusta beans, through purchases on the open market, would allow the relaxation of one of the constraints. Consider Figure 4.10. The figure illustrates an increase by one unit in the quantity of the arabica beans (the beans which most severely constrain production of the premium product). It can be seen that the optimal vertex is now at D; total profits increase to 11.387. Thus, the *marginal product* of one unit of arabica beans is $11.387 - 10.31 = 1.077$. To consider whether it would be worthwhile purchasing arabica beans on the open market, we simply compare the net profit gained with the cost of the market transaction.

The general form of the solution for dual values involves *minimizing* an objective function which is made up of the value of inputs used in production. Consider the inputs initially available for use in production. In order to maximize profits it is necessary to minimize costs. The costs which are elements of a linear programming problem are the *opportunity costs* of the inputs in production. The revised aim is to

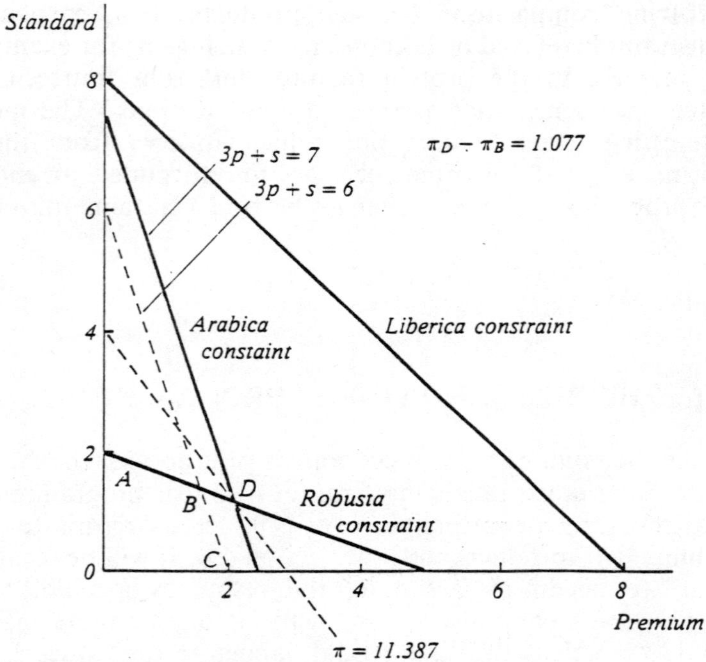


*Figure 4.10: The shadow value of one unit of arabica*

minimize $Z$, the cost function, given:

$$Z = 6V_1 + 10V_2 + 8V_3 \tag{4.26}$$

where $V_1$ is the value of arabica beans at the margin, $V_2$ is the value of robusta beans and $V_3$ is the value of liberica beans. We are concerned with marginal values and we expect that a change in the composition of production or in the inputs available might alter input values. For instance, we know that additional liberica beans would be of no use to our producer given production at the vertex B (or at D). Indeed, some liberica beans could be withdrawn from production without affecting production. Clearly, at the margin, $V_3 = 0$.

The constraints of dual problems are found by reference to the inputs which are required in the production of the two products. It will be recalled that beans in the ratio 3 : 2 : 1 are needed for production of the premium coffee and that beans in the ratio 1 : 5 : 1 are needed for standard coffee. Thus, our objective is to minimize:

$$Z = 6\,V_1 + 10\,V_2 + 8\,V_3 \tag{4.27}$$

subject to:

$$3\,V_1 + 2\,V_2 + 1\,V_3 \geqslant 4 \tag{4.28}$$

$$1\,V_1 + 5\,V_2 + 1\,V_3 \geqslant 3 \tag{4.29}$$

Equation 4.28 may be read as 'in order to obtain a net profit of 4 from the production of premium coffee, *at least* 3 units of arabica, 2 of robusta and 1 of liberica must be combined'. Before continuing, note the striking similarities and differences between the primal and dual problems.

| *Primal* | *Dual* |
|---|---|
| Max $4p + 3s$ | Min. $6\,V_1 + 10\,V_2 + 8\,V_3$ |

Subject to:

| | |
|---|---|
| $3p + 1s \leqslant 6$ | $3\,V_1 + 2\,V_2 + 1\,V_3 \geqslant 4$ |
| $2p + 5s \leqslant 10$ | $1\,V + 5\,V + 1\,V_3 \geqslant 3$ |
| $1p + 1s \leqslant 8$ | |

We know that $V_3 = 0$ but that $V_1$ and $V_2$ have positive 'shadow values' since the arabica and robusta constraints are effective whilst the liberica constraint is not. At the margin, net profits are accounted for only in terms of these inputs. Converting equations 4.28 and 4.29 into equalities, the solution for $V_1$ and $V_2$ is straightforward:

$$3\,V_1 + 2\,V_2 + 0 = 4$$

$$1\,V_1 + 5\,V_2 + 0 = 3$$

$V_1 = 1.077$; $V_2 = 0.385$. The value of arabica beans obtained by solving for the dual is the same as the value derived when the graphical method is applied. Moreover, considering the marginal value of the inputs, we find:

$$Z = 6\ (1.077) + 10\ (0.385) + 8\ (0)$$

$$= 10.31$$

Evidently, $Z = \pi$: the entire value of the net profits from production is accounted for by the value of the inputs used in production.

Before continuing it is worthwhile reconsidering the procedure which has been adopted. We assume that fixed coefficients were necessary in production. However, we have introduced the possibility of additional units of just *one* input. This allows profit to increase. But, given the assumption of fixed input proportions, how was an increase in production possible? From Figure 4.10, it is clear that at D there is an increase in the production of premium and a reduction in the production of standard coffee. This may be confirmed by reference to the revised primal solutions. The aim remains to maximize $(4p + 3s)$ but the effective constraints now take the form: $3p + s = 7$; $2p + 5s = 10$; $p$ increases from 1.539 to 1.923 and $s$ falls from 1.385 to 1.231. It is concluded that larger quantities of both the constraining inputs are not required for production to increase. The solution for the shadow values is a by-product of the decision on the combination of goods produced. LP can assist accountants and economists in finding out whether resources are used effectively and in recommendations on purchasing policy. Comparisons can be made between current policy and the policies which might be adopted if various constraints were relaxed.

## 4.9 LINEAR PROGRAMMING AND CONTINUOUS SUBSTITUTION PRODUCTION FUNCTIONS: HISTORICAL NOTE AND SOME COMPARISONS

Economic analysis provides many examples of the form taken by the scarcity problem, defined as the problem relating to resources which are both scarce and limited relative to the demands for them. In the context of production decisions, theories of decision making have developed against the background of physical and human resource data. In the history of economic thought, two distinct lines of enquiry have developed. One has its origins in Ricardian analysis, where the concept of diminishing returns is central; the other has its origins in the theory of Soviet type economies, where the problem is what goods should be produced, how they should be produced and what value should be placed on the resources used. LP shows how problems in cost accountancy might be viewed since costs do not consist only of inputs which are physically used up in production. The concept of opportunity cost is central to cost analysis. In different subjects, the mathematical concept of the dual is recognized and this has led to many strands of thought in economics, accountancy and engineering coming together. These developments have allowed writers in different disciplines to communicate in terms of a common language; the disciplines support each other. LP provides practical tools for analysis and calculation. The rules by which solutions are obtained (the algorithms) are applicable to a wide range of problems. In this chapter we have decided against describing the rules in detail as they are more adequately dealt with in specialist texts. Also, an LP program has not been included since it would need to be very long and several excellent packages are available; see, for instance, University Software (1985).

## SUMMARY

1. Production functions can be classified as additive, multiplicative or linear. In the case of additive functions there is no interaction reflecting the multiplication of inputs as with the Cobb-Douglas and CES functions. Linear production functions typically involve more than one product or production goal and physical constraints upon the objective function are specified.
2. When multiplicative functions have been used in empirical studies, it is commonly found that diminishing returns apply to the variable factor inputs, all other inputs being held constant.
3. Lagrange's method can be used to solve problems involving the maximization of a function subject to a budget constraint. Alternatively, a computer program involving the 'nested loop' principle may be employed. If the budget constraint is relaxed, it is often possible to obtain a larger

value of the objective function and profits can be increased.
4. When the focus is upon cost minimization using multiplicative functions an important concept is the elasticity of substitution.
5. The Cobb Douglas function is a special case of the CES function.
6. Graphical methods can be used to solve linear programming problems when there are two products and several constraints.
7. Constraints may be effective or non-effective. If they are non-effective they play no part in reaching solutions.
8. LP provides information for contingency planning by managers.
9. The dual represents one of the most interesting features of LP since the concepts of marginal values and opportunity costs apply.

## FURTHER READING

A concise account is provided by Heathfield (1971). Bosworth (1976) considers whether there exists a realistic theory of production. Johansen (1972) examines alternative concepts of the production function and considers their use in empirical work. Baumol (1977) may be referred to on the several different forms taken by linear programming. Laidler (1981) provides an introductory account of Lancaster's theory of consumer/producer choice. Cohen (1985) is recommended as an introduction to integer programming and University Software (1985) as a software package. Dorfman *et al* (1958) is possibly the strongest book on linear programming for students of economics. Lawler and Seddighi (1986) may be referred to on the mathematics and estimation of production functions. For an excellent but rather dated survey of the empirical literature see Walters (1963). Wallis (1979) considers econometric issues. For a report on price/cost/production relationships in the manufacture of animal feedstuffs, see the Price Commission (1978).

# 5 Uncertainty and the Firm

A distinction is drawn in economics between situations where decisions are taken involving risk and those taken in a state of uncertainty. If a decision maker is able to calculate the probability that a particular outcome will result if any given action is taken, then the decision model is a risk model. If a decision maker is unable to formulate the probabilities that specific outcomes will correspond to particular actions, but instead is only able to indicate the range of outcomes which might follow from any action, then the decision model is an uncertainty model.

Sections one to four of this chapter concern decision making within the firm in conditions of uncertainty. Sections five and six apply conditional probability analysis, specifically a Markov process model, to determine the shares of a market which might arise following a period of active competition between firms.

In the orthodox textbook model of the firm, uncertainty is kept in the background. This allows three or four variable models to be developed but it has the disadvantage that the number of decisions which are discussed are too few for the models to be realistic. In fact, the problem most often reduces to a single decision: the output to produce since, once output is determined, the corresponding price level and other variables follow automatically. Introductory textbook accounts are both simple and elegant. Following the marginal cost/marginal revenue rule price and output are determined. But the question of trade-offs between different objectives is seldom raised even through they are a central part of decision making in actual firms.

## 5.1 UNCERTAINTY AND PRICE FORMATION

In the first part of this chapter, at the cost of sacrificing very little in simplicity, an extra dimension is added to the decision process. The demand function used in calculating the optimal price is specified within a range of plausible values. Adding this complication allows the decision to rest between a relatively certain but low profit figure and a relatively uncertain but higher profit figure.

We begin by examining a firm which is a price maker. Its demand is uncertain but can be specified within limits. It is assumed that once a price level is set it must apply throughout the period of time to which the data relate. The variables used in the model are as follows:

$\pi$ = profit
$q$ = quantity of demand per period of time
$p$ = price level
$a$ = demand curve intercept
$b$ = gradient of the demand curve
c = unit costs
$s$ = stocks available for sale
$hc$ = unit cost of unsold stocks per period of time (holding cost)

$c$ and $hc$ will be assumed to be known in advance; $p$ and $s$ are under the control of the firm. The value of $a$ is assumed to lie within certain limits.

In the orthodox textbook model of the firm, solutions are obtained for $p$ and $q$ by finding the value of $q$ which maximizes $\pi$ in the equation:

$$\pi = q(p - c) \tag{5.1}$$

$qp$ is total revenue and $qc$ is total cost. In the model developed here, the problem is to find the value of $q$ which maximizes $\pi$ in the equation:

$$\pi = q(p - c) - (s - q)hc \tag{5.2}$$

The expression $(s - q)hc$ refers to the cost of unsold stocks. Unsold stocks are particularly likely if a relatively high price is fixed. The quantity sold is a function of price. Adopting a linear demand function, $q = a - bp$. For simplicity, let $b = 1$. Substituting $(a - p)$ for $q$ in equation 5.2:

$$\pi = (a - p)\,(p - c) - [s - (a - p)]hc \tag{5.3}$$

If the quantity demanded, $(a - p)$, equals the stock of goods available for sale, equation 5.3 reduces to $\pi = (a - p)(p - c)$. Given that demand is uncertain, 'losses' through unsold stocks and through charging an inappropriate price must be taken into account. Uncertainty makes it advisable to consider, for different values of $p$ chosen, both the expected level of profit and its variability.

Consider Figure 5.1. Here, both minimum and maximum possible demand functions are illustrated together with the associated marginal revenue and marginal cost functions. Demand is assumed to lie within the limits given by functions: $q = 10 - 1p$; $q = 14 - 1p$. Assume costs are constant, hence the marginal cost curve is horizontal. Let $c = 4$. Assume that a value for $s$ is selected so as to ensure that demand can always be met. How is the value of $s$ to be determined? Given the most pessimistic demand forecast it can be seen that the profit-maximizing price is $p = 7$. This price must be included as one of the possible prices. If this,

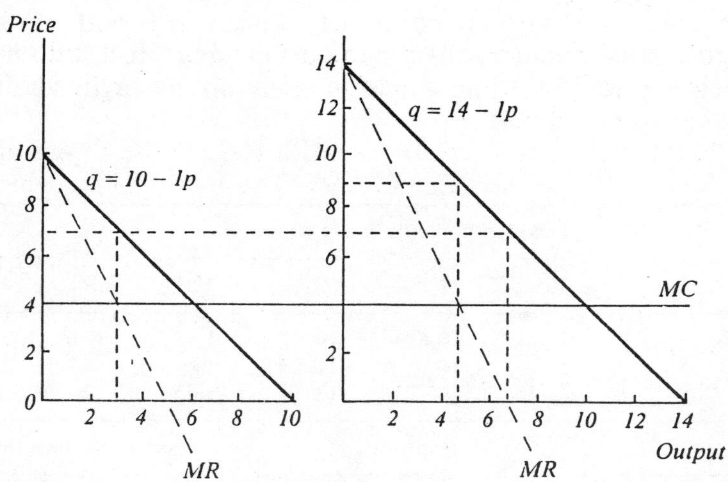


*Figure 5.1: Marginal analysis applied to determine the feasible lower and upper limits to the quantities demanded*

the lowest price, is charged and the demand out-turn is the most favourable the quantity demanded will equal 7 units. Thus, a stock of 7 units is sufficient to guarantee that demand never exceeds supply. Now, assume the holding cost of each unit of unsold stocks (*hc*) is 0.5. When the complete set of feasible demand levels and prices is tabulated, a pay-off matrix is obtained. This is shown in Table 5.1. In the absence of further information, each level of demand may be considered to be equally likely. Indeed, over the period of time to which the data relate, each level of demand might be experienced (i.e. $q = 14 - p$; $q = 13 - p$, etc.). If this is so, which price should be chosen? If a price equal to 7 is fixed, for instance, the mean expected profit is 14; its standard deviation is 4.95. Table 5.1 displays the solutions for whole number prices. Depending on the decision maker's utility function (where expected income and income variance are the considerations) relatively low or high prices might be selected. However, prices exceeding 8 would be rejected since they involve lower *and* more variable profits.

One of the interesting implications of the modification above to the conventional textbook model is that it can be used to support the neoclassical (marginalist) approach to the firm. This approach often has been criticized for being remote from the experience of actual firms. It is said that its information requirements are too demanding. Real firms are supposed to find it impossible to apply profit maximization

*Table 5.1: Profit levels for different levels of a* and *p*

| | Demand curve intercept ($a$) | | | | |
|---|---|---|---|---|---|
| Price ($p$) | 10 | 11 | 12 | 13 | 14 |
| 7 | 7 | 10.5 | 14 | 17.5 | 21 |
| 8 | 5.5 | 10 | 14.5 | 19 | 23.5 |
| 9 | 2 | 7.5 | 13 | 18.5 | 24 |

| | Mean profit | Standard deviation |
|---|---|---|
| $p = 7$ | 14 | 4.95 |
| $p = 8$ | 14.5 | 6.36 |
| $p = 9$ | 13 | 7.78 |

criteria; they are supposed to prefer cost-plus pricing. However, it has been shown that, if various demand functions are postulated, marginal analysis can be applied in the determination of prices provided only that firms are able to consider the likely lower and upper limits to demand levels. It is also clear that firms which fail to apply rational decision-making criteria are likely to experience 'opportunity losses'.

## PROGRAM 5.1

This program is used to obtain the solutions presented in the upper half of Table 5.1. The upper and lower limits to the price selected and the value of the demand curve intercept are explained in the text and by reference to Figure 5.1. The stock level which ensures that demand will not exceed supply can also be understood by reference to Figure 5.1. The program shows how uncertainty can be allowed for in price formation. It is unnecessary to assign probabilities to the various possible outcomes. Only the upper and the lower limits to the levels of demand need to be known.

```
 10 REM5.1
 20 C=4:S=7:hc=.5
 30 PRINT"PRICE   DEMAND INDEX      PROFIT"
 40 FOR P= 7 TO 9:REM PRICE RANGE IF PROFIT MAX. POLICY
 50 FOR A=10 TO 14:REM LOWER AND UPPER LIMITS TO DEMAND
 60  PROFIT = (A-P)*(P-C)-(S-(A-P))*hc
 70 PRINT;P;".........";A;"............";PROFIT
 80 NEXT A
 90 NEXT P
100 STOP
```

Lines 40, 50 80 and 90; the loop FOR *A*, NEXT *A* lies within the loop FOR *P*, NEXT *P*. Hence, the first set of calculations involve $P = 7$, $A = 10$. The next set involves $P = 7$, $A = 11$, etc., until $P = 7$, $A = 14$. Once calculations within the inner loop, FOR $P = 7$, have been completed, the value of *P* is increased to 8 and solutions FOR $A = 10$ TO 14 are obtained.

Line 60: Corresponds to equation 5.3.

## PROGRAM 5.2

This program calculates the mean profit level and standard

deviation for a given price. It is useful if a large number of calculations are needed although here there are only five items of data. This is the only program in the book involving the 'reading' of data. Since the DATA are to be read twice they must be 'restored' after having been accessed the first time. The program operates in the following way: FOR $N = 1$ TO 5 (the number of items), the data are READ. The data is then stored. Each item of data is subscripted [READ $A(N)$] and the mean value is obtained. The data is accessed a second time and the standard deviation of profit is calculated. The lower half of Table 5.1 presents the solutions.

```
 10 REM 5.2
 20 DIM A(5)
 30 sum=0
 40 FOR N=1 TO 5
 50 READ A(N)
 60 sum = sum + A(N)
 70 NEXT N
 80 av = sum/5
 90 RESTORE
100 total=0
110 FOR N=1 TO 5
120 READ A(N)
130 VAR =(A(N)-av)^2
140 total = total + VAR
150 NEXT N
160 STA = SQR(total/5)
165 PRINT
170 PRINT "MEAN = ";av
180 PRINT "STANDARD DEVIATION = ";STA
190 DATA 7,10.5,14,17.5,21
200 STOP
```

Line 20: An amount of memory is reserved to allow items of data to be stored. The array $A(5)$ is set up.

Line 30: The initial sum total of the values is equal to zero.

Line 60: The sum total of the items of data equals each of the individual items READ from the database (line 190).

Line 80: The mean is calculated.

Line 120: The data are read again after they have been restored.

Lines 130, 140 and 160: The standard deviation is calculated.

## 5.2 CLASSICAL OLIGOPOLY THEORY

In oligopoly industry the main sources of uncertainty within the long and short periods are competition from entrants and competition from existing firms. The latter is the main subject of this chapter, oligopolistic price rivalry is discussed. We begin by considering some of the classical approaches to the oligopoly problem. In order to emphasize the main principles we consider the simple model of two firms (duopoly) making interdependent decisions. This case draws attention to the fact that each firm knows that its profits partly depend on its rival's reactions to its own actions. Hence, a duopolist's pricing problem is one of determining a policy to ensure an optimum profit given the policy of its rival. Profit maximization without regard to the rival's output and price decision is not possible. The problem is a strategic one. A large number of solutions exist depending upon the rival's strategy.

Cournot's pioneering work on oligopoly, which provides a useful basis for more advanced work, is discussed first. Following the approach of Cournot (1831), assume each firm seeks to maximize profit, taking rival's output as constant. Assume that each firm has identical costs, $c$, and that the market demand curve is linear with $p = a - bq$. Distinguish between the outputs of firm 1 and 2: $q_1$ and $q_2$. Firm 1 seeks to maximize profits:

$$\pi_1 = pq_1 - cq_1 \tag{5.4}$$

Market price is inversely related to the combined outputs of the firms. Thus:

$$p = a - b(q_1 + q_2) \tag{5.5}$$

Firm 1's profits equal total revenue minus total cost. Multiply equation 5.5 through by $q_1$ to obtain an expression for 1's total revenue function (shown as equation 5.6) and deduct total costs:

$$pq_1 = aq_1 - b(q_1 + q_2)q_1 \tag{5.6}$$

$$\pi_1 = aq_1 - bq_1^2 - bq_1q_2 - cq_1 \tag{5.7}$$

Differentiating equation 5.7 with respect to $q_1$,

$$\frac{\partial \pi_1}{\partial q_1} = a - 2bq_1 - bq_2 - c = 0 \tag{5.8}$$

Equation 5.8 concerns the output which firm 1 must produce and sell if its profits are to be maximized. Firm 2's output, $q_2$, is assumed to be constant. Expressing $q_1$ in terms of the variables upon which it depends:

$$2bq_1 = a - bq_2 - c$$

$$q_1 = \frac{a - bq_2 - c}{2b} \tag{5.9}$$

Before continuing, let us pause to assess what is involved in the mathematics of equations 5.4 to 5.9. Equation 5.9 is described as firm 1's *reaction function*. It measures how firm 1 would react to changes in $q_2$, given $a$, $b$ and $c$ as constants. In Cournot's model, it is assumed that firm 1 has no control over its rival's output. Indeed, it is assumed that firm 1 imagines that firm 2 will hold its output constant irrespective of its own decision. Reaction functions express the optimal output of each firm as a function of the rival's output. These functions are illustrated in Figure 5.2. Cournot equilibrium is

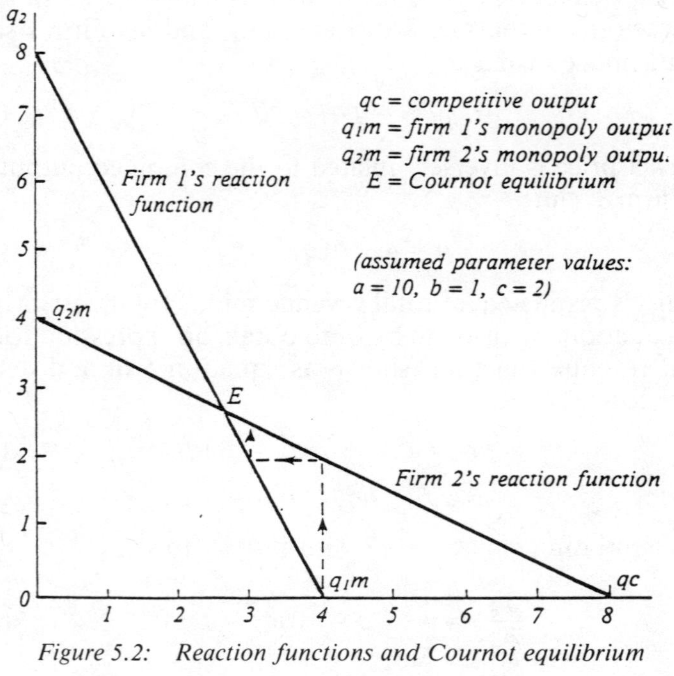


Figure 5.2: Reaction functions and Cournot equilibrium

at E where the curves intersect. Clearly, the model suggests a dynamic adjustment process (i.e. an adjustment process involving responses over time). The major difficulty with the model, and a common criticism of it, is that it implies that neither firm has the capacity to learn from experience or to take advantage of the information on their rival's behaviour pattern. These criticisms may be harsh. Some firms are slow to learn because of managerial limitations. Other firms, because of contractual obligations, do find it difficult to amend their production levels, particularly in the short run. For further discussion of the role of learning in oligopoly models, see Section 5.4. We consider further the logic behind the *Cournot equilibrium* later in this section.

One of the hallmarks of a good model is that it can be amended or built upon to obtain new insights. Cournot's model meets this requirement. Consider the amendment introduced by Stackelberg (1934). In his model, one firm continues to behave in the manner described by Cournot but the other recognizes the mode of behaviour of its rival and builds its output function into his own function. That is, one firm discovers the reactions of his rival and allows for them in his own decisions. Recall that firm 1's reaction function is:

$$q_1 = \frac{a - bq_2 - c}{2b}$$

Assume firms 2's reaction function is:

$$q_2 = \frac{a - bq_1 - c}{2b} \tag{5.10}$$

Suppose, now, that firm 1 learns from his experiences and builds equation 5.10 into his own profit function. Substituting equation 5.10 into equation 5.7, we have:

$$\pi_1 = aq_1 - bq_1^2 - bq_1 \left(\frac{a - bq_1 - c}{2b}\right) - cq_1$$

$$\frac{\partial \pi_1}{\partial q_1} = \frac{a}{2} - \frac{c}{2} - bq_1$$

$$q_1 = \frac{a - c}{2b} \tag{5.11}$$

We can see what this means in terms of Figure 5.2 if a numerical example is considered. Suppose $a = 10$, $b = 1$, $c = 2$. In the absence of competition firm 1 would produce at the point along its reaction function where $q_2 = 0$ (i.e. $q_1$ would equal 4). This is half the competitive output, which equals 8. A Cournot duopolist would produce that output level where the reaction functions intersect (i.e. $q_1 = 2\frac{2}{3}$ units). A Stackelberg duopolist, however, sees that a contraction of his own output will encourage an expansion in his rival's output. The Stackelberg duopolist, to discourage his rival from expanding output, *maintains* output at four units after the rival produces two units. The Stackelberg duopolist is a market leader; once he makes an output decision he sticks to it. The leader comes to accept the existence and output decisions of the follower. A particular price applies and the market settles provided the rival is prepared to act as a follower by continuing to produce two units and not starting a price war.

## PROGRAM 5.3

This program is based upon reaction function analysis in the model of duopoly. The output levels for two firms are reported together with the market price. Output changes time period by time period but the solution converge upon their equilibrium values. The model upon which the program is based does not allow for 'learning' by the rival firms.

```
 10 REM5.3
 20 CLS
 30 DIM Q1(30):DIM Q2(30)
 40 A=10:B=1:C=2:Q1=4:Q2=0
 50 PRINT"TIME....Q1....Q2.....PRICE"
 60 PRINT
 70 PRINT;1;"......";Q1;".......";Q2
 80 FOR T = 2 TO 20
 90 REM FIRM 2 MAKES ITS OUTPUT DECISION ...
100 REM ... FOLLOWING FIRM 1´S DECISION
110 REM FIRM 1´S DECISION IN T DEPENDS ON Q2(T-1)
120 Q1 = (A-B*Q2-C)/2
130 Q2 = (A-B*Q1-C)/2
140 PRICE = A-B*(Q1+Q2)
150 PRINT;T;".......";INT(100*Q1)/100;
160 PRINT;".......";INT(100*Q2)/100;"......";
165 PRINT; INT (100*PRICE)/100
170 NEXT T
180 STOP
```

Line 40: The values of the parameters and the initial output levels of the two firms.

Line 80: The iterative process commences.

Lines 120 and 130: Correspond to equations 5.9 and 5.10.

Line 140: Corresponds to equation 5.5.

Line 150: Solutions to two decimal places.

## 5.3 SOME RECENT DEVELOPMENTS IN OLIGOPOLY THEORY

In this section we develop the work of Cowling and Waterson (1976), Clarke and Davies (1982), Clarke (1985) and Nash (1950, 1953). Reaction function analysis is developed and the conditions for three alternative states in an (initially) oligopolistic environment are described. The key relationship is each firm's 'conjectural variation' defined as:

$$r_1 = (\mathrm{d}q_2/\mathrm{d}q_1) \qquad \text{for firm 1,}$$
$$r_2 = (\mathrm{d}q_1/\mathrm{d}q_2) \qquad \text{for firm 2.}$$

These relationships refer to the conjecture of each firm concerning the *rival's* reaction to a change in *own* output. For ease of exposition, suppose $r_1 = r_2 = r$. The limit values for $r$ are minus and plus one. If $r$ is positive the rival is expected to change its output in the same direction as the change in own output. If it is negative (and this is the most interesting case in a non-collusive environment), the rival is expected, for instance, to increase its output if one's own output is reduced. If $r$ equals zero (the Cournot case), the rival is expected to maintain its output constant irrespective of the change in one's own output.

It will be shown that the following conditions apply:

| | |
|---|---|
| If $\mathrm{d}q_2/\mathrm{d}q_1 > 0$ | solutions approximating joint profit maximization will apply and if $r = 1$ joint monopoly profits are obtained. |
| If $\mathrm{d}q_2/\mathrm{d}q_1 = 0$ | the Cournot equilibrium is obtained. |
| If $\mathrm{d}q_2/\mathrm{d}q_1 < 0$ | solutions approximating competitive states will apply and if $r = -1$ the perfectly competitive solution is obtained. |

The mathematics which follows is somewhat involved and readers may safely proceed to equation 5.17 if they wish. Equation 5.17 concerns market output for different values of $r$.

Examine the policy options from firm 1's viewpoint. Recall that:

$$\pi_1 = pq_1 - c_1 q_1 \qquad \text{(firm 1's profit function)}$$

where:

$$p = a - b(q_1 + q_2) \quad \text{(price function)} \tag{5.12}$$

$$q = q_1 + q_2 \qquad \text{(total output)}$$

Now, in place of the Cournot assumption where $dq_2/dq_1$ is assumed equal to zero (firm 1 does not expect the rival to adjust its output in response to changes in own output), let:

$$q_2 = \bar{q}_2 + (dq_2/dq_1)dq_1 \tag{5.13}$$

where $\bar{q}_2$ = the initial output of firm 2 and $(dq_2/dq_1)dq_1$ measures the total change anticipated by firm 1 in firm 2's output resulting from a change in firm 1's output. The function given by equation 5.13 is illustrated in Figure 5.3.

Differentiating firm 1's profit function:

$$\frac{d\pi}{dq_1} = \left(\frac{dp}{dq_1}\right) q_1 + \left(\frac{dq_1}{dq_1}\right) p - c_1 \tag{5.14}$$

Substituting for $q_2$ in equation 5.12, using equation 5.13, and differentiating the amended price function with respect to $q_1$:

$$\frac{dp}{dq_1} = -\, b\left(1 + \frac{dq_2}{dq_1}\right) \tag{5.15}$$

Substituting for $dp/dq_1$ in equation 5.14, using (5.15), we find:

$$\frac{d\pi_1}{dq_1} = -\, b\left(1 + \frac{dq_2}{dq_1}\right) q_1 + p - c_1 = 0$$

Finally, substituting for $b$, it follows that:

$$\frac{d\pi_1}{dq_1} = \frac{dp}{dq}\left(1 + \frac{dq_2}{dq_1}\right) q_1 + p - c_1 \tag{5.16a}$$

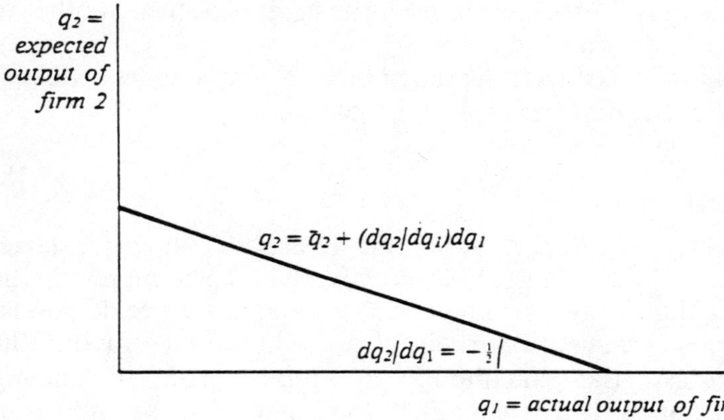


*Figure 5.3:* *Firm 1's conjecture on the anticipated response of firm 2 to changes in firm 1's output when $r_1 = -\frac{1}{2}$.*

Similarly, for firm 2, it will be found that:

$$\frac{d\pi_2}{dq_2} = \frac{dp}{dq}\left(1 + \frac{dq_1}{dq_2}\right)q_2 + p - c_2 \tag{5.16b}$$

By addition of (5.16a) and (5.16b), substituting for $dp/dq$, $dq_1/dq_2$, $dq_2/dq_1$ and $p$, and assuming $c_1 = c_2$, we find that:

$$0 = 2a - 2bq - b(1 + r)q - 2c$$

$$q = \frac{2\,(a - c)}{(3 + r)b} \tag{5.17}$$

By inserting various values of $r$ in equation 5.17, the propositions concerning monopoly, Cournot duopoly and competitive tendencies may be confirmed. Set $r = -1$ in equation 5.17. Given $a = 10$, $b = 1$, $c = 2$ and $r = -1$, output = 8 (i.e. the competitive output). By contrast, if $r = 1$, or if $r$ varies between zero and + 1, either complete or partial *coordination* of output adjustments is expected by each of the firms. In this instance, a situation resembling the joint monopoly solution is obtained. From equation (5.17), if $r = 1$, $q = 4$ (i.e. the monopoly output). The reader should appreciate that if $r = 1$, in our model, neither firm believes that its rival will seek to take advantage of a contraction in its own output. In fact, when $r = 1$ the firms expect each other to match any output adjustment.

Arguments concerning the price level may also be deduced. From equation (5.17) we find that:

$$p = \frac{a(1 + r) + 2c}{(3 + r)} \tag{5.18}$$

Evidently, the larger is $r$, the greater is the price level. Antitrust bodies in the UK and US take a keen interest in the degree that firms coordinate their output and price decisions. If firms *believe* that their rivals will adopt 'favourable responses' the likelihood of joint profit-maximizing behaviour is increased. The dominant view in industrial economics is that certain structural characteristics in a market are likely to promote or inhibit collusion between firms. See Clarke (1985) for a recent text on this subject.

We have still to consider the form which *individual firm* output functions take given various values of $r$. From equation 5.5, 5.16a and 5.16b, it can be shown after substitution of terms that:

$$q_1 = \frac{a - c}{b(2 + r)} - \frac{1}{(2 + r)} q_2 \tag{5.19}$$

$$q_2 = \frac{a - c}{b(2 + r)} - \frac{1}{(2 + r)} q_1 \tag{5.20}$$

Equations 5.19 and 5.20 refer to the reaction functions of each of the firms. These expressions involve the same line of reasoning as applied in the case of equations 5.9 and 5.10.

We can make immediate observations on 'favourable', ($r > 0$), and 'unfavourable', ($r < 0$), responses from equations 5.19 and 5.20. We have noted that when $r < 0$ each firm believes that at least part of the deficiency in its own supplies to the market will be made up by the rival. When this suspicion exists, it is profitable for firms established in the market to offer a larger volume for sale compared with the situation where there is no threat of competition. Thus, for instance, from equation 5.19, for $r = -0.75$, if $q_2 = 0$ then $q_1 = 6.4$; if $q_2 = -1$ then $q_1 = 5.6$. When $r = -0.50$, if $q_2 = 0$ then $q_1 = 5.33$; if $q_2 = 1$ then $q_1 = 4.66$. It is concluded

*Table 5.2: Actual market adjustments given $r = 0$*

| Time period | $q_1$ | $q_2$ | Price |
|---|---|---|---|
| 0* | 4 | 0 | 6 |
| 1 | 4 | 2 | 4 |
| 2 | 3 | 2.5 | 4.5 |
| 3 | 2.75 | 2.625 | 4.625 |
| 4 | 2.687 | 2.656 | 4.656 |
| 5 | 2.672 | 2.664 | 4.664 |
| 6 | 2.668 | 2.666 | 4.666 |
| 7 | 2.667 | 2.667 | 4.667 |

(* Note: the first set of solutions, row 0, for all possible values of $r$, refers to output and price levels when firm 1 is not affected by competition.)

that when $r < 0$ market prices will be lower, because of the marketing of a larger volume of goods, in the *disequilibrium* as well as in the equilibrium state, compared with situations where $r > 0$. This may be confirmed by considering output levels for $r > 0$. For instance, if $r = +0.5$ and $q_2 = 0$ then $q_1 = 3.2$. When $r > 0$, each firm effectively *signals* that it is prepared to accept a rival by producing less than the profit-maximizing output (which equals four units).

By differentiation of equations 5.19 and 5.20, or by observation of any of the sets of solutions such as those given in Table 5.2, it should be clear that the relationship between $r$ and the size of the *actual* response is measured by:

$$\frac{\Delta q_1}{\Delta q_2} = \frac{\Delta q_2}{\Delta q_1} = \frac{-1}{(2 + r)} \tag{5.21}$$

Only in the limiting case when $r = -1$ is the actual response by firms consistent with the expected response. In all other cases, what actually happens in the market differs from what was expected. In this respect the model resembles Cournot's. Does the same criticism that firms are irrational for disregarding outcomes apply?

We need to answer this question in two stages. Firstly, in connection with the Cournot model, the strongest objections are to reaction function analysis and not to the concept of Cournot equilibrium. The latter applies to a *single-period* decision framework whereas the objections relate to the multiperiod model. We return to this point shortly. Secondly, a distinction should be drawn between the mathematical certainty of a formal model and the 'real world' where many factors make it difficult to know exactly what is occurring in a market or even the motivation behind individual firms' decisions. The Cournot model and its later developments concern non-cooperative oligopoly. When $r < 0$ each firm expects non-cooperative decisions to be made by other firms. When $r < 0$ a *small* numerical difference is found between the actual market responses of firms and their expected responses, but the adjustments are in the same direction. When $r > 0$ the problem of consistency is apparent (see Bresnahan (1981) on this issue), but we might ask whether the model should be applied to situations where evidence of cooperation is found. The subject of cooperative oligopoly and market signals is taken up in the next section.

Returning to the first point, the single-period model is concerned with the conditions for, and the stability of, the state of equilibrium. In recent literature the Cournot equilibrium is discussed within the context of game theory where the contribution of Nash is significant. In the single-period model each firm has a given set of independent strategies from which it can choose. This concept of strategy is to be distinguished from a firm's best plan of action over several periods (its 'battle plan' as Friedman (1983) calls it) when each output decision can be looked upon as a *move*. The 'Cournot-Nash' equilibrium has the characteristic that once a strategy has been chosen, no firm could obtain higher profits by changing its decision. In this sense we have a state of equilibrium. Table 5.3, which involves a single-period Prisoner's Dilemma game, should help to explain the issue. The game is examined from firm 1's viewpoint. The environment is duopolistic. The best option available to firm 1 is to cut its prices. Given that an identical pay-off matrix applies to firm 2, it will also cut its price. We can see from the table that the cut-price/cut-price option is the *third* best outcome and yet it cannot be improved upon unless there is collusion. Each firm will consider, in retrospect, that it could not have made a better decision given the decision of the competing firm.

*Table 5.3: Single period pay-off matrix in the Prisoner's Dilemma game*

| | | Firm 2's choices | |
|---|---|---|---|
| | | Hold price constant | Cut price |
| Firm 1's choices | Hold price constant | 0 | − 3 |
| | Cut price | + 2 | − 1 |

Comparing the option to cut prices with the option to hold prices constant (i.e. comparing the solution in row 2 with those in row 1) the pay-offs for firm 1 are higher whether firm 2 opts to hold prices constant or to cut prices (two is greater than zero and minus one is greater than minus three). A little thought will confirm that the pay-off figures are sensible given the situation we are describing. Each firm will wish to cut its prices and the outcome is collectively unfavourable but each firm makes an optimal decision given the decision of its rival. In a more complex version of this model, a different pay-off matrix applies to each possible price reduction. In our simple model, all that can be inferred is that the cut-price option remains the preferred alternative until the Cournot-Nash equilibrium is reached, when a new pay-off matrix applies and the *cut-price* option is no longer preferred. In conclusion, the theory above implies the existence of competitive tendencies in oligopolistic environments. In Section 5.4 we further discuss the multiperiod model.

## PROGRAM 5.4

This program develops reaction function analysis to allow for different conjectures concerning the response of a rival to changes in own output. In Program 5.3 the assumption was that the rival (firm 2) holds its output constant. In Program 5.4 the user selects the value of $r$, the conjectural variation, where $r = \mathrm{d}q_2/\mathrm{d}q_1 = \mathrm{d}q_1/\mathrm{d}q_2$.

```
 10 REM5.4
 30 DIM Q1(100):DIM Q2(100)
 40 B=1:C=2:Q1(1)=4:Q2(1)=0:A=10
 50 PRINT´´"ENTER THE VALUE OF R"
 60 PRINT:INPUT R
 70 IF R>1 OR R<-1 GOTO 50
 80 REM IF R>0 "FAVOURABLE" REACTIONS EXPECTED
 90 REM IF R<0 RIVALS EXPECTED TO INCREASE OUTPUT...
100 REM ..IF OWN OUPUT CUT
110  CLS: PRINT´´"TIME......Q1......Q2.....Q1´S PROFIT"
120 PRINT
140 FOR T = 2 TO 20
150 Q1(T) = (A-C)/(2+R)*B-(1/(2+R))*Q2(T-1)
160 Q2(T) = (A-C)/(2+R)*B-(1/(2+R))*Q1(T)
170 REM Q1(T) IS A FUNCTION OF Q2(T-1)
180 REM Q2(T) IS A FUNCTION OF Q1(T)
190 REM Q1 AND Q2 BOTH DEPEND ON PAST RIVAL BEHAVIOUR
200 REM *** DISCRETE time intervals are involved ***
210 P = A - B*(Q1(T)+Q2(T))
220 PRINT;T;"........";INT(100*Q1(T))/100;".....";
230 PRINT;INT(100*Q2(T))/100;".....";
240 PRINT; INT(100*(Q1(T)*P-Q1(T)*C))/100
250 NEXT T
260 STOP
```

Lines 150 and 160: Correspond to equations 5.19 and 5.20

Line 240: Levels of profit through time depend upon the value of $r$. If the program is run more than once, note the sensitivity of profit to the value of $r$ chosen.

## 5.4 ITERATIVE PRISONER'S DILEMMA GAMES

In this section we apply the Prisoner's Dilemma framework to a multiperiod model of behaviour. We intentionally blur the distinction between cooperative and non-cooperative models. Iterative Prisoner's Dilemma games involve two participants who are faced with the question whether to stick to a certain course of action or to defect. There is no single best strategy to follow. What is best depends on the decision of the other player. How a fellow player is likely to act depends on what he expects *you* to do. The most interesting games involve repeated trials since these games model real situations involving interaction between people or institutions over a period of time. Much has been learned from computer tournaments between machines which have been programmed to behave and respond to past experiences in a certain way.

As Prisoner's Dilemma games progress actors are able to learn something about their fellow participants. Initial reactions may be misleading as a guide to the future since players who see the game for the first time are unlikely to appreciate its complexity and richness or to have discovered the character of fellow players. Formally, the pay-off matrix is quite simple (see previous section) but the range of possible outcomes and responses to each other's decisions over time is enormous. Players or 'prisoners' are separated and do not know their fellows' responses until after a decision has been made. Players may seek to cooperate or they may pursue their own interests selfishly. In oligopolistic situations, rewards and penalties take the form of monetary sums gained or lost depending upon the collective outcome of the decision taken. In two-person games there are just four possible outcomes in each trial. Participants *learn* through experience whether the fellow player generally adopts a cooperative or a selfish strategy. The learning process takes time and changes in the behaviour adopted are more common than a set pattern. Hostile reactions by one player might take place in retaliation to apparently selfish actions by the other player but this behaviour might be due to inexperience, fear or the failure of subtle communication mechanisms to have developed.

The model discussed in Section 5.3 concerned how firms react to the output decisions of closely related firms. The model predicted various joint production levels depending upon the perceived value of $r$, defined as the *expected* adjustment in a rival's output in response to changes in own output. (Consider, for instance, the attempts within OPEC to limit production and the decision of individual members.) These models are applicable over that period of time during which participants believe their fellow producers will behave in a certain way; if circumstances change or if beliefs are revised in the light of experience, a different behaviour pattern will be predicted.

Recent work in mathematics and social science has enriched our knowledge of game theoretic situations and has contributed to a greater understanding of the range of possible reaction functions. When behaviour modification is possible, it is no longer appropriate to focus in a model on the options which are open in a single time period, nor should just two kinds of actors be distinguished. In the single-time-period model the actors either adopt a 'cooperative' mode of behaviour (group welfare is aimed for) or a 'selfish' mode (decision makers pursue their own interests). Agreements made in the past are either adhered to or broken. In such situations 'cheats' (those who deviate from the unwritten rules of acceptable behaviour) and 'suckers' (those who are betrayed) emerge. But in a multiperiod model a third kind of actor might be distinguished. This actor was given the name 'the grudger' by the biologist Richard Dawkins in a television programme for the BBC (1986) *Horizon* series. Grudgers remember those who have behaved selfishly in the past. Grudgers adopt hostile attitudes to actors who have chosen to ignore group welfare. In a world inhabited only by cheats and suckers, suckers would be eliminated but cheats would eventually bring about their own downfall as a time would come when they are unable to exploit others. In a world inhabited by cheats, suckers and grudgers, however, cheats would find themselves isolated. In a cartelized oligopolistic market, for instance, collective action to boycott wayward firms might take place. In other situations cheats might find it impossible to form mutually beneficial alliances. Whether cartels are likely to endure through time will depend on the character of their members and the quality of the signalling mechanisms which develop. However, the most important conclusion of the above theory of the outcome of group interaction is that ruthless individualistic behaviour is unlikely to reap long term rewards.

Robert Axelrod (1984), an American political scientist, in a series of experiments using computers to act out Prisoner's Dilemma games (with the computers programmed in many different ways), has found that the most successful *long run* strategy is one in which the actors believe that their fellow participants will cooperate. This strategy fails when cheats are encountered but it succeeds if grudgers are encountered. The grudger does not seek to defeat the other actor; he does not see the other actor as an opponent but as an accomplice. Successful environments are environments where there are a sufficient number of suckers and grudgers. Professor Axelrod's findings were based on two computer tournaments which took place at the University of Michigan. Entrants included players from several disciplines: psychology, political science, sociology, economics and mathematics. In the first tournament fourteen players competed in a round-robin event (all play all). An entrant called TIT FOR TAT was the winner. The program upon which TIT FOR TAT was based was the simplest of the entrants. TIT FOR TAT starts with a cooperative move and thereafter it follows the same move as its fellow player. In the second tournament there were sixty-three entries and some very complex programs. TIT FOR TAT won again after 3,969 paired combinations and 200 moves in each game.

Considering these results in terms of a model of oligopolistic firms, firms which adopt cooperative strategies are likely to perform well in the long term even though optimal results are not obtained in the short term. Such firms are more likely to be represented in the population of surviving firms in future generations. Firms may try different strategies through time and stick with those which seem to work best. Another possibility is that cartels might be founded upon one set of rules but members become aware of and switch to another, more successful, set of rules. A further possibility is that leading spokesmen in cartels which are not performing well might be replaced by others who promise better results.

Figure 5.4 is taken from Axelrod (1984). It demonstrates the ranking of entries over time with points scored in games determining the representation in the total population. To begin with, all sixty-three entries had the same share in the population. Entry 1 is TIT FOR TAT; entry 8 is HARRINGTON, an aggressive entrant which performed well provided it could exploit but which could not function successfully in a cooperative environment. The lowest-ranking entrants fell to half their initial size by the fifth generation (iteration); by the fifteenth iteration several entrants practically disappeared. Cartels which survive, perhaps, are those which develop the most sophisticated form of signalling arrangements, where the penalties for not cooperating are high and where profits can be made by remaining within existing markets. Change in the state of the market

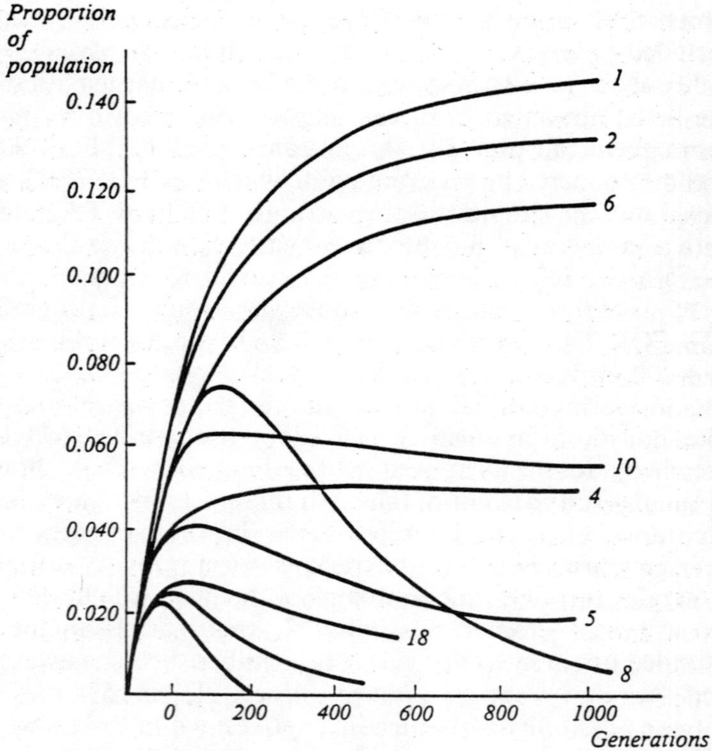


*Figure 5.4: Simulated ecological success of the decision rules. (Source: Axelrod, R. (1984): The Evolution of Cooperation, p. 5, Basic Books)*

(e.g. a recession) might disrupt a well-established order and antitrust policy might be effective. If cartel members adopt policies which favour their fellows and if they believe that others will match their own behaviour, the most successful group outcome will be realized. Just such an outcome is obtained in the Cowling and Waterson, Clarke and Davies models when $r > 0$.

## 5.5 MARKET SHARES THROUGH TIME

The final two sections in this chapter employ Markov chain analysis. This may be used to make predictions on the basis of existing trends. For instance, prior competition between three oligopolists might have resulted in one firm increasing its market share at the expense of the other two. Over a period of time, past and present sales levels are known to all participants. Given the change in spending patterns, how could shares after a number of time periods be calculated? Imagine that competition results in customers switching between firms and that the trends will continue unless drastic changes in policy are adopted.

The idea is most easily communicated by means of a numerical example. Consider a market which has three major firms—call them A, B and C. The firm which is growing is B. The industry could be the tabloid newspaper industry where total daily sales of newspapers are constant. On the basis of a detailed survey of readers, the management of any of the firms might be able to identify a national trend. This would involve an analysis of switches between the newspapers. Let average sales of tabloid newspapers in the model amount to 1,000 per time period. Consider firstly the figures in Table 5.4 at the end of each row and at the foot of each column. A's sales, which were 400 in period 1, fall to 365 in period 2; B's, which were 300, increase to 370, and so on. Reading down column B, 40 of B's current customers previously purchased from A, 270 of B's customers traded in the past with B and 60 of their customers previously traded with C. Reading down Column A, 320 of A's customers previously traded with A, 15 of their customers previously traded with B and 30 traded with C. From Table 5.4, Table 5.5 is derived. Table 5.5 is often described in texts as the transition probability matrix.

*Table 5.4: Customer switch and loyalty data*

| | | Supplying firm in period 2<br>A | <br>B | <br>C | Period 1<br>sales |
|---|---|---|---|---|---|
| Supplying firm in period 1 | A | 320 | 40 | 40 | 400 |
| | B | 15 | 270 | 15 | 300 |
| | C | 30 | 60 | 210 | 300 |
| Period 2 sales | | 365 | 370 | 265 | 1,000 |

*Table 5.5: Customer switch and loyalty data as a proportion of the beginning of period totals*

| | | To | | |
|---|---|---|---|---|
| | | A | B | C |
| From | A | 0.8 | 0.1 | 0.1 |
| | B | 0.05 | 0.9 | 0.05 |
| | C | 0.1 | 0.2 | 0.7 |

On the basis of the original market shares—40 per cent for A, 30 per cent for B, 30 per cent for C—and the switches taking place, conditional probability estimates of future shares can be made.

Applying conditional probability notation and considering B's position, the figures in column B of Table 5.5 are used to illustrate the switches taking place and to assess their relative importance during the first period.

| *Switch* | | *Probability* |
|---|---|---|
| B | B | $P$ (buy B \| bought B) × $P$ (bought B) = (0.9) (0.3) = 0.27 |
| A | B | $P$ (buy B \| bought A) × $P$ (bought A) = (0.1) (0.4) = 0.04 |
| C | B | $P$ (buy B \| bought C) × $P$ (bought C) = (0.2) (0.3) = 0.06 |
| | | $P$ (buy B) = 0.37 |

The expression $P$ (buy B | bought A) simply means the probability that B will be bought when A has been bought in the past. It refers to the probability of one event given that another event has occurred previously.

Drawing up the complete table and arranging the information in a form suitable for computer modelling gives:

$P$ (buy A | bought A) = 0.8 $P$ (buy A | bought B) = 0.05
$P$ (buy A | bought C) = 0.1
$P$ (buy B | bought B) = 0.9 $P$ (buy B | bought A) = 0.1
$P$ (buy B | bought C) = 0.2
$P$ (buy C | bought C) = 0.7 $P$ (buy C | bought A) = 0.1
$P$ (buy C | bought B) = 0.05

Anticipated changes in sales week by week can now be calculated. B's sales, for instance, are determined by the probability that its customers will remain loyal, multiplied by the number of its original customers, plus the probability that customers will transfer from A, multiplied by the customers who originally traded with A, etc. After one time period has passed, period 2 shares will be as shown in Table 5.6. $P_A$, $P_B$ and $P_C$ denote the *proportions* of the market held. After a further period, forecasted sales will be as shown in Table 5.7. The table changes in one way only: the figures used for forecasting purposes will be the shares which are known to apply after one transition has been completed. Of course, these shares will change continuously until a steady state is reached. In equilibrium the market shares consist of 23 per cent of the market for A, 59 per cent for B and 18 per cent for C.

*Table 5.6: Market shares from probability data, period 2*

| | A | B | C |
|---|---|---|---|
| A | $0.8 \times 0.4$ = 0.32 | $0.1 \times 0.4$ = 0.04 | $0.1 \times 0.4$ = 0.04 |
| B | $0.02 \times 0.3$ = 0.015 | $0.9 \times 0.3$ = 0.27 | $0.05 \times 0.3$ = 0.015 |
| C | $0.1 \times 0.3$ = 0.03 | $0.2 \times 0.3$ = 0.06 | $0.7 \times 0.3$ = 021 |
| | $P_A = 0.365$ | $P_B = 0.37$ | $P_C = 0.265$ |

*Table 5.7: Market shares from probability data, Period 3*

| | A | B | C |
|---|---|---|---|
| A | $0.8 \times 0.365$ = 0.2920 | $0.1 \times 0.365$ = 0.0365 | $0.1 \times 0.365$ = 0.0365 |
| B | $0.05 \times 0.37$ = 0.0185 | $0.9 \times 0.37$ = 0.333 | $0.05 \times 0.37$ = 0.0185 |
| C | $0.1 \times 0.265$ = 0.0265 | $0.2 \times 0.265$ = 0.053 | $0.7 \times 0.265$ = 0.1855 |
| | $P_A = 0.337$ | $P_B = 0.4255$ | $P_c = 0.2395$ |

## 5.6 APPLICATIONS OF MARKET SHARE ANALYSIS TO MARKETING STRATEGY

In the example of Section 5.5 we have seen that the shares of firms A and C are predicted to fall from 40 per cent and 30 per cent respectively to 23 per cent and 18 per cent if no action is taken to reverse downward trends. How might either company respond to this situation? The following discussion indicates how Markov process analysis can be used to assist decision makers in evaluating alternative marketing strategies. Two strategies are discussed: (1) retention and (2) acquisition.

The first alternative might be to attempt to retain a larger percentage of own's own newspaper readership. This strategy might be achieved by reducing price, offering bingo competitions to readers, a better coverage of sport, and so on. Suppose that A could retain more readers by reducing the *loss rate* to B from 10 per cent per period (see Table 5.5) to 2.5 per cent per period; in period two its losses to B would fall from forty to ten units. The new transition matrix would be as shown in Table 5.8. After approximately twenty periods, the final equilibrium solutions would then be: A's share = 35 per cent, B's share = 46 per cent and C's share equal to 19 per cent. A's share would be approximately 12 percentage points higher than if it failed to take action. Of course, this strategy could not be achieved without cost. The management of *A* would have to analyze other possibilities before proceeding.

*Table 5.8: Customer switch and loyalty data following retention policies by* A

| | | To | | |
|---|---|---|---|---|
| | | A | B | C |
| From | A | 0.875 | 0.025 | 0.1 |
| | B | 0.05 | 0.9 | 0.05 |
| | C | 0.1 | 0.2 | 0.7 |

*Table 5.9: Customer switch and loyalty data following the acquisitions policies of* A

| | | To | | |
|---|---|---|---|---|
| | | A | B | C |
| From | A | 0.8 | 0.1 | 0.1 |
| | B | 0.05 | 0.9 | 0.05 |
| | C | 0.2 | 0.2 | 0.6 |

A second possible strategy would be to concentrate on taking customers away from rival newspaper companies. The acquisitions strategy might be to try to force C into an insignificant market position. This might be achieved by increasing the customer switch rate from C to A from 10 per cent period to 20 per cent per period. (Suppose currently it is not possible to prevent some readers from switching from A to C as they appear to enjoy a regular change.) In tabular form the new switch and loyalty table would be as shown in Table 5.9. In the final equilibrium, A would have 28 per cent of the market.

The two alternative strategies would result in different long term sales levels and different costs. The decision as to which of the alternative strategies to implement would depend on a comparison of the anticipated benefits and costs of the strategies involved.

## PROGRAM 5.5

The usefulness of a computer is demonstrated by this program. To obtain equilibrium solutions for a Markov process model using mathematics requires many tedious calculations. Program 5.5 illustrates in a small number of lines the main principle involved in reaching solutions time period by time period.

```
 10 REM5.5
 30 DIM A(20):DIM B(20):DIM C(20)
 40 PRINT"TIME     A´S SHARE    B´S SHARE  C´S SHARE"
 50 PRINT
 60 FOR T=1 TO 19
 70 PAA=.8:PAB=.05:PAC=.1
 80 PBB=.9:PBA=.1:PBC=.2
 90 PCC=.7:PCA=.1:PCB=.05
100 A(1)=.4:B(1)=.3:C(1)=.3
110 A(T+1)=A(T)*PAA + B(T)*PAB + C(T)*PAC
120 B(T+1)=B(T)*PBB + A(T)*PBA + C(T)*PBC
130 C(T+1)=C(T)*PCC + B(T)*PCB + A(T)*PCA
140 PRINT;T;"......";INT(100*A(T))/100;"......";
150 PRINT;INT(100*B(T))/100;"....";INT(100*C(T))/100
160 NEXT T
170 STOP
```

Lines 70 to 90: The transition probabilities. *PAA* denotes, for instance, the probability that A will be bought, A having been purchased previously.

Line 100: The shares of A, B and C in period one.

Lines 110 to 130: Shares at the end of each time period $[A(T+1)]$, etc., depend on the shares at the start of each period multiplied by the transition probabilities.

Lines 140 and 150: End of time period shares are reported.

## SUMMARY

1. A distinction is drawn between models involving risk and uncertainty. Risk models involve the probability of various outcomes. If probabilities cannot be assigned it is useful to consider the range of alternative outcomes and the associated distribution of returns.
2. Classical oligopoly models involve uncertainty. In order to make progress in specifying the nature of firms' price/output decisions, classical models are based upon assumptions on how firms behave in an interdependent market environment. Reaction function analysis plays a prominent part and has been developed by recent theorists. A key relationship is each firm's 'conjectural variation' defined for a given firm by $r_1 = (dq_2/dq_1)$ where $r_1$ measures firm 1's beliefs concerning the adjustment of a rival's output to changes in its own output.
3. Cournot equilibrium analysis does not require the restrictive assumptions of reaction function analysis. Using

game theory models it is possible to explain how the state of Cournot equilibrium can be reached.

4. Iterative Prisoner's Dilemma games are based upon the behaviour of rivals over time when interdependence is recognised. Computer tournaments have shown that selfish or individualistic modes of behaviour score badly compared with cooperative modes. The interaction between participants in the long run is recorded and the performance, scorewise, of alternative strategies is measured.

5. Markov chain analysis is useful in predicting the relative long run market shares of companies which compete. Customer switch and loyalty data (transition probabilities) can be used to calculate the likelihood of different outcomes. Firms which find their shares falling may adopt retention and acquisition strategies. These may be costed and evaluated in terms of the potential effects upon long run shares.

## FURTHER READING

Henderson and Quandt (1980), Horowitz (1970) and Naylor and Vernon (1969) are useful for readers interested in a mathematical approach. Thompson (1985) includes many interesting case studies of rivalry such as that between the manufacturers of Coca Cola and Pepsi. Pickering and Kinloch (1984) discuss the management of risk and uncertainty. Rapoport (1974) provides one of the clearest accounts of two person non-constant sum games. Bacharach (1976) and Neumann and Morgenstern (1944) discuss game theory models. McLaughlin and Pickhardt (1979) is clear and readable on Markov process models.

# 6 Investment Appraisal

Suppose a firm is faced with the choice between three alternative investment projects. Let the investments involve the same outlay and their lifetime expectancy (the time period over which profits are generated) be the same. Let each investment have a different time profile of profits. To illustrate the point, consider Figure 6.1. Project A is preferred if the early years are focused upon but project B provides the more steady flow of profit whilst project C might be judged the best from the standpoint of total profit, as measured by the area beneath the three curves. How should the firm decide between these alternatives? Clearly, some criteria involving time is necessary before a decision can be made. This is even more important if the investments involve different initial outlays and different lifetime expectancies. In this chapter we concentrate upon discounted cash flow (DCF) criteria as opposed to non-discounting approaches such as the pay-back, average profit rate and peak profit methods. Alternative DCF techniques are described and the concept of capital as foregone consumption is used to help to explain the basis of the calculations when investment decisions involve resources committed over more than one time period. The returns from investment are seldom known with certainty. However, if probabilities are attached to the possible cash flow values, risk can be reduced. In the final section we consider one of the most promising approaches to risk management—portfolio analysis as applied to investments in more than one project.

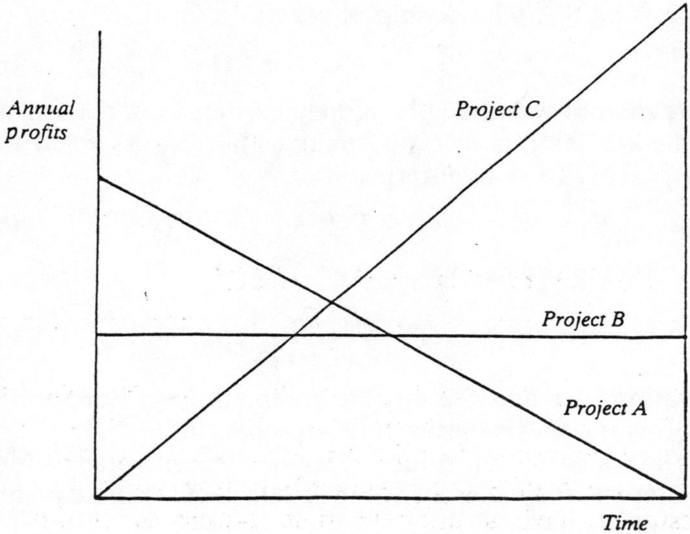


*Figure 6.1: Annual profits from three alternative investments*

## 6.1 DISCOUNTING TECHNIQUES—SINGLE PERIOD INVESTMENTS

In this section the most commonly applied DCF techniques—the present value and internal rate of return methods are discussed. Single period investments are considered. Section 6.2 concerns the general case where resources are committed over several time periods.

The principle of discounting is quite clearly illustrated by looking at how a sum accumulates through time when interest is paid on a deposit and then by examining the reverse procedure which concerns the 'present value' of a sum which will accrue at some time in the future. Suppose we have currently available a sum of £100. Its present value or $PV$ is £100. Suppose this sum could be deposited in a bank at an interest rate, $r$, of 10%. After one year we could withdraw both the original deposit and the accumulated interest. The receipt in year one would be: $R_1 = 100 + 0.1\ (100) = 110$.

Expressing this relationship in general terms:

$$R_1 = PV + r(PV) = PV(1 + r) \qquad (6.1)$$

If we did not withdraw the money but left it on deposit then at the end of the year we could withdraw: $R_2 = 110 + 0.1$ $(110) = 121$. In general terms:

$$R_2 = R_1 + r(R_1) = R_1(1 + r) = PV(1 + r)^2 \qquad (6.2)$$

By cross multiplication:

$$PV = \frac{R_2}{(1 + r)^2} \qquad (6.3)$$

Equations 6.1 and 6.2 involve compounding. Equation 6.3 involves the reverse procedure—discounting.

When a series of future receipts are generated through investment, their present value is calculated using equations 6.4 and 6.5.

$$PV = \frac{R_1}{(1 + r)} + \frac{R_2}{(1 + r)} + ,\ldots, \frac{R_n}{(1 + r)^n} \qquad (6.4)$$

$$PV = \sum_{t=1}^{n} R_t/(1 + r)^t \qquad (6.5)$$

$$NPV = PV - I_0 \qquad (6.6)$$

$R_t$ is the annual revenue, $t = 1, 2, \ldots, n$; $I_0$ is the initial investment; $NPV$ is the net present value of the investment; $r$ is the rate of discount.

Since the present value method is easily understood, we devote most of this section to the meaning of the internal rate of return. But firstly it is useful to note that if annual net revenues are constant and in perpetuity equation 6.5 simplifies to:

$$PV = R_t/r \qquad (6.7)$$

This can be proved by multiplying (6.4) through by $(1 + r)$ and deducting the expression derived from (6.4). Equation 6.7 applies, for instance, to the value of British government stock. If between two moments in time the market rate of discount (e.g. the *Minimum Lending Rate*) doubles, the value of stocks which yield an annual income, $R_t$, is halved. Perpetuities are rare but many shares in companies (e.g. preference shares) are similar in that they return to their owners a constant income provided nothing unforeseen like bankruptcy happens. Moreover, if an asset yields income many years into the future (say twenty or twenty-five), given the high rates of interest which have been normal because of inflation in the 1970s and 1980s, distant incomes play an insignificant part in the calculation of present values. In such cases (6.7) can be used to calculate the approximate value of many assets.

The internal rate of return (IRR) is obtained by solving for $r^*$ in the equation:

$$\sum_{t=o}^{n} R_t \frac{1}{(1 + r^*)^t} - I_0 = 0 \qquad (6.8)$$

It is the rate of discount which equates the value of future revenues to the initial cost of the investment. The following numerical example should make the point clear. In the example, $I_0$ is £100 and £100 of revenue is generated in years one and two. Setting the net present value of the investment equal to zero: $(100)/(1 + r^*) + (100)/(1 + r^*)^2 - 100 = 0$, it will be found that the value of $r^*$ is 0.618. Putting this another way, if the revenues obtained in each of the years are discounted with $r = r^* = 0.618$, the net present value of the investment equals zero. Provided that funds could be borrowed to finance the investment at a cost of less than 61.8 per cent, the investment would be worth undertaking. The relationship between the present value of the investment and the rate of discount shown in Figure 6.2.

To appreciate further the meaning of the IRR, consider a commonly used definition:—the IRR is the rate of return that is earned on tied up capital, while it is tied up, after allowing for the recoupment of the initial investment. Consider table 6.1. The investment generates net revenues which allow the capital debt to be repayed over two years. Given an interest rate of 61.8 per cent, if no income was earned the outstanding debt would grow to 161.8 at the end of year one. However, deducting income earned the debt is 61.8. In year two, if no income was earned the debt would be

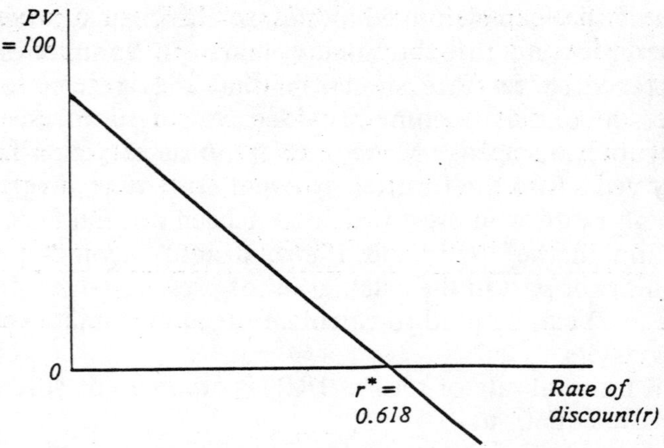


*Figure 6.2: Relationship between PV and r, measurement of the internal rate of return, r**

$(61.8 \times 0.618) = 38.2$. Since an income is earned, this debt does not arise and the surplus of 61.8 cancels the debt which was outstanding at the end of year one. The surplus of undiscounted income over costs is 100. When interest is charged at 61.8 per cent on the initial capital, total interest payments equal 100 thus cancelling the surplus income.

There are various problems with this method including the purely numerical difficulty of obtaining solutions. One substantive point needs emphasising. Basing investment decisions upon comparisons between rate of return figures (however defined) is invalid when differences exist in the size

*Table 6.1: Calculation of the internal rate of return as the return on tied up capital*

| Year | Capital debt outstanding at the beginning of the year | Cash flow | Interest on capital outstanding | Capital repayment (2–3) |
|---|---|---|---|---|
| | (1) | (2) | (3) | (4) |
| 1 | 100 | 100 | 61.8 | 38.2 |
| 2 | 61.8 | 100 | 38.2 | 61.8 |
| | | 200 | 100 | 100 |

of the initial capital outlays. A larger IRR for a project X, compared with a project Y, is not proof of the superiority of X. Rate of return figures are percentages. A large percentage return on a small outlay, obviously, might return a smaller profit than a small percentage return on a larger outlay. In Table 6.2, where a 10 per cent discount rate is used for

*Table 6.2: Comparisons between mutually exclusive investments.*

| Years | 0 | 1 | 2 | 3 |
|---|---|---|---|---|
| Project X | | | | |
| Annual Undiscounted Income | – 100 | 100 | 100 | 0 |
| Annual Discounted Income at 10% | – 100 | 90.9 | 82.6 | 0 |
| Annual Discounted Income at 61.8% | – 100 | 61.8 | 38.2 | 0 |
| *PV* at 10% = 73.5 | | | | |
| IRR = 61.8% | | | | |
| Project Y | | | | |
| Annual Undiscounted Income | – 400 | 205 | 205 | 205 |
| Annual Discounted Income at 10% | – 400 | 186.4 | 169.4 | 154.0 |
| Annual Discounted Income at 25% | – 400 | 164.0 | 131.2 | 105.0 |
| *PV* at 10% = 109.8 | | | | |
| IRR = 25% | | | | |
| Project Y – X | | | | |
| Annual Undiscounted Income | – 300 | 105 | 105 | 205 |
| Annual Discounted Income at 10% | – 300 | 95.4 | 86.8 | 154.0 |
| Annual Discounted Income at 16% | – 300 | 90.5 | 78.0 | 131.3 |
| *PV* at 10% = 36.2 | | | | |
| IRR = 16% | | | | |

calculating PVs, a 61.8 per cent IRR on an outlay of £100m. yields a smaller profit than a 25 per cent IRR on £400m. This point is particularly important in the case of mutually exclusive projects. Suppose a large land reclamation and water resource project is under consideration. X might involve the building of a small dam, Y a larger dam. Only one dam can be built. Suppose the smaller dam allows income to be generated over two years whilst the larger dam has a longer life and the returns are over three years. The correct procedure is to calculate the incremental return on the difference between the cost of X and Y. Provided that the discount rate measures the opportunity cost of the funds, if a profit can be made on the incremental investment it is worth undertaking. In Table 6.2 a discount rate of 10 per cent is adopted. Since a *PV* figure of £36m. applies to the additional funds committed, (Y – X), it follows that a profit is made on the incremental investment. Also, the IRR on the additional funds is 16 per cent. Since this exceeds the assumed market rate the return is greater than the opportunity cost of the funds required.

## 6.2 INVESTMENT OVER TIME

Section 6.1 concerned investment in a single time period. The cost of capital was the sum invested initially. Investment, however, often involves a commitment of funds over several time periods before any receipts are obtained. Investment by individuals or the state in education is one example. Calculating the rate of return on education with respect to the initial outlay would be quite arbitrary. Equally, the replacement of old equipment by new or the displacement of one long established product line by a new line involves costs other than the development, initial capital and production costs. One stream of income through time is often sacrificed before another stream is established. Volkswagen discontinued production of the Beetle, for instance, at the same time as the Golf and Polo became available. A decision was taken to produce only so many models at any one time. In such cases we recognize two things: immediate income is renounced for future income and new investment involves outlays over several years. In the case of investments over time calculating the rate of return involves estimating the difference in earnings for every year, including the investment years. The rate of discount which equates to zero the present value of the stream of net income differences is the internal rate of return. Alternatively, if the lower incomes in the early years are regarded as the costs of the investment and the larger incomes in the future are the returns, then the rate of discount which equates the present value of the returns to the present value of the costs is the internal rate of return. It is also known as the rate of return over costs. The costs of an investment are the initial costs, plus the earnings which could have been obtained from old plant and equipment, product lines, occupations, etc., plus accumulated interest charges on costs incurred and on the returns which are foregone. In any given year, $t$, after a decision is taken to replace old equipment, etc., earnings $Y_t$ are achieved; earnings $X_t$ are sacrificed. Let $t = 1$ denote the first year. The cost of the investment in the first year is $C_1 = X_1 - Y_1$. In the second year costs are $C_2 = (X_2 + rC_1) - Y_2$, where $r$ refers to the rate of interest. Total costs are made up of the income differential plus the foregone return on past costs. Considering this sum over the lifetime of the alternative income streams, total accumulated costs in any year, $t$, are:

$$C_t = X_t + r\left(\sum_{t=1}^{t-1} C_t\right) - Y_t \tag{6.9}$$

Concepts used in capital theory are helpful in furthering our understanding of the nature of the investment decision. Economists distinguish between consumption and investment. If all income is consumed in any year the stock of capital goods (ignoring depreciation) remains the same. If in an economy consumption exceeds income there is 'disinvestment'. Capital can only be accumulated if consumption is restricted. By not consuming in the present there can be more income in the future.

Consider the rate of exploitation of a fish stock such as North Sea herring. Mankind is the principal predator of fish. If after a period of over-intensive fishing it was decided to

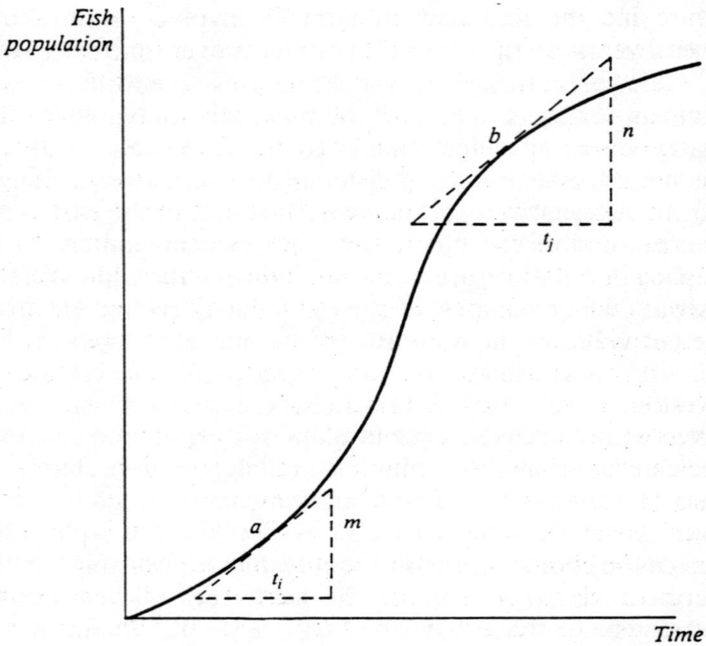


*Figure 6.3: The growth in fish populations with time in the absence of fishing*

allow the population to recover, studies (by the Ministry of Agriculture, Forestry and Fishing) have shown that stocks grow for a time at a constant rate—say 10 per cent per time period. In this example, the marginal product from *not* consuming would be 10 per cent per period. If, at the end of a single time period's fast, fisherman decided to go out fishing their decision would affect the size of the current and future population. Suppose the stock at the beginning of a time period is 100 million fish and without fishing it would grow to 110 million. If fishermen then restricted themselves to catching ten million fish per time period, they could enjoy this catch *forever*. Fishing in excess of this amount would reduce the fish stock; it would be equivalent to consuming capital. The return on not fishing is growth in the stock. If the population is allowed to grow to 200 million and fishing commenced, provided the same growth rate applied, twenty million fish per period could be caught without affecting the fish stock. But there is a limit to the extent that abstaining from consumption can lead to such an increase. Fish stocks, in the absence of fishing, do not grow indefinitely (at a constant exponential rate) because of food limitations, change in the age when breeding commences, etc. In fact, it has been found that the growth curve is as shown in Figure 6.3. In mathematics, this curve is known as the logistic curve. The per-period growth of the stock is proportional to the existing population until a certain limit is reached; thereafter, growth declines. The limit is determined by factors specific to the population and is discovered by empirical enquiry. The growth of the fish stock at any moment of time is given by the slope of the curve. This measures how many fish can be taken without reducing the population. The largest catch can be achieved when the population is close to its limit; when the natural death rate equals the natural birth rate. But this catch could not be sustained. From Figure 6.3, it can be seen that two of the choices over time are to catch $m$ fish over a period $t_i$ or to catch $n$ fish over a period $t_j$. The maximum sustainable yield is to be determined by the reader or computer user. The general point which follows from this argument is that many choices exist between flows of income over time. These correspond to different consumption/investment choices. In many businesses a growth curve resembling the logistic curve can be observed: rapid growth from a small base, with size levelling off asymptotically as the firm becomes more mature. Of course, a natural law does not apply as in the fish example but changes in a firm's financial policy can have predictable consequences. A firm's share value largely depends on the use it makes of its funds relatively to the opportunities available. A company with significant growth prospects appreciates in value if profits are retained. Well-established companies with little scope for growth, however, might have to distribute dividends to their shareholders if their market value is to be sustained.

## PROGRAM 6.1

Program 6.1 illustrates the consequences for present and

future generations of decisions taken now. Total yields from fishing over a time interval fifty time periods ahead are measured. The initial stock is assumed to be equal to ten million fish. The program's users are recommended to experiment with alternative values for the fishing rate and the time ahead when fishing should recommence after a moratorium for conservation. It is assumed growth is at 10 per cent per time period until limits imposed by the food supply are experienced. The total catch after a given number of years is the *yield*; the catch in a single year is the *catch*. When the computer prompts you to 'enter the year when fishing begins', the user should select a number of time periods into the future, say ten or fifteen. When the user is asked to decide upon the size of the catch, select a number between, say, two and twenty which represents the fish to be caught per time period. Suppose that your aim is to maximize the cumulative yield fifty + $N$ time periods ahead. In order to discover the size of the fish-stock without fishing, enter zero to each of the questions on the chosen fishing levels and the year when fishing is to commence. Complete several runs of the programs and make a note of the totals achieved. Use Figure 6.4 in conjunction with Program 6.1.

```
 10 REM6.1
 15 CLS
 20 DIM YIELD(200)
 30 YIELD(1)=0
 40 PRINT
 50 PRINT"ENTER WHEN FISHING SHOULD RECOMMENCE"
 60 PRINT"-i.e. the NUMBER of time periods ahead"
 70 INPUT"into the future";N
 80 INPUT'"ENTER THE SIZE OF THE CATCH ";CATCH
 90 PRINT
100 FOOD = 1000
110 PRINT
120 STOCK = 10
130 PRINT"TIME AHEAD    STOCK        YIELD"
140 FOR T = 1 TO N
150 REM WITHOUT FISHING POP. GROWTH IS EXPONENTIAL..
155 REM PROVIDED FISH < 100
160 IF STOCK < 100 GROWTH = .1*STOCK
165 IF STOCK>=100 THEN GROWTH = FOOD/STOCK
170 STOCK=STOCK+GROWTH
180 PRINT;T;"...........";INTSTOCK;".........";INTYIELD(T)
190 A$=INKEY$(0):IF A$ = "" THEN 190
200 NEXT T
210 FOR T = N+1 TO 50 :REM POPULATION GROWTH SLOWS DOWN
220 A$=INKEY$(0):IF A$ = "" THEN 220
230 IF CATCH >= STOCK THEN CATCH=STOCK
240 YIELD(T) = YIELD(T-1) + CATCH
250 IF STOCK >=100 THEN GROWTH =(FOOD/STOCK)-CATCH
```

```
260  IF STOCK < 100 THEN GROWTH=(.1*STOCK)-CATCH
270  STOCK = STOCK + GROWTH
280 PRINT;T;"..........";INTSTOCK;".........";INTYIELD(T)
290  CUMMULATIVECATCH = YIELD(T)
300  IF STOCK >=1  THEN NEXT T
310  IF STOCK <1 THEN GOTO 320
320  PRINT´´"CUMMULATIVE CATCH = ";CUMMULATIVECATCH
330 STOP
340  REM **** IBM ****
350  REM LINE 190:-
360  A$ = INKEY$: IF A$ = "" THEN 190
370  REM LINE 220:-
380  A$ = INKEY$: IF A$ = "" THEN 220
```

Line 30: Yield in time period 1 (before fishing commences) = zero.

Lines 50 to 80: The program user determines when fishing will commence and the annual catch which will apply.

Line 100: Food is set equal to 1000 throughout the program but competition for food may reduce growth in the fish stock.

Line 120: Initial size of the fish stock.

Line 140: First loop in the program concerns the period of time when the fish stock is allowed to grow without fishing.

Line 160 and 165: Growth is determined by the size of the fish stock. If the stock is less than 100 it is relatively small compared with the food supply. In this case the fish stock grows exponentially. If the stock is equal to or greater than 100, growth is determined by the food/stock ratio.

Line 210: The second loop in the program. Fishing commences.

Lines 230 and 260: The catch, yield and stock are determined. The catch cannot exceed the stock (line 230), the yield is cumulative (line 240) and growth depends on the food/stock ratio.

Line 280: An update of the program's solutions is reported.

Line 300: If the stock is equal to or exceeds one it is viable and the population can increase.

Line 320: End of program solutions are printed.

## PROGRAM 6.2

Program 6.2 brings together many of the ideas which have been discussed in this chapter. In particular, it shows numerically how a comparison can be made between alternative income streams. It also shows how an investment might be evaluated according to different criteria. The cost of capital, *r*, is to be set by the reader. It could be the market rate of

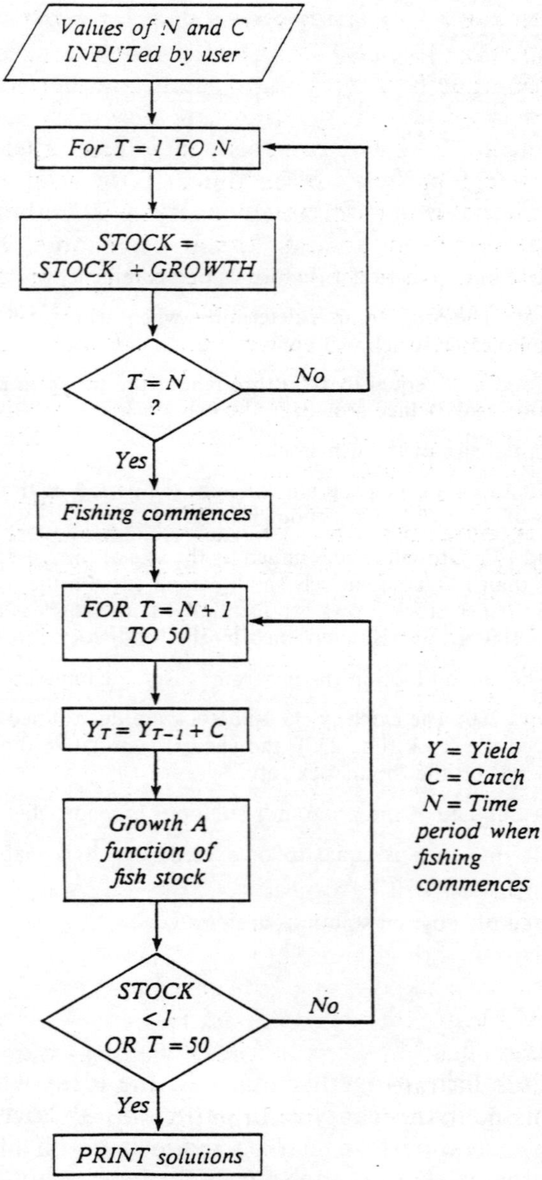


*Figure 6.4: Flow diagram in support of Program 6.1*

interest. To see how the program works, users are recommended to begin with the assumed values for the alternative income streams, the levels of investment, etc. In the first part of the program two streams of undiscounted income are compared. For simplicity, they are assumed to grow at a constant rate. The user can easily introduce other values or consider irregular flows of income. If the user prefers to consider the returns from a new investment, without assuming the existence of an old stream of income, he should simply enter zeros for the variables concerned. In the case of comparisons between two streams, it is clear that, for a typical investment, long after one income stream has overtaken the income which would have been obtained from the alternative investment, the cost of income foregone might not have been recovered. The second part of the program involves income streams which are discounted back to their present values. The third part enables the calculation of the average income per unit of capital employed. This is measured as $(PV/T)/I_0$, where $PV$ is the present value after $T$ time periods. This value is approximately equal to the internal rate of return when discounting takes place over many years (see equation 6.1 and Section 6.1). Here we use a 'short cut' method of the kind often favoured by the business community for its simplicity. Alfred and Evans (1965) examine the basis of such methods.

The notation for and variables adopted in Program 6.2 are as follows:

$A$ = initial cost of capital invested in project $Y$
$B$ = growth rate of income from $X$
$C$ = growth rate of income from $Y$
$D$ = first year's income sacrificed from $X$
$E$ = first year's income obtained from $Y$
$F$ = time ahead in years before $Y$ yields income
$G$ = discount rate
$X$ = income over time from the investment in $X$
$Y$ = income over time from the investment in $Y$
$Z$ = income difference in any one year
$W$ = cumulative income difference or outstanding debt
$N$ = cumulative interest on the outstanding debt

*T* = time
*V* = present value of income difference in year *T*
*U* = cumulative value of income differences discounted back to their present value, i.e. the *PV* of the investment
*R* = average value of discounted net income over twenty years
*S* = average discounted net income per unit of initial capital employed.

```
10 REM6.2
20 DIM Y(30):DIM X(30):DIM Z(30):DIM N(30)
30 DIM W(30):DIM V(30):DIM U(30):DIM R(30):DIM S(30)
40 A=1000:B=.04:C=.06:D=200:E=500:F=4:G=.1
50 X(1)=-D
60 Y(1)=-A
70  CLS
80 Y(F)=E
90 PRINT"The displays which follow concern"
100 PRINT"returns over time (row by row)."
110 REM diff. = difference, Outs. = outstanding
120 A$=INKEY$(0):IF A$="" THEN 120:CLS
130 PRINT"Income   New    Income  Outst.  Current"
140 PRINT"foregone income diff.    debt   interest"
150 FOR T=1 TO 18
160 X(T+1)=X(T)+B*X(T)
170 Y(T+F)=Y(T+F-1)+C*Y(T+F-1)
180 Z(T)=Y(T)+X(T)
190 W(T)=W(T-1)+Z(T)+N(T-1)
200 N(T)=G*W(T)
210 PRINT;INT (X(T));".....";INT (Y(T));"....";INT (Z(T));
220  PRINT;".....";INT (-W(T));"....";INT (-N(T))
230 NEXT T
240 PRINT"Press any key for a display of the"
250 PRINT"present values of the income stream."
260  A$=INKEY$(0):IF A$="" THEN 260
270 CLS
280 PRINT"Time    Discounted       Cummulative"
290 PRINT"          income     discounted income"
300 FOR T = 1 TO 18
310 V(T)=X(T)/(1+G)^T+Y(T)/(1+G)^T
320 U(T)=U(T-1)+V(T)
330 NEXT T
340 R(T)=U(18)/18
350 S(T)=R(T)/A*100
360 FOR T = 1 TO 18
370 PRINT;T;"..........";INT V(T);"..........";INT U(T)
380 NEXT T
390 PRINT"Press any key to continue"
400 A$=INKEY$(0): IF A$="" THEN 400
410 CLS
420  PRINT''"Present value = ";U(18)
430 PRINT''"Average income per unit of capital"
440 PRINT"employed = ";S(T);"% p.a."
450 STOP
460 REM **** IBM ****
470  REM LINE 120:-
480 A$ = INKEY$: IF A$ = "" THEN 120:CLS
490 REM Note also lines 260 and 400
```

Line 40: Initial values of *A* to *G* are established.

Line 50: In period one, income foregone equals 200 units.

Line 60: In period one, the income from new investment is minus 1000 (the initial cost of the investment).

Line 80: The first year's income from the new investment (equals income in period four).

Line 190: Note that this corresponds to equation 6.9.

Lines 210 to 220: Program users should work through the first few sets of solutions manually to confirm their understanding of how they are obtained.

Line 300: The second loop. Discounted values are calculated. The values of each of the variables held in memory are calculated at the rate given by *G*.

## 6.3 MULTI-PROJECT ANALYSIS—THE MARKOWITZ APPROACH

Investors, be they corporations with interests in several markets, or shareholders, or managers of unit trusts and pension funds, assess the risks as well as the returns from investments. In financial analysis the principle of spreading risks by diversifying the composition of a portfolio is well known. It involves dividing investment funds between different holdings with a view to minimising income variance for a given mean expected income. Corporations often consider the impact of new projects upon their risk structure. A project might seem worthwhile when viewed individually but not in terms of its overall consequences. The modern theory behind these issues stems mainly from the contributions of Markowitz (1952, 1959). It applies both to financial and real assets. In essence, the analysis concerns expected returns: variance rules and the trade-off between a 'good' and a 'bad'; efficient portfolios reduce risk and/or increase mean expected returns. In Figure 6.5, efficient portfolios are shown along the south-east boundary of the attainable set of $E(Y)V(Y)$ combinations, i.e. between points *m* and *n*. Searching for these solutions requires an examination of the degree of *correlation* between the assets. One of the interesting findings of portfolio analysis is that it is possible to invest in assets which are more risky (and higher

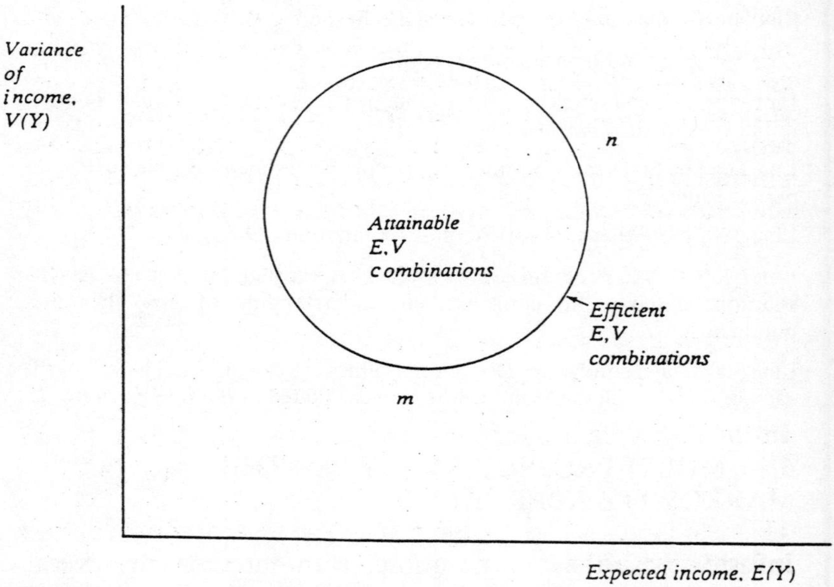


*Figure 6.5: Feasible E(Y), V(Y) solutions and the search for efficient combinations*

earners) than those which are currently held and yet to *reduce* overall risk.

To illustrate the principles involved in portfolio management we restrict ourselves to examples of two asset models. Suppose a firm could invest either in project A or in project B or it could diversify putting half of its funds in A and half in B. For simplicity, assume to begin with that the risks associated with each are identical and that there is no correlation between the projects. If the entire funds are invested in A (or B) assume that there is a 50 per cent chance of making a profit, $\pi$, of £20 and a 50 per cent chance of making a loss, $L$, of £10. The expected return from either project is 0.5(£20) + 0.5( − £10) = £5. If the funds are divided equally between the projects there are four possible outcomes: a profit on both projects, a profit on A with a loss on B, a loss on both projects and a loss on A with a profit on B. Taking account of the size of the investments, given that each of the four outcomes are equally likely, the expected return equals 0.25(£10 + £10) + 0.5(£10 − £5) + 0.25( − £5 − £5);

this sums to £5. Thus, returns are not different from the returns in the single project case but the *extreme* outcomes are less likely. Although the expected return is the same, variance is reduced by diversification. Denote the expected return by $E(Y)$, its variance by $V(Y)$, the returns and probabilities of each outcome by $X_i$, $P_i$, for $i = 1,...,4$ and the expected return by $\bar{X}$. The variance of income is:

$$V(Y) = \sum_{i=1}^{4} P_i(X_i - \bar{X})^2 \qquad (6.10)$$

In the single project case,

$$V(Y) = 0.5(20 - 5)^2 + 0.5(-10 - 5)^2 = 225.$$

In the case of divided funds,

$$V(Y) = 0.25(20 - 5)^2 + 0.5(5 - 5)^2 + 0.25(-10 - 5)^2.$$

This sums to 112.5. Tables 6.3 and 6.4 summarize the information above.

*Table 6.3: Pay-off data for investment in a single project*

| | Project A | | Project B | |
|---|---|---|---|---|
| | Return | Probability | Return | Probability |
| | 20 | 0.5 | 20 | 0.5 |
| | −10 | 0.5 | −10 | 0.5 |
| Expected Return: $E(Y)$ | | 5 | | 5 |
| Variance $V(Y)$ | | 225 | | 225 |
| Standard Deviation of Returns: $\sqrt{V(Y)}$ | | 15 | | 15 |

*Table 6.4: Pay-off data for an investment in two project with independent returns*

| | Return | Probability |
|---|---|---|
| Profit on A and B | 20 | 0.25 |
| Loss on A and B | −10 | 0.25 |
| Profit on A or B | 5 | 0.5 |
| Expected Return | 5 | |
| Variance | 112.5 | |

Let us now consider the case where the proportion invested in each project may be varied and where the projects are correlated. Assume that for each project the expected level of income and its standard deviation have been forecasted. It is reasonable to suppose that the higher the expected income the greater is the variance. If variance did not increase with the expected income there would be no case for considering the more risky project. Denote the proportion of funds invested in A by $pA$ and the returns by $(Y_A, \sigma_A)$, $(Y_B, \sigma_B)$. The expected return is: $E(Y) = pAY_A + (1 - pA)Y_B$.

The variance of the portfolio is:

$$V(Y) = pA^2\sigma_A^2 + (1 - pA)^2\sigma_B^2 + 2pA(1 - pA)R\sigma_A\sigma_B \quad (6.11)$$

where $R$ is the degree of correlation between the projects. (For a proof of this equation, see Koutsoyiannis (1982), Chapter 12). Clearly, if $pA = 1$, $V(Y) = \sigma_A^2$. Variance is reduced if $R$ is negative and it is increased if $R$ is positive. Negatively correlated might be the returns to investment in barbecues and rainware; positively correlated might the returns to snooker and television. Given the forecasted data below, consider the solutions for different values of $pA$ in Table 6.12

| A | B |
|---|---|
| $Y_A = 10$ | $Y_B = 15$ |
| $\sigma_A = 10$ | $\sigma_B = 20$ |

*Table 6.5: E(Y), V(Y) data for different proportions of funds invested in projects A and B.*

| Proportion of funds invested in Project A ($pA$) | E($Y$) | Variance of returns for different values of $R$: $R = 1$ | $R = 0.5$ | $R = 0$ | $R = -0.5$ | $R = -1$ |
|---|---|---|---|---|---|---|
| 0 | 15 | 400 | 400 | 400 | 400 | 400 |
| 0.2 | 14 | 324 | 292 | 260 | 228 | 196 |
| 0.4 | 13 | 256 | 208 | 160 | 112 | 64 |
| 0.6 | 12 | 196 | 148 | 100 | 52 | 4 |
| 0.8 | 11 | 144 | 112 | 80 | 48 | 16 |
| 1 | 10 | 100 | 100 | 100 | 100 | 100 |

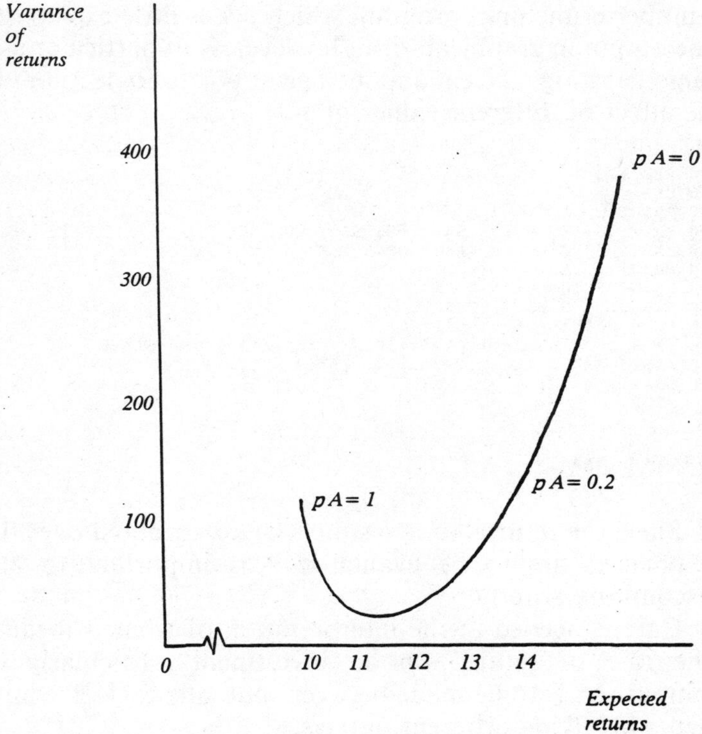


*Figure 6.6: E(Y), V(Y) relationship for different proportions of funds invested in A with R = – 1*

From Table 6.5, if $R$ is negative we see that it is possible by diversification both to increase the expected return *and* to reduce variance by efficiently selecting the proportions invested. See, for instance, the last two columns and the effect of reducing from 100 per cent the percentage of funds in A. The information in Table 6.5 is shown graphically in Figure 6.6 for $R = -1$. The negative section of the graph illustrates inefficient portfolio decisions.

## PROGRAM 6.3

In this program the user is invited to vary the parameters and to consider the impact upon $E(Y)$, $V(Y)$. It is a simple 'number-crunching' program which needs little explanation. The output in graphical form, however, is of particular use in demonstrating efficient and inefficient portfolio decisions and the effect of different values of *R*.

```
 10 REM 6.3
 20 CLS
 30 PRINT
 40 YA = 10: YB = 15: SA = 10: SB = 20
 50 INPUT "ENTER THE VALUE OF R ";R
 60 PRINT
 70 PRINT"Proportion in A      E(Y)       V(Y)"
 80 FOR pA = 0 TO 1 STEP .2
 90 EY = pA*YA + (1 - pA)*YB
100 VY = pA^2*SA^2+(1-pA)^2*SB^2 + 2*pA*(1-pA)*R*SA*SB
110PRINT;pA;"..................";EY;"......";VY
120 NEXT
130 STOP
```

## SUMMARY

1. Since the returns to investment are distributed over time, if projects are to be evaluated it is important to apply discounting criteria.
2. Care is needed in the interpretation of what is meant by 'the rate of return' on an investment particularly if a comparison is to be made between mutually exclusive investments involving different outlays.
3. Investment often requires the commitment of resources over several time periods and/or comparisons between alternative income streams. In measuring cost an allowance should be made for the return which is foregone on funds which could have been employed elsewhere.
4. The resources available for capital accumulation depend on consumption levels over time. Current consumption depends on past investment.
5. Risks in investment can be reduced if firms diversify. Diversification is particularly effective if projects are negatively correlated.

## FURTHER READING

A concise yet quite thorough book is Hawkins and Pearce (1971). Koutsoyiannis (1982) covers may neglected areas and includes a strong section on risk-return analysis. Levy and Sarnat (1982) is widely adopted. Elton and Gruber (1979) consider recent developments in investment analysis particularly in connection with the contribution of Markowitz. Dewey (1965) provides many insights into the cost of capital and Anderson (1977) concerns the theory and practice of fishing policy.

# 7 Time Series Forecasting

Many decisions require forecasts to be made. The main purpose of forecasting is to provide as much information as possible to assist decision makers. In this chapter we restrict ourselves to a data series for a single variable. Unlike in Chapter 9, which is also concerned with forecasting, no attempt is made to relate data for one variable to data for another. The method adopted for carrying out calculations is the Holt-Winters procedure following from the work of C.C. Holt (1955) and P.R. Winters (1960). In Section 7.1 we examine methods based on averaging aimed at eliminating random disturbances. In Section 7.2 we seek patterns in previous observations and consider how trend and seasonal influences can be included.

Forecasting based on time series data essentially involves extrapolation of a curve fitted to a series of observations. In one respect forecasting shares with regression analysis the idea that visual observation of data plotted on a graph can be improved upon and estimates subject to precise statistical tests. Assessment 'by eye' can be misleading as different people may reach different conclusions. Further, study of forecasting methods helps the forecaster to question his or her own procedures and opens a wider range of criteria for evaluation than might otherwise be employed.

The first step in deciding upon a forecasting method is to plot a graph of the data. This will show if the data follow a recognizable pattern. Examination of the graph for a particular data series will reveal whether it is necessary to build seasonal variations, trends and possibly cyclical factors into a forecast. Of course, even if the past has always provided a reliable guide to the future, forecasters must exercise their judgement and recognize that relevant external conditions must continue as in the past if predictions are to be made. (The word *prediction* is useful in describing the 'subjective' aspect of forecasting when the analyst adopts other than a purely mechanical or mathematical approach to his or her work.) In some cases a graph can be fitted very successfully to data (with little deviation of the fitted curve form the observations), but the past still proves a very unreliable guide to the future. For instance, if unemployment is forecasted using time series methods, the election of a new government with different policies is likely to change drastically the pattern of unemployment over time (at least in the short term). This does not mean that forecasting based on this series is impossible; it simply means that more complex relationships must be sought.

## 7.1 SIMPLE FORECASTING METHODS

In this chapter, we concentrate upon short term forecasts. Long term forecasts require great stability in the determining factors and are rarely successful. Short term forecasts typically have the property that a relatively high value for a variable is more often than not followed by another high value, whilst a low value is commonly followed by another low value. The simplest forecasting rule is to base the forecasting for time $T+1$ upon the observation in $T$. (It is the forecast used by many British holiday-makers when deciding between holidaying at home or abroad!) It takes the form:

$$\hat{Y}_{T+1} = Y_T \tag{7.1}$$

where $\hat{Y}_{T+1}$ is the forecast, $Y_T$ is the observed value and $\hat{Y}_{T+1}$ is read '$Y$ hat $T+1$'. This is the standard notation for the difference between estimated and observed values. Different notation will be used when we apply the computer. This method relies on the most recent observation as the best forecast of the immediate future. Better forecasts are usually obtained by taking the average of the last $N$ observations:

$$\hat{Y}_{T+1} = \frac{1}{N}(Y_T + T_{T-1}, \ldots, + Y_{T+1-N}) \tag{7.2}$$

This method is known as the simple moving average of order $N$. It is a moving average because each new observation is included when it becomes available and the most distant observation is discarded each time a new one is added.

Most often, time series forecasting involves a combination of the approaches above. The relation:

$$\hat{Y}_{T+1} = \alpha Y_T + (1 - \alpha)\hat{Y}_T \tag{7.3}$$

where $\alpha$ is a constant satisfying $0 \leqslant \alpha \leqslant 1$ is commonly applied. The value of $\alpha$ is selected by the forecaster according to his or her own judgement of past events. It may be adjusted when different constants are tried in search of a better fit. If $\alpha$ is zero, forecasts are not affected by the existing observation; the forecast depends on past forecasts. If $\alpha$ equals one, equation 7.3 simplifies to equation 7.1. The forecast given by equation 7.3 involves a *weighted moving average*. If $\alpha > 0$, the greatest weight is attached to recent forecasts. The forecast involves an exponentially weighted moving average and the method is known as *exponential smoothing*. The weight attached to the most recent forecast is $(1 - \alpha)$, to the previous forecast is $(1 - \alpha)^2$, to the one before that is $(1 - \alpha)^3$, etc. By substitution for $\hat{Y}_T$ in equation 7.3, $\hat{Y}_{T+1} = \alpha Y_T + (1 - \alpha)(\alpha Y_{T-1} + (1 - \alpha)\hat{Y}_{T-1})$, it will be apparent that for any value of $\alpha$ other than 0 or 1 the weights attached to the current and past observations and past forecasts add up to one. As they add up to one, the method is based on the assumption that the observed data are fluctuating randomly around some fixed value which we aim to estimate. If the sum of the weights did not add up to one, the forecasts would tend to increase or decrease.

In order to use this method, we have to make an initial forecast, $\hat{Y}_1$. This is not critical provided a sufficiently long series of observations are available. The value of $\hat{Y}_1$ most often used is the first observation in the series. Exponential smoothing is best understood from an example. Consider Table 7.1. Here, $\alpha = 0.5$ and $\hat{Y}_1 = Y_1 = 100$. The reader is left

*Table 7.1: Exponential smoothing a data series with $\alpha = 0.5$*

| | | | | | |
|---|---|---|---|---|---|
| $T$ | 1 | 2 | 3 | 4 | 5 |
| $Y_T$ | 100 | 112 | 124 | 136 | 120 |
| $\hat{Y}_T$ | 100 | 100 | 106 | | |
| $\alpha Y_T$ | 50 | 56 | 62 | | |
| $(1-\alpha)\hat{Y}_T$ | 50 | 50 | 53 | | |
| $\alpha Y_T + (1-\alpha)\hat{Y}_{T+1}$ | 100 | 106 | 115 | | |

to complete columns 4 and 5. Of course, in order to forecast with any confidence, it would be necessary to have observations for more than four time periods. When this table was drawn up a value of 0.5 for $\alpha$ was chosen arbitrarily. A value for $\alpha$, generally, is obtained by trial and error with the aim of obtaining the closest fit between $Y_T$ and $\hat{Y}_T$ over the period observed. Once it is found it is used for forecasting future values. We calculate the difference between the forecasts and observations: $e_1 = Y_1 - \hat{Y}_1$, $e_2 = Y_2 - \hat{Y}_2$, ..., and determine their total size for different values of $\alpha$. When selecting $\alpha$ the aim is to minimise the forecasting error, $V$, where:

$$V = \sum_{T=1}^{N} e_T^2 \tag{7.4}$$

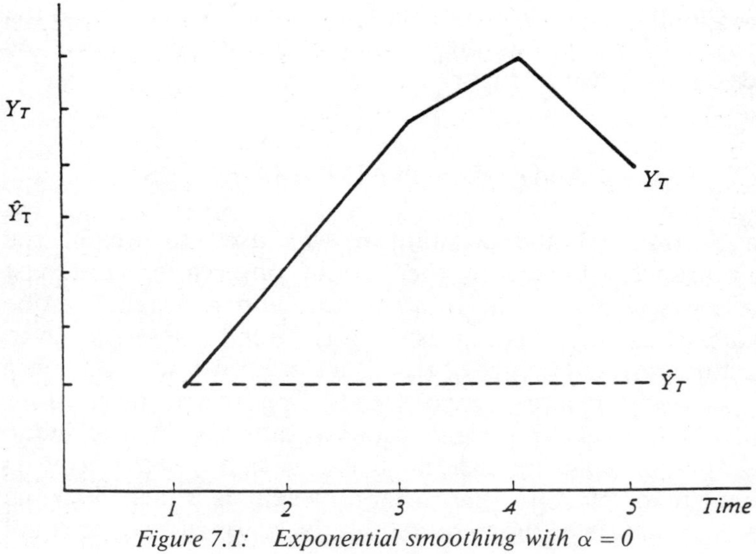


*Figure 7.1: Exponential smoothing with $\alpha = 0$*

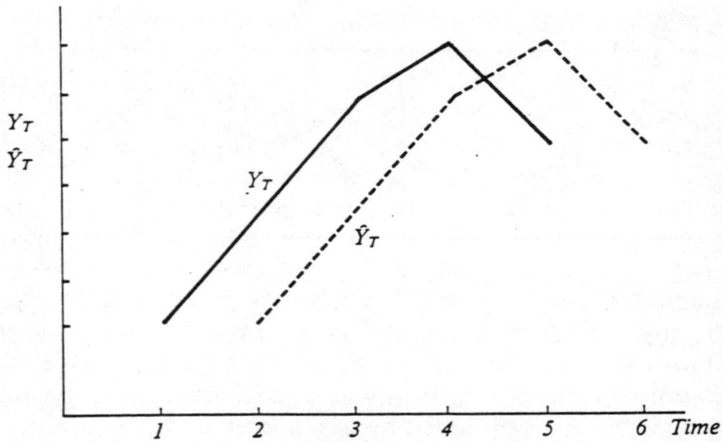


*Figure 7.2: Exponential smoothing with* $\alpha = 1$

To consider the impact of alternative extreme values of $\alpha$, examine Figures 7.1 and 7.2. If $\alpha = 0$, no weight is attached to the current observation in the series. Current forecasts depend only on past forecasts and the current value has no part to play. The forecast made at the beginning of the time period is the forecast for all subsequent time periods.

If, on the other hand, $\alpha = 1$, if follows that past forecasts have no part to play; in terms of equation 7.3 $\hat{Y}_{T+1} = Y_T$: the forecasted value lags the current observation by one time period as shown in Figure 7.2.

## 7.2 TREND AND SEASONAL INFLUENCES

In Section 7.1 the constant $\alpha$ was used to weight the importance attached to the current observation and past forecasts of a variable. In a similar manner, weights can be attached to the current measure of the trend in a series and to past measures. The size of trends is not known with certainty hence we refer to measure of trends. Denote $\beta$ as the constant used in the analysis of trends and $\gamma$ as the constant used in the analysis of seasonal factors; $0 \leqslant \beta \leqslant 1$; $0 \leqslant \gamma \leqslant 1$. If $\beta$ is equal to or close to one, a large weight is attached to the recent measure of the trend. Similarly, if $\gamma$ is close to or equal to one of the most recent seasonal variation is considered to be the most important. Before discussing the mathematics of the arguments involving $\alpha$, $\beta$ and $\gamma$, consider the following problems: (1) how could future human populations be forecasted? (2) what is the likely future demand for electricity? (3) how many people are likely to attend football matches in the future? Is it likely that trend and seasonal influences will have a part to play in all three forecasts? Should high or low weights be attached to the most recent measures? The answers to these questions no doubt depend on which human populations are considered, over which period of time—weeks, months or years—the demand for electricity is measured and for which football clubs attendance is to be recorded. Once the questioner has specified a more detailed line of enquiry, he or she will be in a stronger position to think about the initial values of the constants $\beta$ and $\gamma$. Readers might already consider themselves in a position to select such values in connection with a problem which has come to mind. If there is no *a priori* reason why high or low values should be selected it might be thought reasonable to attach an equal weight to the most recent observation and to all previous forecasts. In this case, $\beta$ would equal 0.5 in the case of the trend. This would have the status of an initial trial value. If it proves unsatisfactory, others could be tried.

The trial and error procedure we are describing might be considered unsatisfactory either because it involves guess-estimates, which have no theoretical justification, or because it seems laborious in that many combinations of $\alpha$, $\beta$ and $\gamma$ would need to be tried. To the first objection it is conceded that time series analysis involves the crudest form of empiricism. However, this method of obtaining forecasts is preferable to drawing a rough line through a scatter of observations. The latter inevitably involves greater inaccuracy, given the forecasting error, $V$, than the selection and rejection of alternative constants. Furthermore, if a line is fitted 'by eye' the investigator in all likelihood will have made up his mind about what is likely to happen in the future regardless of analysis. The algorithms used within professional forecasting packages, such as the one applied by the animal foodstuffs manufacturer BOCM, enable the alternative constants to be assessed in terms of their forecasting performance. Alternative models of the economy involving time series methods are applied. Many thousands of comparisons between the alternative values are carried out without any human labour necessarily being involved. When the best combination of values for $\alpha$, $\beta$, $\gamma$, etc. have been found, they are reported to the program user along with the measure of the forecasting error. Thus, a numerical value for the trend and seasonal variation is available. This is not so easy by rough curve sketching since it is difficult to sort out the influence one from another. In professional packages, confidence intervals for forecasts several time periods ahead are also provided. It is then up to the researcher to decide whether to use the *ex post* values of $\alpha$, $\beta$, $\gamma$, etc. in forecasting. Professional packages are based on a forecasting method known as the Box-Jenkins methods (1976). The information relating to BOCM's forecasting problem was obtained from the Open University (1981b).

## PROGRAMS 7.1, 7.2 AND 7.3

These programs are discussed together since they are similar in structure and apply the same data series. They were written as separate programs in order to illustrate how progressively more complex forecasting procedures can be built up. Program 7.1 involves exponential smoothing, Program 7.2 smoothing with trend and Program 7.3 smoothing with trend and seasonal variations. The forecasting problem concerns levels of unemployment in the UK. The data for the variable $X(t)$, the recorded unemployment level at time $t$, is contained in Table 7.2 and Figure 7.3. Equations 7.5 and 7.6 provide the basis for Program 7.1.

$$Y(t+1) = Y(t) + a[X(t) - Y(t)] \tag{7.5}$$

$$R(t) = Y(t) + a[X(t) - Y(t)] \tag{7.6}$$

The terms are defined as follows:

*Table 7.2: Unadjusted unemployment levels including school leavers, 1983 to 1985, in millions*

| | | | |
|---|---|---|---|
| Nov. 1983 | 3.06 | Nov. 1984 | 3.22 |
| Dec. | 3.08 | Dec. | 3.22 |
| Jan. 1984 | 3.2 | Jan. 1985 | 3.34 |
| Feb. | 3.19 | Feb. | 3.33 |
| March | 3.14 | March | 3.27 |
| April | 3.11 | April | 3.27 |
| May | 3.08 | May | 3.24 |
| June | 3.03 | June | 3.12 |
| July | 3.10 | July | 3.23 |
| Aug. | 3.12 | Aug. | 3.24 |
| Sept. | 3.28 | Sept. | 3.35 |
| Oct. | 3.22 | Oct. | 3.28 |

*Source: CSO Economic Trends,* Jan. 1986

$Y(t+1)$ = forecast of unemployment one period ahead
$Y(t)$ = previous forecast of unemployment
$X(t)$ = observed unemployment figure
$R(t)$ = forecast of unemployment after smoothing the data series
$a$ = constant selected by the forecaster

The similarity between equations 7.5 and 7.3 should be noted. By rearrangement of the terms it will become clear they involve the same mathematical relationship. From Table 7.2, and adopting the initial value $a = 0.5$, Table 7.3 is derived. In Table 7.3, only the observations and forecasts from May 1985 to September 1985 are shown . In Table 7.3 $X(1)$, if displayed, would correspond to recorded unemployment in November 1983; $X(2)$ to unemployment in December 1983; $Y(2)$ to forecasted unemployment in December 1983. In the first period, $Y(1) = X(1)$. With or without Program 7.1, set $a = 0.5$ and determine the value of $Y(t)$ over the time periods 22 to 24. Confirm that $Y(25)$ equals 3.28. The last row is included in order to assess how good the forecasts $Y(t)$ are of $X(t)$. Different values of $a$ may be selected to see if improved *ex post* forecasts can be obtained. Experiment with different values for $a$ until *past* forecasts are as close as possible to actually observed values. When a value for $a$ has been chosen which seems to enable

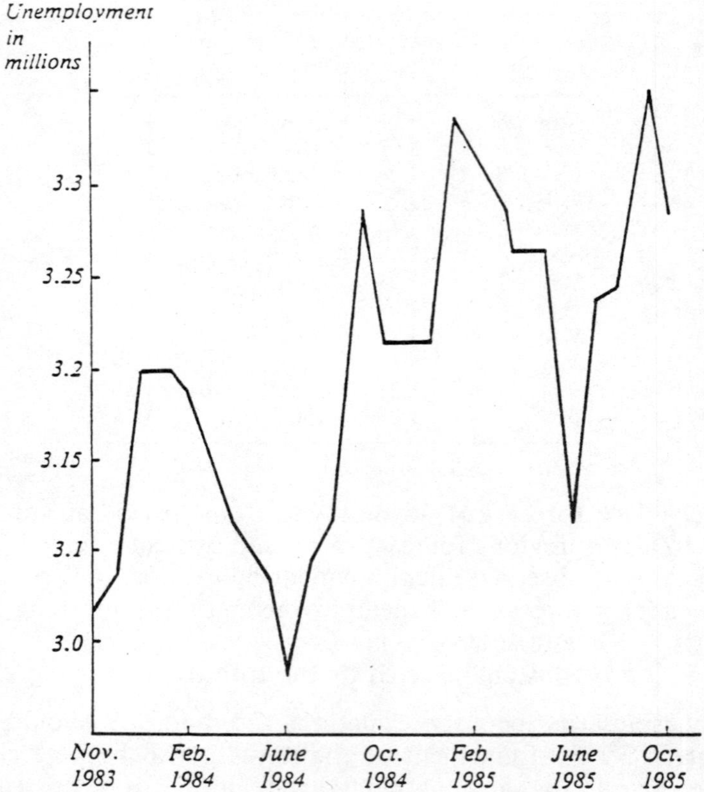


*Figure 7.3: Total unemployed, including school leavers, UK, Nov. 1983–Oct. 1985, Unadjusted data. (Source: CSO (Jan. 1986) Economic Trends, HMSO)*

*Table 7.3: Corrections for random disturbances with* $a = 0.5$

| $T$ (1985) | 19 (May) | 20 (June) | 21 (July) | 22 (Aug) | 23 (Sept) | 24 |
|---|---|---|---|---|---|---|
| $X(t)$ | 3.24 | 3.12 | 3.23 | 3.24 | 3.35 | 3.28 |
| $Y(t)$ | 3.27 | 3.25 | 3.18 | | | |
| $a(X(t) - Y(t))$ | – 0.02 | – 0.07 | 0.02 | | | |
| $R(t)$ | 3.25 | 3.18 | 3.20 | | | |
| $Y(t+1)$ | 3.25 | 3.18 | 3.20 | | | |
| $X(t) - Y(t)$ | | | | | | |

Forecasted unemployment level in period 25 (Nov. 1985) is 3.28 millions.

the closest overall fit between $Y(t)$ and $X(t)$, use this value in *ex ante* forecasting.

The equations for Program 7.2 are:

$$Y(t+1) = R(t) + T(t+1) \tag{7.7}$$

$$T(t+1) = T(t) + b[D(t) - T(t)] \tag{7.8}$$

$$D(t) = R(t) - R(t-1) \tag{7.9}$$

$$R(t) = Y(t) + a[X(t) - Y(t)] \tag{7.10}$$

The additional terms used in the program are defined as follows:

$T(t+1)$ = measure of the trend in unemployment per month to be used in forecasting future unemployment
$T(t)$ = past measure of the trend in unemployment per month
$D(t)$ = difference between two forecasts after exponential smoothing. This is the measure of the current trend in unemployment
$b$ = constant used in weighting the current and previous measures of the trend

By working back through the equations it should be appreciated that $T(t+1)$ is determined by the weight attached to the past measure of the trend in unemployment and the current measure of the trend after exponential smoothing. To help to understand the full system of equations, assume for simplicity $a = 0$, $b = 0$. It follows that $Y(t+1) = T(t) + Y(t)$. In other cases, some further explanation is necessary on how the forecasts involving $T(t+1)$ are performed. From equation 7.8, if $b = 1$, $T(t)$ equals zero: the measure of the trend in unemployment is based upon the current measure alone. Equation 7.9 concerns two forecasts of unemployment: one which is made for period $t$, the other which is made for period $(t-1)$, after exponential smoothing. The difference between these two forecasts is the most recent or current measure of the trend.

Table 7.4 provides a breakdown of the solutions for Program 7.2 given $a = 0.5$, $b = 0.8$. Given these weights, are improved forecasts obtained? By comparison of Figures 7.4

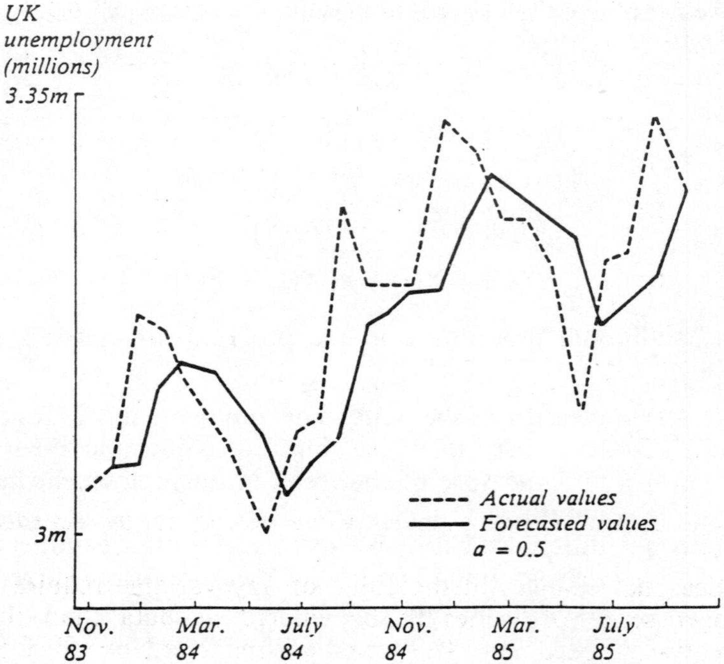


*Figure 7.4:* *Forecasted unemployment adjusted for random disturbances*

and 7.5 it is apparent they are not. The difference between the series $X(t)$, $Y(t)$ is approximately 30 per cent greater in Figure 7.5. This is a by eye approximation and, of course, a fully developed program is needed for numerical solutions involving equation 7.4. But why does the forecast deteriorate so markedly when $b = 0.8$? Attaching a weight of 0.8 to the most recent trend involves attaching considerable weight to the most recent measure. From Table 7.4 (row eight) it will be seen that this amounts to supposing that the trend in unemployment was *falling*. This erroneous deduction is explained by the simple fact that period 20, for instance, corresponds to the month of June which is always a month when relatively low unemployment is recorded. Also, the preceding months are months of relatively low unemployment. A trend based on these months will suggest *falling* unemployment. If a low value for $b$ is set, the overall trend

*Table 7.4: Corrections for random disturbance and trend,* $a = 0.5$ $b = 0.8$

| 1 | $t$ | 20 | 21 | 22 | 23 | 24 |
|---|---|---|---|---|---|---|
| 2 | $X(t)$ | 3.12 | 3.23 | 3.24 | 3.35 | 3.28 |
| 3 | $Y(t)$ | 3.22 | 3.09 | 3.14 | 3.21 | |
| 4 | $X(t) - Y(t)$ | − 0.10 | 0.14 | 0.10 | | |
| 5 | $0.5 * (X(t) - Y(t))$ | − 0.05 | 0.07 | 0.5 | | |
| 6 | $(3) + (5) = R(t)$ | 3.17 | 3.16 | 3.19 | | |
| 7 | $R(t) - R(t-1) = D(t)$ | − 0.09 | − 0.01 | 0.03 | | |
| 8 | $T(t)$ | − 0.04 | − 0.08 | − 0.02 | | |
| 9 | $D(t) - T(t)$ | − 0.05 | 0.07 | 0.05 | | |
| 10 | $0.8 * (D(t) - T(t))$ | − 0.04 | 0.06 | 0.04 | | |
| 11 | $(8) + (10) = T(t+1)$ | − 0.08 | − 0.02 | 0.02 | | |
| 12 | $(6) + (11) = Y(t+1)$ | 3.09 | 3.14 | 3.21 | | |

would be upward and *negative values would not be recorded in row 8.*

Seasonal changes in the value of any variable require a longer series of values to be entered as data than the twenty-four used here. If a forecast is made in November of unemployment which will be found in December it is necessary to compare the change which occurred in the previous December over the previous November. The adjustment for this change is shown in line 300 of Program 7.3 as $S(t+1) = R(t-11) - R(t-12)$. This line is read as 'the anticipated change in next month's unemployment due to seasonal factors is equal to (the adjusted value of) the difference between unemployment eleven and twelve months previously'. Thus, in the final calculation, line 310 of Program 7.3: $Y(t+1) = R(t) + T(t+1) + S(t+1)$. In program 7.3 only the values over one full season are considered. Earlier seasons might have provided a better guide or a weighted average might have been used setting $0 \leqslant c \leqslant 1$. However, .it was decided to ignore earlier seasonal adjustments so as to reduce the amount of data which would need to be read into the computer. The most recent seasonal influence is assumed to be representative, hence $c$ is set equal to one. In the case of the data used in Program 7.3, a seasonal influence is present but it is not strong and a

*Figure 7.5: Forcasted unemployment adjusted for random disturbances and trend*

seasonal influence is only taken account of in the second half of the series.

## PROGRAM 7.1

This program may be used in connection with any data for a single variable over time. It is assumed that the data fluctuates randomly around some fixed value which we aim to estimate by applying weights to past forecasts and the current observation. The program listing only provides solutions in tabular form. To obtain a clearer impression of the forecasting error, for different values of the constant chosen for weighting purposes, it is preferable to refer to the program on disk where graphical solutions are provided.

```
10 REM7.1
20 CLS
30 DIM S(30):DIM X(30):DIM Y(30):DIM R(30)
40 INPUT "ENTER THE VALUE OF a "´"(BETWEEN 0 AND 1)";a
50 REM LINES 60-100 = OBSERVED UNEMPLOYMENT DATA
60 X(1)=3.06:X(2)=3.08:X(3)=3.2:X(4)=3.19:X(5)=3.14:X(6)=3.11
70 X(7)=3.08:X(8)=3.03:X(9)=3.1:X(10)=3.12:X(11)=3.28
80 X(12)=3.22:X(13)=3.22:X(14)=3.22:X(15)=3.34:X(16)=3.33
90 X(17)=3.27:X(18)=3.27:X(19)=3.24:X(20)=3.12:X(21)=3.23
100 X(22)=3.24:X(23)=3.35:X(24)=3.28
110 PRINT´"t          X(t) Y(t) a*(X(t)-Y(T)) R(t)"
115 PRINT
120 Y(1)=X(1):Y(2)=X(2)
130 R(1)=Y(1):R(2)=Y(2)
140 FOR t=2 TO 24
150 R(t)=Y(t)+a*(X(t)-Y(t))
160 Y(t+1)=R(t)
170 PRINT;t;"...";INT(100*X(t))/100;"..";
180 PRINT;INT(100*Y(t))/100;
190 PRINT;".....";INT(100*a*(X(t)-Y(t)))/100;
200 PRINT;"....";INT(100*R(t))/100
210 A$=INKEY$(0):IF A$=""THEN 210
220 NEXT t
230 PRINT´"THE FORECAST Y(t) IN THE NEXT"´"PERIOD IS ";
240 PRINT;Y(25)
250 STOP
260 REM **** IBM ****
270 REM LINE 210:-
280 A$ = INKEY$: IF A$ = "" THEN 210
```

Lines 60 to 100: Monthly unemployment data.

Lines 120 and 130: Forecasts for the first two months equal the observed values.

Lines 150 and 160: Corresponds to equations 7.5 and 7.6. The value of $R(t)$ is revised month by month. The forecast for one month ahead, $Y(t+1)$ equals $R(t)$.

Lines 170 to 200: Solutions to two decimal places. The numerical value of the terms within the brackets are calculated first, their integer values are obtained and are then divided by 100.

## PROGRAM 7.2

The expression $R(t) = Y(t) + a[X(t) - Y(t)]$ applies once more. It is included to allow for random fluctuations. However, if for a given year $Y(t) = X(t)$, it follows that $R(t) = Y(t) = X(t)$. Hence the forecast for the next period is made up of the current observation plus the adjustment for the trend; line 190 in this case becomes $Y(t+1) = X(t) + T(t+1)$.

```
 10 REM7.2
 20 CLS
 30 DIM S(30):DIM X(30):DIM Y(30):DIM R(30):DIM D(30):DIM T(30)
 40 INPUT "ENTER THE VALUE OF a "´"(BETWEEN 0 AND 1)";a
 50 INPUT´ "ENTER THE VALUE OF b "´"(BETWEEN 0 AND 1)";b
 60 X(1)=3.06:X(2)=3.08:X(3)=3.2:X(4)=3.19:X(5)=3.14:X(6)=3.11
 70 X(7)=3.08:X(8)=3.03:X(9)=3.1:X(10)=3.12:X(11)=3.28
 80 X(12)=3.22:X(13)=3.22:X(14)=3.22:X(15)=3.34:X(16)=3.33
 90 X(17)=3.27:X(18)=3.27:X(19)=3.24:X(20)=3.12:X(21)=3.23
100 X(22)=3.24:X(23)=3.35:X(24)=3.28
110 PRINT´"X(t)  Y(t)  R(t)   D(t)  T(t)  T(t+1)"
120 Y(1)=X(1):Y(2)=X(2)
130 R(1)=Y(1):R(2)=Y(2)
140 T(1)=0:T(2)=X(2)-X(1)
150 FOR t = 2 TO 24
160 R(t)=Y(t)+a*(X(t)-Y(t))
170 D(t)=R(t)-R(t-1)
180 T(t+1)=T(t)+b*(D(t)-T(t))
190 Y(t+1)=R(t)+T(t+1)
200 PRINT;X(t);"..";INT(100*Y(t))/100;
210 PRINT;"..";INT(100*R(t))/100;
220 PRINT;"..";INT(100*D(t))/100;"...";
230 PRINT;INT(100*T(t))/100;"..";
240 PRINT;INT(100*T(t+1))/100
250 A$=INKEY$(0):IF A$=""THEN 250
260 NEXT t
270 PRINT´"THE FORECAST Y(t) IN THE NEXT"´"PERIOD IS "
280 PRINT;Y(25)
290 STOP
```

Line 140: The trend in time period one is assumed to equal zero. No data is available before time period one, hence the assumption. The trend in time period two equals $X(2) - X(1)$. This is the first measure of the trend. Depending on the value of $b$ selected, the first measure of the trend may or may not play a part in the subsequent measure. In the limiting case when $b = 0$, the first measure is the only measure used in forecasting.

Lines 160 to 190: Correspond to equations 7.7 to 7.10.

## PROGRAM 7.3

If seasonal variations over several years are to be used in forecasting, a very large number of items of data would be needed in the program. Here we have just twenty-four observations. This enables the influence of one previous year's data to be accounted for in arriving at a measure of the seasonal variation. In a calendar year January to December there are twelve months. The forecast for November of the current year of the seasonal influence depends on the difference between the observations for November and December of the previous year. Program 7.3 is divided into two halves. For the time periods 13 to 24 an allowance is made for seasonal variations in the data. In the earlier period no data is available for calculating the seasonal influence.

```
 10 REM7.3
 20 CLS
 30 DIM S(30):DIM X(30):DIM Y(30):DIM R(30):DIM D(30):DIM T(30)
 40 INPUT "ENTER THE VALUE OF a "´"(BETWEEN 0 AND 1)";a
 50 INPUT´ "ENTER THE VALUE OF b "´"(BETWEEN 0 AND 1)";b
 60 X(1)=3.06:X(2)=3.08:X(3)=3.2:X(4)=3.19:X(5)=3.14:X(6)=3.11
 70 X(7)=3.08:X(8)=3.03:X(9)=3.1:X(10)=3.12:X(11)=3.28
 80 X(12)=3.22:X(13)=3.22:X(14)=3.22:X(15)=3.34:X(16)=3.33
 90 X(17)=3.27:X(18)=3.27:X(19)=3.24:X(20)=3.12:X(21)=3.23
100 X(22)=3.24:X(23)=3.35:X(24)=3.28
110 PRINT´"X(t)  Y(t)  R(t)  D(t)  T(t+1)  S(t+1)"
120 Y(1)=X(1):Y(2)=X(2)
130 R(1)=Y(1):R(2)=Y(2)
140 T(1)=0:T(2)=X(2)-X(1)
150 FOR t = 2 TO 12
160 R(t)=Y(t)+a*(X(t)-Y(t))
170 D(t)=R(t)-R(t-1)
180 T(t+1)=T(t)+b*(D(t)-T(t))
190 Y(t+1)=R(t)+T(t+1)
200 PRINT;X(t);"..";INT(100*Y(t))/100;"..";
210 PRINT;INT(100*R(t))/100;"...";INT(100*D(t))/100;
220 PRINT;"..";INT(100*T(t+1))/100;"...";
230 PRINT;INT(100*S(t+1))/100
240 A$=INKEY$(0):IF A$=""THEN 240
250 NEXT t
260 FOR t = 13 TO 24
270 R(t)=Y(t)+a*(X(t)-Y(t))
280 D(t)=R(t)-R(t-1)
290 T(t+1)=T(t)+b*(D(t)-T(t))
300 S(t+1)=R(t-11)-R(t-12)
310 Y(t+1)=R(t)+T(t+1)+S(t+1)
320 PRINT;INT(100*X(t))/100;"..";INT(100*Y(t))/100;
330 PRINT;"...";INT(100*R(t))/100;"..";
340 PRINT;INT(100*D(t))/100;"..";
350 PRINT;INT(100*T(t+1))/100;"..";INT(100*S(t+1))/100
360 A$=INKEY$(0):IF A$=""THEN 360
370 NEXT
380 PRINT´"THE FORECAST Y(t) IN THE NEXT"´"PERIOD IS ";
390 PRINT; Y(25)
400 STOP
```

## 7.3 FORECASTING: AN ASSESSMENT

The forecasting methods we have discussed have been simple in form and only appropriate to certain kinds of data. They cannot be used with much confidence to forecast, say, future raw material prices even if strong trend and seasonal factors have proved important in the past. The methods are not reliable if the expectations of individuals play a major part in determining current and future values. By contrast, unemployment levels and trends are slow to change in the short period unless there is a very significant change in economic policy. The data on soya or coffee prices (see Chapter 4), however, can be strongly influenced by a small number of market traders. If recent prices have shown an upward trend, traders are likely to incorporate this information into their bids for supplies and into their decisions on how much to buy. A particularly important part of modern economic analysis is rational expectations theory. A readable introductory account is provided by Shaw (1984).

## SUMMARY

1. Time series forecasting involves the analysis of data for a single variable over time. Past data are used as the guide to future values.
2. The aim is to smooth out fluctuations in the data in order to establish the equation which provides the best estimate for the series. Measures of trends, seasonal variations and cyclical factors might be included. Alternative equations are fitted to past data until the best estimate is found *ex post*. This estimate is then used in forecasting *ex ante*. The shorter the time period ahead when forecasts are made, the more reliable the forecasts.
3. Visual assessment of a scatter diagram is unreliable as a means of forecasting. Forecasting errors can be reduced by the application of procedures such as the Holt-Winters method.
4. The Holt-Winters method involves the smoothing of a data series according to weights which are attached to current and past data; the higher the weights the more importance which is attached to recent observations. The weights are determined by trial and error by the forecaster. In professional programming packages the computer is involved in finding the equation which provides the best fit and the most suitable weights to apply in future forecasting work.
5. Forecasting using time series methods is likely to prove more successful with certain kinds of data than with others. Rational expectations theory places a question mark against

forecasting economic data over which individuals have a degree of control.

## FURTHER READING

Harvey (1981a, 1981b) are at an advanced level for students of economics. Harvey considers what time series models are capable of and ways they can be applied. Wheelwright and Makridakis (1980) and Firth (1977) are readable sources. Box and Jenkins (1976) is widely recognised as one of the most important texts in the field. Lilien (1986) and Stewart (1985) have written software packages which include forecasting.

# 8 Keynesian Macroeconomics

Income and expenditure models are closely linked with John Maynard Keynes and his followers. Aggregate demand is emphasised as the most important determinant of income and employment. Before Keynes, variations in income and employment were largely explained in terms of cycles of activity brought about by population changes, geographical expansion or uneven rates of technological innovation. Monetary variables and changes in the level of bank credit, associated with movements in gold and the gold standard, also played a major part but the possibility of continuously insufficient demand was denied. In this chapter, no attempt is made to consider the role of factors 'outside the system', or money, or interest rates in a theory of economic activity, nor is an attempt made to consider the debate on the fundamental contribution of Keynes. The aim of this chapter is more modest. We seek to demonstrate how certain concepts introduced (or more correctly, emphasized) by Keynes, such as the multiplier and the accelerator, have played a part in shaping our understanding of national income, employment and instability. In this chapter, we concentrate upon a two sector model of an economy. Sections 8.1 and 8.2 concern comparative static models and Section 8.3 a dynamic model. Comparative static analysis involves comparisons between solutions following shifts in certain parameter values. Dynamic analysis involves *rates* of change of key variables over time. The chapter is written primarily for first year students.

## 8.1 A SIMPLE MODEL

Imagine an economy where there is no investment, government expenditure or exports. Suppose the economy in the recent past has experienced something disastrous like defeat at war or a catastrophic earthquake and people are able to sustain themselves only by selling their assets like jewellery and gold. Suppose ten million units of consumption are financed in this way. Since consumption is not financed out of income currently earned, it represents a form of *negative saving*. The suppliers of basic necessities who accept such a medium of exchange provide a basis for economic activity. The ten million units of consumption are *autonomous* expenditure. These become ten million units of income in the hands of the suppliers. These individuals in turn are likely to spend at least part of their newly acquired income. Thus, total consumption will in part be autonomous of current production and wealth creation and in part it will depend on current production and wealth creation. Let the latter component represent three-quarters of all income obtained from the sales activity; in conventional terminology, let the marginal propensity to consume equal 0.75. After two time periods, the total value of expenditure and income will equal 17.5 million units. Note that *some* positive saving now takes place but saving in total equal minus 7.5 million units. The process by which income would change time period by time period is illustrated in Figure 8.1. Assuming for simplicity that the rate of expenditure out of income remains equal to 0.75, income continues to increase but the increments get smaller. Denoting equilibrium income and consumption by asterisks, $Y^* = C^* = 40$ million units. In equilibrium, saving is neither positive nor negative; negative saving which once equalled 10 million is eliminated over time through the process of income creation.

In the model which we have just described, the level of income depends on total spending. In the most simple version of Keynesian economics, demand is made up of consumption and investment. If consumers spend a larger proportion of any increase in income (in our model, their propensity to save

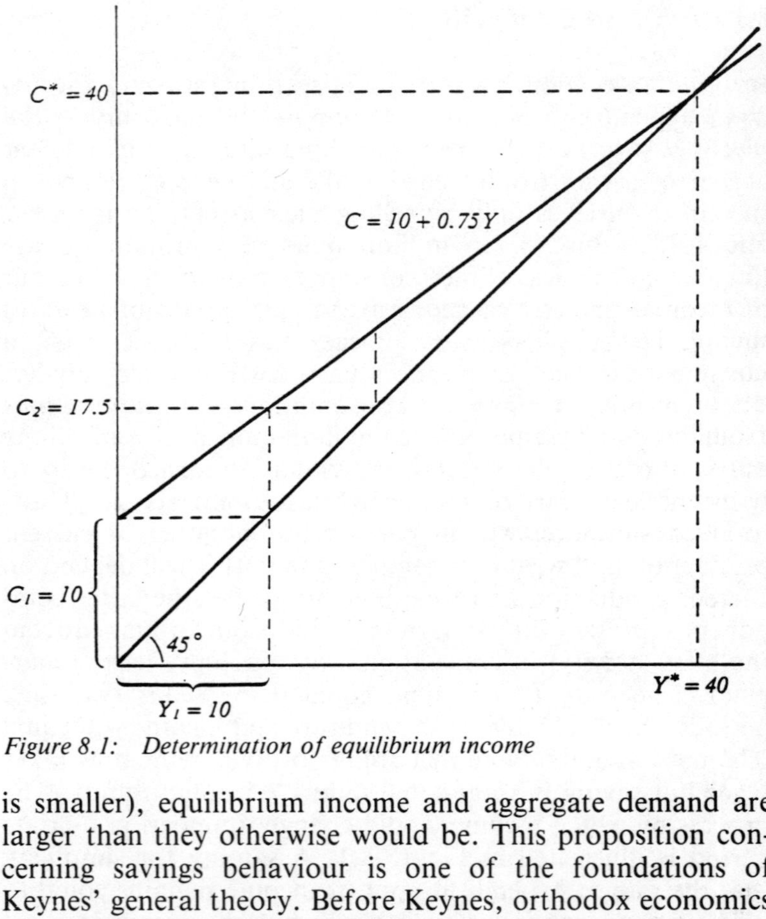


*Figure 8.1: Determination of equilibrium income*

is smaller), equilibrium income and aggregate demand are larger than they otherwise would be. This proposition concerning savings behaviour is one of the foundations of Keynes' general theory. Before Keynes, orthodox economics did not include a theory of aggregate demand. Following 'Say's Law', as described by Napoleoni (1972), p. 65,:

> 'whatever the volume of production, the aggregate value of demand is exactly equal to, and therefore cannot be less than, the value of all goods produced, that is, of aggregate supply'.

In our simple model, we do not allow for investment, government expenditure or foreign trade. A truly catastrophic event has brought down the level of production and income and there is no basis for recovery other than to a meagre standard of life. It was Keynes' contention that whatever caused a decline in aggregate demand, no mechanism existed which would allow a recovery to take place *automatically*. He provided a theory of equilibrium and demand which was quite different from the orthodox or classical theory of the time.

## PROGRAM 8.1

The process of convergence towards an equilibrium level of income might be understood using Program 8.1. Levels of consumption and income over several time intervals are determined. Consumption and income are found to increase from ten to forty units. Given the initial basis for income (the autonomous expenditure) and the marginal propensity to consume, equilibrium income equals forty units.

The notation used in Program 8.1 is

$a$ = autonomous consumption
$C_t$ = total consumption per time period
$b$ = the marginal propensity to consume
$Y_t$ = income per time period
$Y^*$ = equilibrium income

The equations of the model are:

$$Y_t = C_t$$
$$C_t = a + bY_t$$
$$Y^* = a/(1 - b)$$

```
10 REM 8.1
20 CLS :a=10:b=.75:C=a:Y=C
25 PRINT"TIME       CONSUMPTION      INCOME"
30 FOR time = 1 TO 20
45 PRINT;time;".......";C;"...........";Y
50 C=a+b*Y
60 Y=C
70 NEXT time
80 STOP
```

Line 20: The initial values are set. These values correspond to the situation where autonomous spending only takes place.

Line 30: The course of income over twenty time intervals is recorded.

Line 50: Consumption in each time interval is partly a function of autonomous spending and partly a function of the income which is created by that spending.

Line 60: Income equals consumption. Income increases time interval by time interval but at a progressively decreasing rate.

Line 70: The program loops back to line thirty.

Computer users are recommended to consider the following development of the model.

For a given 'injection', $J$, of expenditure into the economy, the expenditure multiplier, $K$, defined as $K = \Delta Y / \Delta J$, equals four. This follows since $b = 0.75$. Increased expenditure might come in the form of aid by a foreign government, domestic investment or a newly established export sector. The equilibrium condition in the model is that total injections equal total 'withdrawals'. Withdrawals sometimes also known as 'leakages' take the form of saving, and possibly taxation, imports, etc. A new value for equilibrium income is established when $\Delta W = \Delta J$. Program users might consider this development of the model before proceeding to Section 8.2.

## 8.2 KEYNESIAN ECONOMIC POLICY

Keynesian economic policy is widely covered in nearly all the mainstream introductory textbooks, alternatively under the heading of fiscal or budgetary policy; see, for instance, Begg *et al* (1987). Our account is primarily in support of Program 8.2.

In the post-war period, until the early 1970's, Keynesian thinking dominated in both the UK and the USA. Its influence has waned since partly in response to concern over inflation and partly because the more open nature of both economies has exerted greater restraint upon the freedom of action of their governments. Nevertheless, the concept of the consumption function continues to play a major part in the analysis of policy options. In this section, we consider a simple open economy model with tax and government spending. The key issue discussed is the likely effect upon the value of the multiplier of taxation and imports. If government policy is designed to regulate the economy by reducing 'inflationary and deflationary gaps', to what degree must account be taken of such leakages?

Figure 8.2 shows the relationship between consumption and income in the UK between 1974 and 1985. It relates to time series data. The relationship between the multiplier, $K$, and the marginal propensity to consume, in elementary analysis, follows from the equations:

$$Y = C + I + G$$
$$C = a + bY$$
$$Y = \frac{a + I + G}{1 - b} \tag{8.1}$$

where $I$ and $G$ are the measures of real investment and government spending. Considering the multiplier effects of government spending we simply differentiate (8.1) with

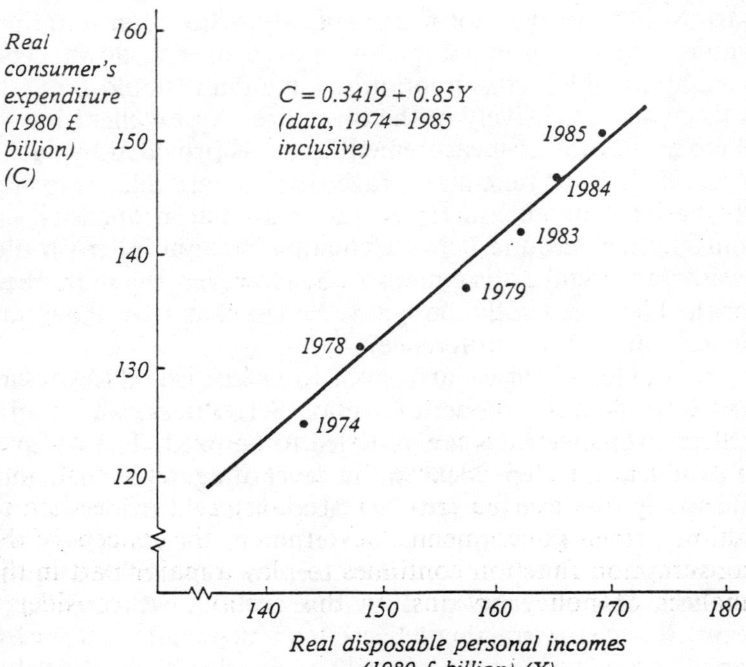


*Figure 8.2: The relationship between consumption and income (Source: CSO (Dec. 1983 and Nov. 1986) Economic Trends, Table 10, HMSO)*

respect to $G$:

$$K = \frac{\Delta Y}{\Delta G} = \frac{1}{(1 - b)} \tag{8.2}$$

Given equation 8.1, investment and government spending have the same multiplier effect upon income. If the multiplier was calculated on the basis of the data displayed in Figure 8.2, where $b = \mathrm{d}C/\mathrm{d}Y$, its value would be equal to 6.66. Time series data of the form presented in Figure 8.2 is not generally used in the analysis of short run behaviour, that is in analysing how consumers would respond to an increase in their incomes at a given moment of time. Is cross section data any better? Cross section data shows how consumption varies between households with different incomes. It is published annually in the *Family Expenditure Survey*. Since cross section data concerns the behaviour of individuals within a given time interval it is useful for a variety of purposes but it does not necessarily show how consumption would vary if household income moved up and down. The issue as to which consumption/income data should be used is discussed extensively in the literature. An excellent introductory account of measurement issues is provided by Jackson (1982). If we take an average (for no particular reason!) of the various measures of the marginal propensity to consume it is around 0.7. Calculating the multiplier on the basis of this figure it is equal to 3.3. However, the multiplier for the UK is generally thought to be less than two. How can we account for this difference?

The model which we are about to use is little different in structure from the model of section 8.1. Prices, wages and foreign exchange rates are assumed to be fixed. The volume of production is dependent on the level of aggregate demand and many of the equations are accounting identities. Consider the role of government. Government spends money on goods and services and this increases the level of aggregate demand. But government also raises revenue through taxation. If government spending, $G$, equals taxation, $T$, is its impact on the economy neutral? Similarly, if the level of exports, $X$, equals imports, $M$, does foreign trade have no net effect upon aggregate demand and income?

Let us build a model by specifying equations for some of the key variables. Considering taxes and transfer payments, we can arrive at an expression for consumption as a function of *disposable* income. Let net income taxes, $T$, equal a constant fraction, $t$, of income:

$$T = tY \tag{8.3}$$

Let disposable income, $D$, equal income minus net income taxes:

$$D = Y(1 - t) \tag{8.4}$$

and consumption, $C$, equal autonomous expenditure, $a$, plus a constant fraction, $b$, of disposable income:

$$C = a + b(D)$$

$$C = a + b[Y(1 - t)] \tag{8.5}$$

Assume government expenditure, $G$, is constant. Considering the foreign sector, let import, $M$, equal a constant fraction, $m$, of income:

$$M = mY \tag{8.6}$$

Assume exports, $X$, are exogenously determined. Given the national income accounting identity between income and total expenditure, it follows that:

$$Y = C + I + G + X - M \tag{8.7}$$

By substitution for $C$ and $M$ we find that:

$$Y = \frac{(a + I + G + X)}{(1 - b + bt + m)} \tag{8.8}$$

PROGRAM 8.2

Program 8.2 can be used to assess many of the implications of these developments of the simple model. They can be introduced without difficulty since the dependent variables, $C$, $T$, and $M$ are all a function of income, the value of which is given at the commencement of each iteration. Solutions converge upon their equilibrium values after ten iterations.

The values adopted for the marginal propensities to import and tax, $m = 0.25$, $t = 0.28$ are close to actual estimates for the UK economy. The value of the multiplier which we obtain by observing the solutions for Program 8.2 is 1.34. Coincidentally, this is close to the figure which has been obtained by empirical analysis. (See for instance, Figure 9.1 in the next chapter.) Our result, of course, is no different from the solution which can be arrived at using equation 8.8. Also of interest is the relationship between the government's budget balance $(G-T)$ and the trade balance $(X-M)$. For a five units increase in $G$ the trade balance deteriorates by 1.7 units. A five units increase in $G$ increases $(G-T)$ by three units; when $G$ increases, $Y$ and hence $T$ increases.

We have written Program 8.2 so that only the equilibrium solutions are displayed. This enables the results of comparative static analysis to be assessed more easily.

```
 10  REM8.2
 20  CLS
 30  a=10:C=a:Y=C
 40  PRINT
 50  FOR time= 1 TO 50
 60  b=.7:t=.28:m=.25:D=Y*(1-t):C=a+b*D:M=m*Y
 70  G=5:X=10:I=10:J=I+G+X
 80  Y=C+J-M
 90  NEXT
100  PRINT"Equilibrium solutions are:"
110  PRINT'"CONSUMPTION = .........";C
120  PRINT "INJECTIONS = ..........";J
130  PRINT "IMPORTS = .............";M
140  PRINT"EXPORTS - IMPORTS = ..";X-M
150  PRINT"GOV. EXPEN. - TAXES = ";G-t*Y
160  PRINT"INCOME = ..............";Y
170  STOP
```

Line 60: The marginal propensities to consume, tax and import.

Lines 60 and 80: It is essential that all variables have been assigned a value before they are accessed within a computer program. The dependent variables are calculated as a function of the independent variables, line by line. Program users should confirm this by reading the program in a 'top-down' sequence.

Line 70: Given the assumptions adopted in the model, government expenditure, investment and exports have the same effect upon income.

## 8.3 MULTIPLIER-ACCELERATOR MODELS

Attempts to explain the trade cycle have a long history in economics. But until Keynes provided an explanation based upon aggregate demand individual writers were able only to shed light on particular aspects of the trade cycle. A general theory was lacking. Orthodox economics was based on Say's Law (see Section 8.1), hence it was difficult to explain how an economy could experience recession after a period of prosperity. Attempts to explain the 'upper turning point', that is the transition from expansion to contraction, rested upon factors which lay *outside* the system. The explanation for interrupted expansion was based upon factors such as the exhaustion of some fundamental resource, the termination of geographical expansion or the reduction in the opportunities for profitable investment following a period of technical dynamism. A failure in the banking system, such as excessive credit relative to a nation's gold reserves and the subsequent problems this would create, also played a part in the theories of orthodox economists. A combination of factors was needed to precipitate a collapse but different writers emphasised different factors.

Central to Keynesian analysis is the concept of the consumption function. Keynes postulated that an increase in income will cause a rise in consumption expenditure but the rise in consumption will be less than the increase in income. In Keynes' analysis this relationship applies in the short and long run. As income grows, savings grow in absolute terms and as a fraction of income. Unless there is growth in investment, or some other form of exogenous expenditure, a problem of insufficient demand arises. For continued expansion there must be sufficient demand. Investment is profitable only if the rate of return is greater than the cost of capital. The rate of return, in turn, depends on the expected yield from capital equipment (see Chapter 6) which in its turn depends on long run perceptions of the rate of growth in the economy. In Keynesian analysis, a very important component of total investment is 'induced' by the rate of change of income. Investment is undertaken for the purpose of satisfying a demand which is expected to increase at a certain rate. Firms estimate future demand by extrapolating past demand:

$$I_t = v(Y_{t-1} - Y_{t-2}) \qquad (8.9)$$

Investment functions of this kind are known as accelerator

functions. $v$ is a constant which is normally assumed to be greater than one; it is known as the incremental capital—output ratio. The volume of investment in any year is some multiple of the growth income in earlier years. As income grows, more capital goods are needed to meet the additional demand. Investors are prepared to invest more in monetary terms (if $v$ exceeds one) than the growth in demand; they are prepared to invest, say, £3 in new equipment within a given year to produce £1 in new goods within that year. Why are they prepared to do so?—because the returns to an investment over its lifetime are very different from returns in a single year. From equation 8.9, constant output *growth*, $\mathrm{d}Y$, leads to a constant *level* of investment per year, $\mathrm{d}I$. A remarkable implication of this proposition is that if the rate of growth slows down, even though income may still be increasing, investment falls by comparison with its previous level. Thus, the capital—goods—producing sector contracts if there is a levelling off in the pace of expansion.

In the model, the pace of growth might level off for many reasons. Within a given span of years over which expansion is taking place, productive resources will be used more intensively in the later than in the earlier years. Adopting Keynes' terminology, this leads to a decline in the *marginal efficiency of capital* (Keynes [1936], pp. 315–320). In the earlier years, the presence of underutilised resources allows unrestrained growth. A decline in the marginal efficiency of capital is likely to bring a fall in profitability. Further investment is discouraged and the growth of income begins to slow down. As a result, that part of total investment which is induced by growth also declines. Just when investment needs to increase to absorb the increased volume of saving, due to the decline in the average propensity to consume following the past growth in income, it begins to slow down. The growth in disposable income which has taken place is not accompanied by a corresponding growth in aggregate demand. The expansionary process becomes weaker and weaker until growth is brought to a halt. In a zero growth economy there is no incentive to invest. A crucial source of income and employment is removed and contraction follows. The account above enables the upper turning point in the trade cycle and the *crisis* in the state of a capitalist economy to be explained.

An equation system which summarises many of the issues is given by equations 8.10 to 8.14. $A_t$ is autonomous expenditure (e.g. autonomous investment), $I_t$ is induced investment, $s$ is the marginal propensity to save. Particular combinations of $v$ and $s$ are necessary before *cycles* occur in the model. However, what is most important from a theoretical viewpoint is that a general theory of *instability* can be provided using the multiplier–accelerator interaction model. Interestingly, this model does not depend upon Keynes' argument concerning the marginal efficiency of capital which certain writers have suggested is too close to classical analysis. For an account of the mathematics of cycle theory, the reader is referred to Allen (1983).

$$Y_t = C_t + I_t + A_t \tag{8.10}$$

$$C_t = bY_t \tag{8.11}$$

$$s = (1 - b) \tag{8.12}$$

$$I_t = v(Y_{t-1} - Y_{t-2}) \tag{8.13}$$

$$Y_t = A_t/s + v(Y_{t-1} - Y_{t-2})/s \tag{8.14}$$

$$Y_t \geqslant A_t$$

$$I_t \geqslant 0$$

Summarizing, there are two relationships at work in multiplier–accelerator models: (1) in a single time period, changes in induced investment are greater than changes in the level of income, because the value of new machinery is assumed to be in excess of the value of its annual production; and (2) over several time periods, increased (decreased) investment has a cumulative upward (downward) effect on national income because income recipients do not save all of any increase in their incomes.

## PROGRAM 8.3

This program is based upon equations 8.10 to 8.14. Cyclical solutions apply. In order to limit the amplitude of the cycles, quite a large value for $s$ and a small value for $v$ have been selected. This will prevent the display from becoming too cluttered with numbers. The floor to the level of income is given by $A_t/s$, that is, it is given by autonomous spending divided by the rate of saving.

```
 10  REM8.3
 20  CLS
 30  DIM C(60): DIM I(60):DIM A(60):DIM Y(60)
 40  s=.8: v =2
 50  I(1)=0:I(2)=0:A(1)=75:A(2)=76:Y(1)=A(1)/s:Y(2)=A(2)/s
 60  PRINT"TIME    A      C      I        Y"
 70  FOR T = 3 TO 19
 80  A(T)=74+T
 90  I(T)=v*(Y(T-1)-Y(T-2))
100  Y(T)=v*(Y(T-1)-Y(T-2))/s+A(T)/s
110  IF I(T) <0 THEN LET I(T)=0
120  IF Y(T) <50 THEN LET Y(T)=A(T)/s
130  NEXT T
140  FOR T = 1 TO 19
150  PRINT;T;".....";A(T);".......";INT (A(T)+Y(T)-s*Y(T));
160  PRINT;".....";INT (I(T));".......";INT (Y(T))
170  NEXT T
180  STOP
```

Line 50: Levels of $I$ and $A$ in periods one and two. Since $I =$ zero, income is determined by the multiplier relationship involving $A_t$ only.

Line 70: Since values in periods one and two are set by line 50, the calculations commence in period three.

Lines 110 and 120: floor values.

Table 8.1 and Figure 8.3 demonstrate solutions from the program given particular values of $v$, $s$ and $A_t$.

*Table 8.1: Solutions for Program 8.3 given $v = 2$. $s = 0.8$ $A_t > A_{t-1}$*

| Time | Autonomous Expenditure | Induced Investment | Income |
|---|---|---|---|
| 1 | 75 | 0 | 93 |
| 2 | 76 | 0 | 95 |
| 3 | 77 | 2 | 99 |
| 4 | 78 | 8 | 108 |
| 5 | 79 | 18 | 121 |
| 6 | 80 | 25 | 132 |
| 7 | 81 | 22 | 128 |
| 8 | 82 | 0 | 93 |
| 9 | 83 | 0 | 103 |
| 10 | 84 | 20 | 130 |
| 11 | 85 | 54 | 173 |
| 12 | 86 | 86 | 215 |

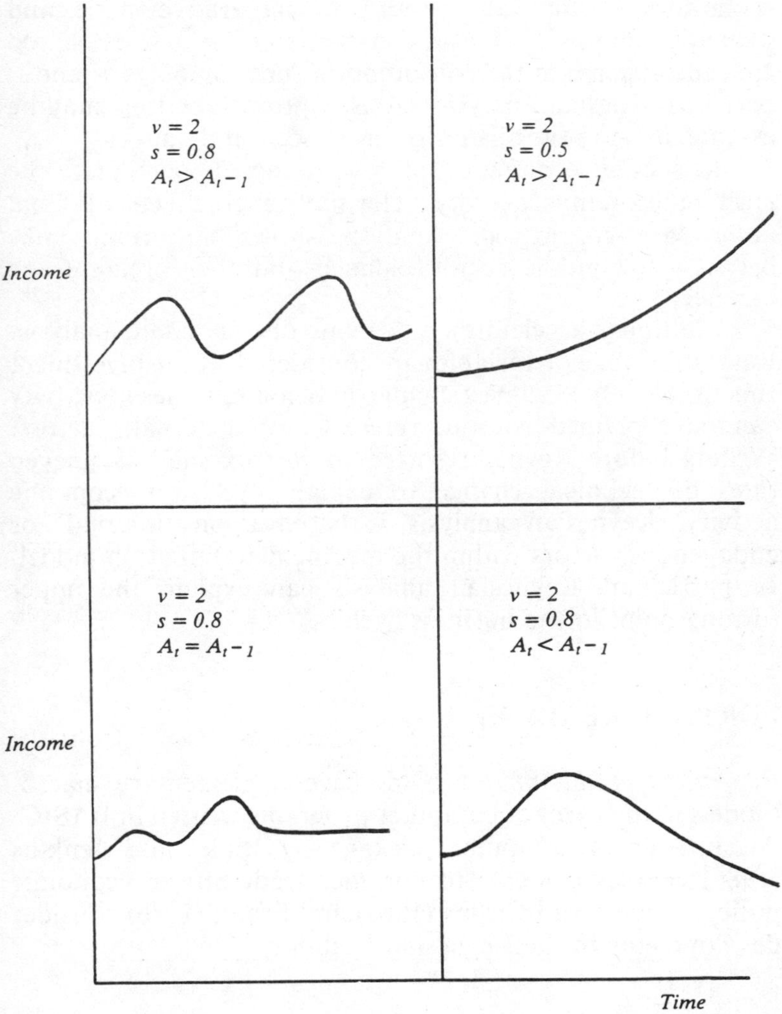


*Figure 8.3: Solutions for Program 8.3 given alternative values for v, s and $A_t$*

## SUMMARY

1. Keynesian economics is based upon aggregate demand as the most important determinant of the level of economic activity. In contrast to classical economics, the possibility of continuously insufficient demand is explained. Keynesian

economics is applicable both to comparative static and dynamic analysis.
2. The concept of the consumption function plays a central part in Keynesian analysis. Consumption functions may be estimated using time series or cross section data.
3. Keynesian economic policy is designed to regulate the level of economic activity. The multiplier effects of fiscal policy are considered. Analysis shows important links between the public sector balance and the foreign trade balance.
4. Multiplier-accelerator models involve dynamic analysis. Rates of change of variables are considered. If the investment function is linked to past change in income, cycles in activity can be explained without reference to 'external' factors. Writers before Keynes resorted to factors such as uneven rates of technical change to explain cycles in economic activity. Keynesian analysis is based upon 'internal' or endogenous factors within the income determination model. In particular, Keynesian analysis can explain the upper turning point in the business cycle.

## FURTHER READING

Brownless *et al* (1985) provide several elementary macro-models in the form of computer programs written in BASIC. An interactive computer package by Binks and Jenkins (1986) enables students to consider trade-offs in economic policy. Godley and Cripps (1983) and Frank (1986) consider developments in the Keynesian tradition.

# 9 Macroeconometric Forecasting

In Chapter 7 a forecasting model was developed in which economic theory played no part. Forecasts depended on observation of seasonal influences and trends. The past was taken as a guide to the future. Both time series and macroeconometric models can be used for forecasting macroeconomic aggregates. However, the former are only useful in short term estimation and may be totally unreliable if change takes place, for instance, in the government in power or if important developments take place, say, in the international economy. Economic theory is concerned with explaining the systematic relationships underlying observed data and the econometrician's task is to improve our understanding of how the economy works. In this respect macromodelling is superior to time series analysis, always provided that the models are derived from sound theory. The temptation is to adopt models which 'work', that is explain existing data, but to get models to work it is often necessary to make *ad hoc* assumptions concerning the functioning of the economy. At a later date, when the models do not 'work', further *ad hoc* assumptions might be introduced and the model drifts further and further away from its respectable theoretical foundations.

The five main UK forecasting models are HM Treasury model, the National Institute (NIESR) model, the London Business School (LBS) model, the Cambridge Economic Policy Group (CEPG) model and the Liverpool model. The Bank of England has its own econometric model though not much is known of its structure. The underlying arguments of the first four models can be illustrated with *IS/LM* analysis. In this chapter we consider a dynamic version of *IS/LM* analysis and introduce wealth effects and the 'crowding out' debate.

## 9.1 THE PURPOSE OF MACROECONOMETRIC MODELLING

In this chapter the emphasis is upon aggregates such as national income and consumption but it should be recognized that the most successful modelling has often taken place when the focus has been on a single sector, for instance of factors determining investment in the construction industry. However, our concern is with discussing the basis of more ambitious models such as the Treasury model. Such models are used for performing 'simulation experiments' or for forecasting the economy if certain changes take place. These experiments are intended to shed light upon a number of questions: for instance, what is the value of the government expenditure multiplier, what is the likely consequence of exchange rate depreciation? and so on. The procedure for answering such questions runs as follows: a set of variables and equations are drawn up reflecting the modeller's understanding of how the economy works. Using statistical analysis, estimates are obtained for the coefficients and the structure of the model is determined. Equations which 'perform badly' from the viewpoint of their statistical properties are rejected. (This is not always the case as will be explained in Section 9.2.) When the system is closed, that is, there are enough equations to obtain solutions for all the endogenous variables, the values of key variables like GDP are found for particular values of exogenous variables like government expenditure. Ball *et al* (1979), p. 88, describe this process as being akin to

> constructing a set of building blocks which, after completion, are then put together to reveal what sort of building one has ended up with.

The solutions for macromodels are time subscripted and

form the 'control model'. One of the exogenous variables is then changed and the model is solved again. The difference between the sets of solutions reflect the alternative states of the economy, for instance one with and one without a large amount of public expenditure.

The best known macroeconometric models differ in terms of their structure and theoretical rationale but in some cases they can be used to check each other's predictions. Generally it is found that the UK economy works differently under floating and fixed exchange rate regimes. The value of the multiplier is lower and the importance of monetary policy is enhanced under floating rates. Figure 9.1 is reproduced from Shepherd *et al* (1973). It concerns a simulation exercise using HM Treasury model and shows, in particular, the falling values of certain multipliers with time. This is explained by the feedback effects of increases in exports or fixed investment upon exchange rates and the rate of interest. During the time when Keynesian economics was dominant, macro-models were used as a form of technical support for government policy, particularly stabilization policy. Recent developments have contributed to scepticism over the beneficial effects of such policy. This scepticism extends to pro-Keynesian teams of economists. The Cambridge Economic Policy Group, for instance, argue that whilst an expansion of public expenditure will not have significant crowding-out effects, it will lead to a general deterioration in the balance of payments. Readable accounts of the various forecasting models are contained in Holden *et al* (1982) and Ormerod (1979).

Consider the role of models in government planning. The UK government's expenditure plans are published three years ahead and depend heavily upon the course which the economy is expected to take. All western governments, irrespective of their political and economic beliefs, are committed to heavy expenditure and taxation programmes and are therefore dependent upon forecasts. The first step is obtain values for those variables which are regarded as exogenous over the forecasting period. Exogenous variables include government expenditure, exports and overseas interest rates. Endogenous variables include the level of consumer spending and

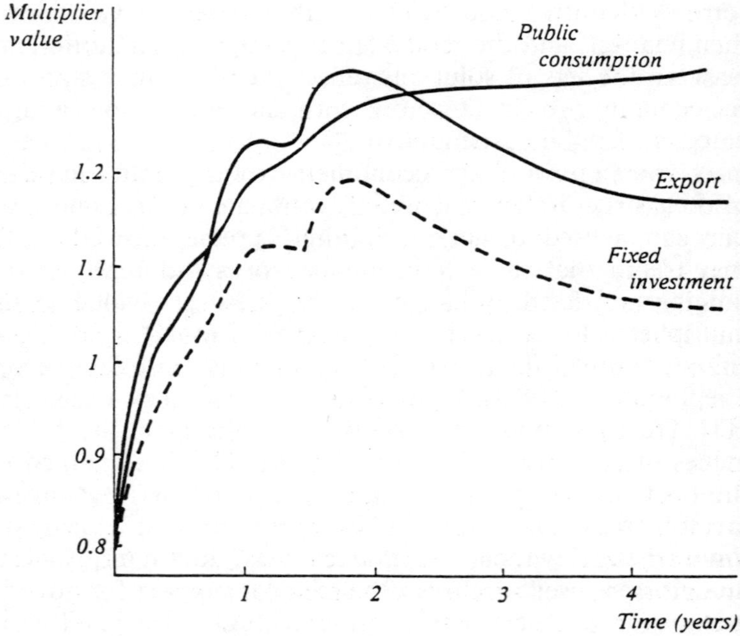


*Figure 9.1: GDP multipliers (Source: Shepherd et al (1974): The Treasury Short Term Forecasting Model, Chart 2, p. 48 HMSO)*

imports. Secondly, *ex ante* solutions are obtained for given values of the policy variables such as the income tax rate. By contrast with simulation modelling where 'within sample' estimates of parameters can be made from past data and *ex post* solutions obtained, forecasting the effects of government planning decisions requires assumptions about the value of unknowns (future values of key variables) and the belief that fundamental relationships, like the slope of the consumption function, will not change. It is the desire of policy makers to change budgetary variables or to implement controlled adjustments in the working of the economy. But operating in a general equilibrium system means that 'almost everything depends on everything else'. From the forecaster's viewpoint, overcoming the problems which this creates means that certain values and relationships must be assumed to be more stable than others. A further difficulty is that the data upon which forecasters depend is imperfect in many respects (highly aggregated, subject to error, etc.) and unquantifiable factors (e.g. business confidence) might be at least as important as information which is measurable. Of course, economists preparing forecasts do not work in a vacuum. Important information is obtainable from investment intentions surveys (published by the DTI), industrial trade surveys (CBI) and monthly surveys of business confidence and consumer opinions (*Financial Times*). Inevitably, forecasts reflect not only formal models but the judgement and intuition of the forecaster. The inherent danger of such methods is clear, but, if public expenditure is to be planned and its impact gauged, is there any alternative?

Econometric modelling need not be confined to the links between the major macroeconomic aggregates. The Treasury model is available as a kind of library for answering questions of a specialist nature. Users include stockbroking firms, investment analysts and tour operators. Tour operators, for instance, are interested in exchange rates. Many tour operators do not surcharge their customers if the domestic exchange rate deteriorates after catalogue prices have been announced. In recent years, interest in simulation exercises has grown considerably. Prior to general elections the programmes of the major political parties are assessed and costed. Private forecasting models have also developed. An example of the latter is the model of the stockbroking firm, Messels.

## 9.2 MODEL STRUCTURE

Although econometric modelling has developed in recent years, with greater emphasis placed on expectations, exchange rates, etc., the basis of the leading models (with the exception of the Liverpool model) remains a form of *IS*/*LM* analysis. However, all models use lagged relationships and partial adjustment mechanisms such as:

$$C_t = \alpha_1 Y_t + \alpha_2 C_{t-1} + \alpha_3 C_{t-2} + \cdots \qquad (9.1)$$

where $C_t$ denotes consumption and $Y_t$ is income. The model which we develop and use in simulation experiments will consist of eight equations and identities and ten variables.

Three of the equations will include lagged variables. However, to provide a link with elementary theory, we begin with a model involving *IS*/*LM* analysis. In this model, the equations:

$$I = 2000 - 100r$$
$$C = 0.4Y$$
$$S = Y - C$$
$$S = I$$

describe the goods market ($I$ = investment; $S$ = savings; $r$ = the interest rate; $C$ = consumption; $Y$ = income). Considering the equilibrium condition, $S = I$, it follows that:

$$0.6Y = 2000 - 100r$$

$$Y = 3333 - 166r \qquad (9.2)$$

Equation 9.2 relates to the *IS* curve. The equations:

$$l_1 = 0.05Y$$
$$l_2 = 200 - 10r$$
$$l = l_1 + l_2$$
$$m = l$$

describe the money market ($l_1$ = transactions demand; $l_2$ = asset or speculative demand; $m$ = money stock). Suppose the money stock is exogenously determined and $m = 150$, clearly, $150 = 0.05Y + 200 - 10r$, and, therefore:

$$Y = -1000 + 200r \qquad (9.3)$$

Equation 9.3 relates to the *LM* curve. Considering equations 9.2 and 9.3, the equilibrium values of $Y$ and $r$ are $Y^* = 1368$, $r^* = 11.84$. The *IS* function and the *LM* curve corresponding to this numerical example are illustrated in Figure 9.2.

This model is similar to mainstream macro-text models. It is comparative static in form and the *IS* and *LM* systems are considered separately. Such models provide an inadequate basis for forecasting even if they are expanded since lagged and partial adjustment mechanisms are ignored. Relationships of the form given by equation 9.1 have strong theoreti-

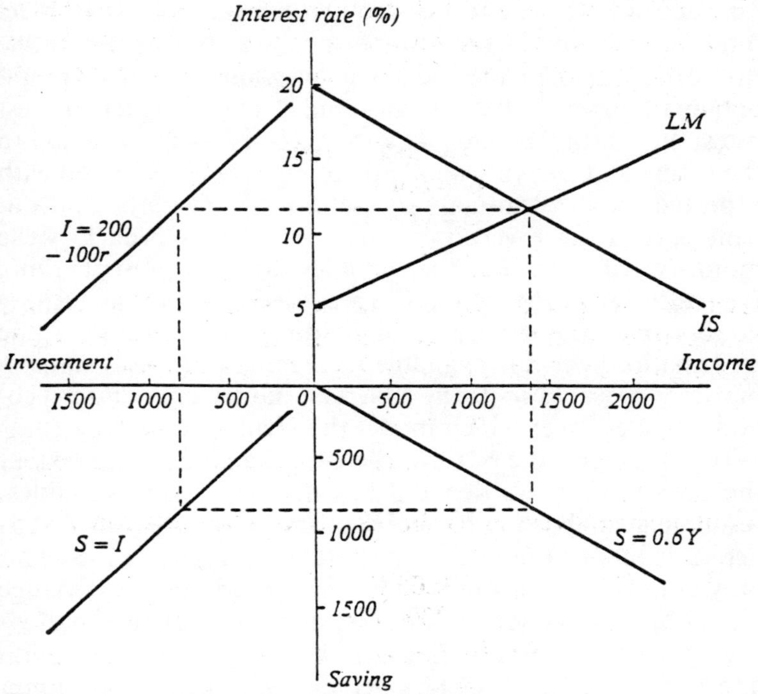


*Figure 9.2: Determination of the equilibrium level of income*

cal foundations and are supported by empirical evidence. However, the system illustrated in Figure 9.2 serves as a useful model of *general equilibrium*. Linkages between the sectors are clear and the magnitude of responses to parameter changes can be measured. The important feature which such systems share with more complex models is that it must be assumed that the behavioural equations do not change over the period of time to which forecasts relate. What this means is that the relationships underlying the model are not influenced by developments in the economy which individuals are able to observe. This assumption is at the heart of the rational expectations controversy. Rational expectations theorists maintain that if a change in government policy is announced, for instance a switch from an anti-inflationary to a reflationary strategy, individuals will revise their plans to take account of the effect of their circumstances. Consumers might anticipate larger future incomes and increase the proportion of their income spent on goods; creditors might anticipate higher inflation rates and demand higher interest rates, etc. In the extreme case the past serves as no guide to the future and current values are unimportant compared with expected values. Rational expectations theory plays a prominent part in the Liverpool model but their approach is the minority view in macroeconomics at the present time. Difficulties with the rational expectations hypothesis include doubts over the ability of individuals to understand the information which is available to them and, always supposing they are able to form coherent judgements about economic issues, over which model they will take notice of.

HM Treasury, the NIESR, the CEPG and to a lesser extent the LBS models are demand based. Supply side variables, resource availability, productivity, and so on are regarded as determinants of the maximum potential output of the economy at any moment of time. It is supposed that they change slowly by comparison with prices, interest rates and employment levels. Demand is the main determinant of production and employment. Aggregate demand is linked to consumption, investment and wealth variables. The consumption function plays a central part, though many different theories of consumption are applied. Investment is disaggregated to allow for the quite different determinants of manufacturing investment and investment in construction. The equations for manufacturing investment in the Treasury and NIESR models are based upon simple accelerator mechanisms, consumer expenditure, capacity utilisation in the macroeconomy and financial variables. Researchers working with both the NIESR model, for example Ormerod (1979) and Savage (1978) and the Treasury model comment upon the difficulties which they face in obtaining a specification of the investment function which provides significant coefficients in the case of financial variables. Nevertheless, both forecasting bodies retain in their models a form of the *IS* system which is consistent with our investment function. HM Treasury team (1979), in the book edited by Ormerod (1979), comment (p. 72) that:

It is not difficult to think of convincing reasons why it should be hard to identify significant interest rate effects in the investment functions. First of all, there is the problem of simultaneity since an improvement in business confidence will increase both the demand for investment funds and the interest rate.

Before one can identify the negative effect of independent interest rate changes on investment demand it is necessary to allow first for the positive association caused by autonomous changes in expectations. In other words, there is likely to be a positive association between investment and interest rates if shifts in the *IS* curve have been larger in magnitude than shifts in the *LM* curve. Secondly, there are the familiar problems of measuring real interest rates.

This quotation touches upon some of the most difficult issues in econometric modelling no matter which model is used. It would be out of place, however, to discuss in this section the details of econometric techniques and in particular the estimation problem. The interested reader is referred to Pindyck and Rubinfeld (1981). A quite different problem is that of obtaining solutions to systems involving a large number of variables and equations when many of the relationships are lagged. In Chapter 8 consumption was modelled as a function of income, investment as a function of changes in income and income as the sum of consumption, investment and government expenditure. By cross multiplication and substitution of terms, *reduced form* equations were quite easily obtained. When faced with more complex problems computers are often required. Applying the language BASIC, and in terms of a sequence of program lines, solutions for the equations are obtained one at a time. This approach may not work when lagged independent variables apply unless a particular solution method is applied. We now turn to the Gauss-Seidel method. This involves successive approximations to the solutions for systems of simultaneous equations. When the difference between two alternative approximate solutions falls within tolerable limits the problem is considered to have been solved.

## PROGRAM 9.1

Consider the data in Table 9.1. Suppose an equation of the

*Table 9.1: Values used in estimating a lagged consumption function*

| Consumption | | Investment | Income |
|---|---|---|---|
| 0 | 10000 | — | — |
| 1 | 14000 | 4000 | 18000 |
| 2 | 19000 | 5000 | 24000 |
| 3 | 24000 | 5500 | 29500 |

form: $C_t = aY_t + bC_{t-1}$ is fitted to this data and a Keynesian model is adopted. Applying regression analysis, it will be found that the value of $a$ equals 0.5 and the value of $b$ equals 0.5. The estimated equation fits the data perfectly in periods one and two and quite well in period three. In Program 9.1 only a very small number of equations are used and there is only one behavioural relationship (the consumption function). When, as in the model underlying Program 9.1, so few equations apply, it is not difficult to arrive at consistent estimates for each of the parameters in the system (in the sense that parameters in a system of simultaneous equations must be consistent with each other). But in a large system, when it is not possible to work with *reduced form* equations, the estimates have to be obtained one at a time. Typically, estimates are obtained for a consumption function, an investment function, and so on. The Gauss-Seidel method involves determining, by computational means, valves for $Y_t$, $C_t$, $C_{t-1}$, etc., several times over, given the estimates obtained for each of the parameters in the system. Each variable is subscripted according to the number of the iteration as well as the time period. Thus, by reference to Program 9.1, readers will observe that certain variables are in the form $Y(T, N)$, $C(T, N)$), etc. Only the variables which have just one dimension, investment in this instance, $I(T)$, are treated as exogenous. Readers will also observe expressions such as: $Y(T, N) - Y(T, N-1)$. The latter means the difference between two solutions for $Y_t$ depending upon the numbered iteration, $N$, which applies. If the absolute value (ABS) of the difference between two solutions, expressed as a fraction of the previous solution, is no greater than a

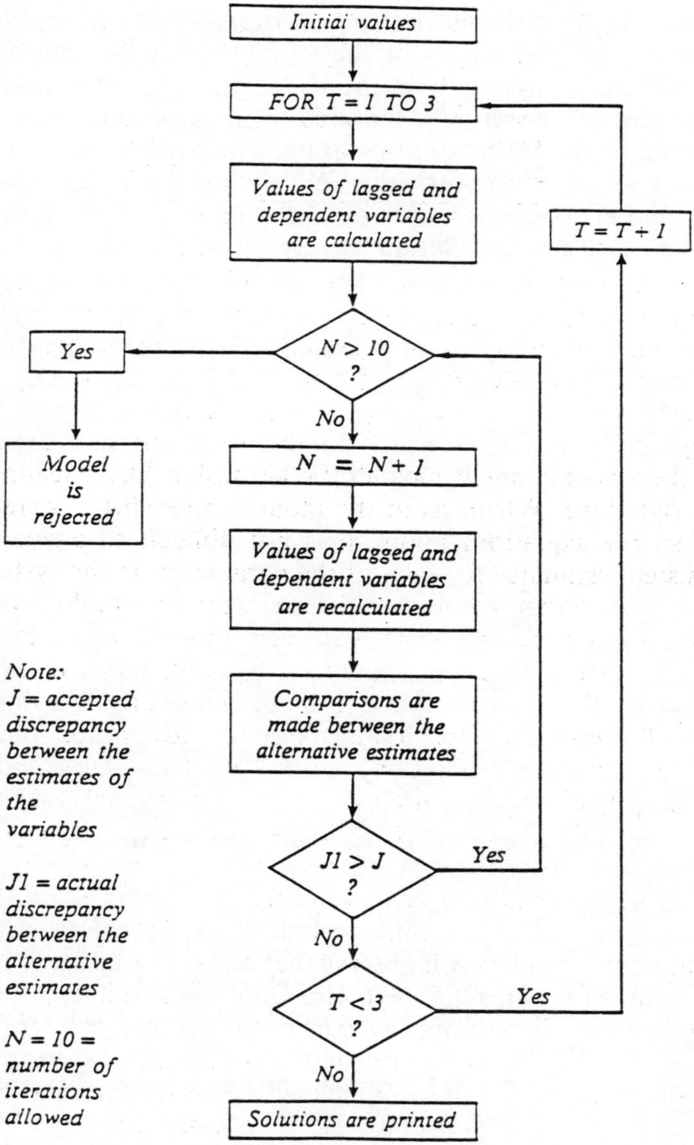


Figure 9.3: *Outline flow chart for Program 9.1*

predetermined limit (0.1% in this case) the solution corresponding to a given iteration is considered acceptable. The smaller the limit the more stringent the test upon the model. Summing up, the values of the variables actually observed are adjusted fractionally in the search for a set of mutually consistent of convergent solutions. (This procedure may be justified by the existence of measurement errors in the data.) Once a set of consistent values are obtained for the dependent and endogenous variables, the equations of the system may be used in a simulation exercise or in forecasting.

```
 10 REM9.1
 20 DIM PC(3):DIM Y(3,10):DIM I(3):DIM C(3,10)
 30 I(1)=4000:I(2)=5000:I(3)=5500
 40 C(1,1)=14000:C(2,1)=19000:C(3,1)=24000:C(0,1)=10000
 50 J=0.001
 60 PRINT"TIME  CONSUMP.   INV.    INCOME  "
 70 FOR T=1 TO 3
 80 N=1
 90 PC(T)=C(T-1,N)
100 Y(T,N)=C(T,N)+I(T)
110 C(T,N)=.5*Y(T,N)+.5*PC(T)
120 N = N+1:IF N >10 PRINT "TOO MANY ITERATIONS":STOP
130 Y(T,N)=C(T,N-1)+I(T)
140 C(T,N)=.5*Y(T,N)+.5*PC(T)
150 J1 = ABS((C(T,N)-C(T,N-1))/C(T,N-1))
160 IF J1 > J  GOSUB 120
170 J1=ABS((Y(T,N)-Y(T,N-1))/Y(T,N-1))
180 IFJ1>J GOSUB 120
190 PRINT;T;".....";INT (C(T,N));".....";I(T);"....";INT (Y(T,N))
200 NEXT T
210 STOP
```

Line 20: Two dimensional arrays are set up for the endogenous variables. $Y(1,2)$, for instance, refers to the value of income in period one, second iteration.

Line 30: The values of the exogenous variable, $I_t$.

LIne 40: Consumption is endogenous to the model. The first set of values for $C$ in periods one to three are the actually recorded values.

Line 50: The accepted difference between alternative solutions for the endogenous variables.

Line 90: $PC(T)$ denotes the lagged component of total consumer expenditure (past consumption).

Line 110: The one and only behavioural equation.

LIne 130 and 140: The values of $Y_t$ and $C_t$ are recalculated since revised values apply each time $N$ is increased.

## 9.3 SIMULATION EXPERIMENTS

Simulation experiments are used to discover the properties of a model. The effect of changing policy variables like government expenditure and the money supply can then be forecasted. In Program 9.2, the following equations and variables apply:

$$Y_t = C_t + I_t + G_t$$
$$C_t = 0.4(Y_t - TAX_t) + 0.5C_{t-1} + 0.01W_t$$
$$I_t = 2000 + 0.5I_{t-1} - 100R_t$$
$$PSBR_t = G_t - TAX_t$$
$$W_t + W1_t + W2_t$$
$$W1_t = (W1_{t-1} + PSBR_t)/R_t$$
$$TAX_t = 0.3Y_t$$
$$R_t = 5 + 0.005\,(PSBR_t) + 0.0005\,Y_t$$

The endogenous variables are:

$Y_t$ – income
$C_t$ – consumption
$I_t$ – investment
$R_t$ – interest rate
$PSBR_t$ – public sector borrowing requirement
$W1_t$ – government bonds
$W_t$ – total wealth
$TAX_t$ – income tax

The exogenous variables are:

$G_t$ – government expenditure
$W2_t$ – component of wealth unaffected by $R_t$

This system is similar in many respects to the model and program used by Holden *et al* (1982), pp. 54–59. Indeed, the idea for the program was first obtained from this source. The main difference is that Program 9.2 takes account of the recent literature on crowding out and investment and interest rates are endogenous variables. Our model, for instance, is in line with the detailed reported results of the LBS model, as reworked by Ball *et al* (1979) simulation two, pp. 108–114. This follows from the specifying of a relationship between investment, the rate of interest and the Public Sector

Borrowing Requirement. (See lines 190 to 220 of Program 9.2). Of course, the LBS model is very much more complex than Program 9.2 and includes international effects, exchange rates and monetary variables. Before considering the detailed results of the model, a consideration of some general issues is necessary. In our model, government expenditure is an exogenous variable in the system. The PSBR equals government expenditure minus taxation and influences the stock of wealth. This follows since we assume that if increased expenditure is not financed by increased taxation, government bonds must be sold. Similarly, if expenditure is reduced whilst taxation remains unchanged, we suppose that bonds are purchased by the central bank and the level of public debt decreases. These assumptions allow money to be 'neutral' in the model. Of course, governments could alternatively finance their expenditure by printing money but possible inflationary consequences would then need to be taken into account in an expanded model. Returning to our model, when government funds its expenditure by bond issue, the stock of wealth increases. Expenditure by government restores the money holdings of individuals to their level prior to the bond issue. Consumer expenditure is related, albeit to a limited degree, to wealth. An important component of wealth is sensitive to the rate of interest. If the interest rate doubles, this component is halved in value. Investment is also affected by interest rate changes. If the government seeks to sell more bonds it generally must offer a higher interest rate, hence the interest rate is partly determined by the PSBR. Finally, we assume that the interest rate is positively related to the level of income. This relationship corresponds to the *LM* curve; given the money supply, an increase in national income causes an increase in the rate of interest. This follows since income growth increases the demand for money. Considering the equation systems as a whole, crowding out occurs through the effects of higher interest rates on investment.

PROGRAM 9.2

Table 9.2 shows the solutions from the Program given the

*Table 9.2: Simulation exercise using Program 9.2*

| Time | Con. | Inv. | Tax | G | Wealth | Income | Int. |
|---|---|---|---|---|---|---|---|
| 1 | 7353 | 1883 | 3926 | 3850 | 8923 | 13088 | 11 |
| 2 | 7539 | 1690 | 4029 | 4200 | 8595 | 13431 | 12 |
| 3 | 7681 | 1438 | 4101 | 4550 | 8105 | 13673 | 14 |
| 4 | 7802 | 1156 | 4159 | 4900 | 7657 | 13863 | 15 |
| 5 | 7908 | 858 | 4208 | 5250 | 7378 | 14029 | 17 |
| 6 | 7984 | 549 | 4243 | 5600 | 5356 | 14143 | 18 |

assumed known values for consumption, investment, wealth etc. in periods one to five; note lines 50 to 80. Given the data, the individual equations for the consumption function, investment function, etc. have been estimated. By means of simulation experiments, the effect upon the economy of different assumed values for the exogenous variables, levels of government expenditure tax rates, etc., may be assessed. Thus, simulation experiments involve asking what would have happened in the economy if different circumstances had applied. Forecasting involves prediction about future values. In the program, forecasts for time period six are made. By reference to line 240 of the program, it can be seen that the (initial) values of *C* and *I* in year six are the values which were determined in year five. In forecasting, assumptions must be made concerning certain values. Values for *C*, *I* may be those which applied in period five or the influence of trends might be included.

Analysis of the effects of economic policy changes involves comparisons between the time paths of income over several years. A change in policy does not, of course, have a once and for all impact on an economy. We could compare the effect of sustaining a relatively light against a heavy government expenditure programme by setting *G* in line 90 at, say, 2,500 instead of 3,500. Alternatively, we might be interested in the implications of holding government expenditure constant over the time period studied by eliminating line 130 from the program. It should not be at all difficult for computer users to make minor alternations to the program in order to explore various questions. An equation for imports as a function of income might be introduced, with exports as an exogenous variable, perhaps.

Program 9.1 should be referred to before Program 9.2 if readers wish to understand how the latter works. Program 9.2 simply involves more behavioural relationships and lagged variables.

```
 10 REM 9.2
 20 DIM W1(6,15):DIM PW1(6):DIM W(6,15)
 25 REM PW1 = past value of gov. bonds
 30 DIM Y(6,15):DIM I(6,15):DIM C(6,15):DIM PC(6):DIM R(6,15)
 35 REM PC = past consumption
 40 DIM PSBR(6,15):DIM IP(6):DIM TAX(6,15)
 45 REM IP = past investment
 50 I(0,1)=2000:C(0,1)=7200:W1(0,1)=5000
 60 C(1,1)=7350: I(1,1)=2000: C(2,1)=7550: I(2,1)=1700
 70 C(3,1)=7700:I(3,1)=1450
 80 C(4,1)=7800:C(5,1)=8000:I(4,1)=1200:I(5,1)=900
 90 G=3500:W2=4000
100 PRINT"CON....INV...TAX....G....WTH....Y....INT"
110 FOR T = 1 TO 6
120 N=1:J=0.01
130 G=G+350
140 PC(T)=C(T-1,N):IP(T)=I(T-1,N):PW1(T)=W1(T-1,N)
150 PC(6)=C(5,N):IP(6)=I(5,N):PW1(6)=W1(5,6)
160 Y(T,N)=C(T,N)+I(T,N)+G
170 TAX(T,N)=0.3*Y(T,N)
180 PSBR(T,N)=G-TAX(T,N)
190 R(T,N)=5+0.0005*Y(T,N)+.005*(G-TAX(T,N))
200 W(T,N)=PW1(T)+PSBR(T,N)+W2
210 W1(T,N)=((PW1(T)+PSBR(T,N))/R(T,N))*10
220 I(T,N)=2000 + .5*IP(T)-100*R(T,N)
230 C(T,N)=0.4*(Y(T,N)-TAX(T,N))+.5*PC(T)+.01*W(T,N)
240 C(6,N)=C(5,N):I(6,N)=I(5,N)
250 N=N+1
260 Y(T,N)=C(T,N-1)+I(T,N-1)+G
270 TAX(T,N)=0.3*Y(T,N)
280 R(T,N)=5+0.0005*Y(T,N)+.005*(G-TAX(T,N))
290 I(T,N)=2000+.5*IP(T)-100*R(T,N)
300 PSBR(T,N)=G-TAX(T,N)
310 W(T,N)=PW1(T)+PSBR(T,N)+W2
320 W1(T,N)=((PW1(T)+PSBR(T,N))/R(T,N))*10
330 C(T,N)=0.4*(Y(T,N)-TAX(T,N))+.5*PC(T)+.01*W(T,N)
340 J1=ABS((C(T,N)-C(T,N-1))/C(T,N-1))
350 IF J1 >J GOSUB 250
360 J1=ABS((TAX(T,N)-TAX(T,N-1))/TAX(T,N-1))
370 IF J1 > J GOSUB 250
380 J1=ABS((R(T,N)-R(T,N-1))/R(T,N-1))
390 IF J1 > J GOSUB 250
400 J1=ABS((Y(T,N)-Y(T,N-1))/Y(T,N-1))
410 J1=ABS((PSBR(T,N)-PSBR(T,N-1))/PSBR(T,N-1))
420 IF J1 > J:GOSUB 250
430 J1=ABS((W(T,N)-W(T,N-1))/W(T,N-1))
440 IF J1 > J:GOSUB 250
450 J1=ABS((W1(T,N)-W1(T,N-1))/W1(T,N-1))
460 IF J1 > J GOSUB 250
470 PRINT;INT (C(T,N));"..";INT (I(T,N));"..";INT (TAX(T,N));
480 PRINT;"..";G;"..";INT (W(T,N));"..";INT (Y(T,N));
490 PRINT;"..";INT (R(T,N))
500 NEXT T
510 STOP
```

Line 120: *J* is set equal to 0.01. Program users are recommended to observe the consequences of reducing this number to, say, 0.001. *J*1 (see subsequent lines) is the difference between two solutions for $Y_t$, $C_t$, etc. When the program is searching for a set of consistent solutions (in the sense that simultaneous equation solutions are consistent with each other), if $J1 > J$, for any of the equations in the program, the program loops back to line 250 and $N$ is increased by one. However, from lines 20 to 40 it will be observed that only enough memory for fifteen iterations has been reserved.

Line 130: G is assumed to increase by 350 in each year. Consider the effect on the program's solutions of setting $G = G$. The results presented in Table 9.2 form the control values.

Lines 140 to 240: The 'first guess' values of the exogenous variables are obtained.

Line 170: The tax rate equals 30 per cent.

Line 240: The levels of consumption and investment to be used in forecasting in period six and the levels which have been obtained for year five after the required number of iterations. In an expanded version of this model trends can be built into the forecasted values.

Line 250: The number of iterations is increased by one each time the calculations in lines 260 to 330 are performed.

Lines 340 to 460: If the absolute difference between particular values of $[C(T,N) - C(T,N-1)]$, etc. is greater than the limit tolerated, the program loops back to line 250.

Line 470: When a consistent set of solutions have been obtained for a given year, they are reported.

Line 500: The program loops back to line 110 and the calculations are repeated for each time period.

## 9.4 ASSESSING FORECASTING MODELS

Have forecasting models improved with their greater sophistication? Which model has the highest rating in terms of its ability to predict economic data and to explain the past? On the face of it, econometric models should be capable of assessment in terms of simple objective tests. Before attempting to consider this question it is important to recognize certain points. First, models are rarely applied mechanically. It would be mindless simply to read data into a programmed computer and to accept the forecasts derived. Forecasters combine the results of computer simulations with other information and take particular note of special circumstances. For instance, a variable which previously had been endogenous might be deemed to be exogenous so that a particular equation is ignored. This might be necessary when an equation performed badly from the viewpoint of the significance of its coefficient or because it is expected to do so in the future as a result of important developments in the economy. Secondly, when considering the performance of single equations in a model or an entire equation system, we must recognize that data relate to a period of time which is continuous. Tests must be carried out over discrete time intervals, but breaking up time in this way is arbitrary. Which period is to be chosen for testing a proposition? If a model performs well initially but subsequently fails what is its status? Thirdly, forecasts are always conditional upon particular circumstances; if a certain inflation rate is forecast on the condition of given money supply figures it would come as no surprise if a different rate applied following a change in the authority's money supply policies. Similarly, a forecasted event might not take place because the authorities decide to change their economic policies in response to the forecasts which have been made. Fourthly, forecasts depend critically upon published data. Balance of payments data, for instance, are very prone to error in the short period. It usually takes three or four years before no further changes take place to previously published figures. Policy decisions, however, have sometimes been forced on government. The decision to devalue in November 1967 was crucial in the management of the UK economy in the late 1960s though it was learned later that exports had been persistently under-reported. Finally, it should be recognized that forecasts relate to several variables. In the period 1980 to 1985, the Liverpool model performed well in its forecast of inflation whilst the CEPG forecast unemployment with great accuracy. Some observers might regard one variable as more important than another. Others might require forecasting models to succeed in several respects.

## SUMMARY

1. Macroeconometric models involve attempts to explain the links between variables in a macro model. Lagged and partial adjustment mechanisms play a part. They are used in simulation exercises and in forecasting the effects of changes in

policy variables such as the level of public expenditure. Forecasting is required by government because of the large share of public expenditure in national income.

2. Four of the five main models involve an expanded version of the *IS*/*LM* system. The fifth applies rational expectations theory. Greater awareness of the limitations of government policy as a counter-cyclical device has emerged as a result of the development of macroeconometric models. Some schools refer to the possibility of 'crowding out', others emphasize the link between the internal (budgetary) balance and the external (foreign trade) balance.

3. The data upon which forecasters depend is imperfect in many respects and unquantifiable factors (e.g. business confidence) might be at least as important as information which is measurable. Forecasting models are not used just in connection with economic policy decisions. Investment analysts, stock broking firms and tour operators make use of them.

4. In addition to the theoretical problems in constructing a macroeconometric model, there is the problem of reaching solutions given the large number of equations involved. Computers alone cannot be used to solve this problem unless particular mathematical procedures such as the Gauss-Seidel method are applied.

5. It is difficult to assess the success of forecasting models. A model may perform well in a particular time period or in explaining the movement of particular variables, but badly in other respects. In general, the forecasting power of a model is assessed by considering the degree of correlation between the results of simulation exercises and the actual course of an economy over time. However, policy decisions are affected by the work of forecasters and the future path taken by the economy might change. It is incorrect, then, to assess the performance of a forecasting model simply by reference to the events which actually take place.

## FURTHER READING

The chapter by Surrey contained in Morris (1985) provides an excellent introductory account. Cuthbertson (1979) considers the ability of alternative policy schools to explain and forecast the behaviour of the economy. Keating (1985) explains how forecasters build and use econometric models. Levacic and Rebmann (1982) contrast Keynesian and monetarist theories and include rational expectations and wealth effects in their analysis. Wallis (1985) considers the properties and performance of models of the UK economy and includes an account of the City University Business School model. A simulation model is also used to assess the relationship between the determination of exchange rates and the impact of North Sea Oil. Fair (1984) discusses techniques for estimating and analyzing non-linear macroeconometric models. Fromm and Taubmann (1968) apply the Brookings Model to the US economy. Chrystal (1979) discusses a forecasting model and provides an account of the crowding out debate. Attfield *et al* (1985) and Begg (1982) consider rational expectations theory. Ramsey (1977) is a useful introductory, though critical, book on economic forecasting. Laury *et al* (1978) compares the properties of macroeconomic models of the UK economy. Probably the most comprehensive books are Holden *et al.* (1982) and Ormerod (1979). For a consideration of wealth effects, see Bennett (1986).

# 10 The Role of Computer Models

One of the purposes of this book has been to develop simulation models. Simulation simply means imitation. The difference between a simulation experiment and a 'real world' experiment is that the former are conducted with a model rather than with an actual system. Simulation models are used to study the potential behaviour of a system, usually over a period of time; computers have come to play an increasingly important part. The problems discussed in Chapter 9, for instance, could not have been solved without a computer. Computers are used when 'analytical' or mathematical procedures cannot be applied or when it is more convenient to use them. We have been interested in the formulation of problems and the inferences which can be drawn rather than pure analytical procedures. On several occasions we have applied computer programs when problems could have been solved using mathematics without too much difficulty. However, only a slight development of the issues discussed would have increased the usefulness of the programming approach. Our aim has been to present a variety of models in their simplest form. Readers no doubt will have considered how the models could be expanded and the programs adapted to deal with more complex problems.

For the most part in this book computer models have been used for two related but clearly distinguishable purposes: (1) in arriving at solutions to optimization problems; (2) in simulation. In the concluding pages we briefly discuss studies involving simulation models of the firm. We have earlier presented five models and programs which could loosely be described as simulation models of the firm but in each case only one decision variable was involved. Program 3.3 concerned the question when a firm should replenish its stocks; Program 5.4, the volume of output which should be placed on the market given the expected decision of a rival; Program 5.5, the acquisition or retention strategy to adopt in a declining market; Program 6.1, when fishing should recommence after a ban to allow stocks to recover and Program 6.2, whether it would be worthwhile switching from one investment to another. Research, particularly in the USA, has applied simulation models of the firm involving several variables. We conclude with a discussion of this work since it presents a promising area for development given the recent reduction in the cost of computing facilities.

The best known work is probably that of Cohen (1960, 1964), Cyert and March (1963) and Cohen and Cyert (1975). Much of this work was directed at stimulating new lines of thinking, particularly in connection with the objectives and mode of operation of firms. Other researchers have developed management games, largely for training personnel and research. Perhaps the most detailed of these games are the Harvard Business School Management Game and the Carnegie Management Game. A large number of corporations such as General Motors, General Electric and IBM have constructed corporate models and use them for simulation exercises. For a discussion of corporate planning and modelling see, in particular, Hussey (1985), Willis (1987), Higgins (1980) and Bell *et al.* (1978).

Corporate models are partly used as a descriptive framework for examining the links in an organization and partly as a tool for policy making. They are developed and updated by their own researchers and are supported by specialists who are brought in from such fields as operations analysis. The models generally are divided into two parts (1) a part which characterizes the structure of the organization and the interrelationships between the variables (controllable and non-controllable) and (2) a part which examines the consequences of particular policy decisions for a corporation's external and internal goals. External goals include profitability, market shares, growth rates, public esteem, etc;

internal goals include the working environment, the aspirations of the employees, product research, and so on. The first part can be referred to as the constraints of the model, the second part as the objectives. Simulation involves examining the values of several variables which make up the objective function given some change in the corporation's mode of operation. The model may be applied to examine the consequences of particular decisions which may be implemented or it may be used for periodic reviews of the corporation's progress. *Actual* performance indicators are inadequate when the focus is upon what might have been achieved. Also, the model can be used to assess the returns and costs associated with *particular* decisions which have been taken; marginal analysis is employed. Simulation may involve the complete corporate model or some extention of it to consider questions of a detailed nature. By contrast with linear programming and optimization models, complex corporate models do not focus upon variables which can be expressed in terms of a single denominator—money. Large corporate models typically do not involve the maximization or minimization of anything in particular; the objectives are multi-dimensional.

When a research team is set to work on a given task, it may not be self evident what the overall objectives of the organization are. These are seldom written down. Furthermore, objectives undergo continuous change in line with each corporation's development and ambitions. It is unlikely that a consensus could ever be obtained upon the weight attached, say, to established compared with new objectives. A corporation is not an individual entirely of one mind. There is always the problem that improving the performance of the organization in one respect will take place at the expense of others. What is needed is some means by which the various objectives can be traded off against each other. Researchers are acutely aware of this problem. When there are many objectives some may be treated as constraints. Readers might well ask, what then is the difference between objectives and constraints? As a rough guide, constraints (for instance in a linear programming problem) must be adhered to in all circumstances. By contrast, certain objectives may be redefined as constraints upon policy making, for instance the minimum required profit level if a policy of maximum sales growth is adopted. There is also the problem of comparing the results of a decision over a long period of time. Here the power of computers is particularly helpful in that equilibrium growth paths, interactions, present values etc. are more readily found. Further, the consequences of a decision are uncertain. Decisions do not have a single predictable outcome but a probability distribution involving many different variables. The researcher's task is to organize data, focus upon issues which relate closely to the known objective function and establish the implications of alternative courses of action. From their point of view, if targets have been set which involve clearly conflicting objectives there is no choice other than to return the problem to management. The research team limits itself to seeking efficient solutions.

Model building is a skill possessed by people trained in many disciplines, including economics. Economists come to corporate planning with many ideas instilled in their mind

> among them an appreciation of the importance of substitution, a sophistication about the objectives of enterprises, an awareness of the importance of trade offs and, most important, a realisation that physical quantities are subsidiary to 'values' in a decision process. Dorfman (1968), pp. 71–72

However, when the research team approaches a problem it cannot expect, even if a well developed corporate model is already in existence, to be able to use the model without difficulty for the purpose which they have in mind. It may be that a particular line of enquiry, prompted by some event, does not involve the kinds of relationships which have already been established by previous study. Fundamental research may be needed before a new line of enquiry can be undertaken. In the course of this research, important gaps in the knowledge of the organization may be filled. The most valuable result of a simulation exercise might be that more is learned about the system. Underutilised resources and promising areas for expansion may be discovered. If, in connection with some new task, research proves to be unsuccessful this does not mean that time has been wasted.

Research may direct an organization towards other, perhaps more limited, goals. Given the incomplete knowledge upon which models are built, it may not be possible to think in terms of maximising a global objective function. It is more often possible to think in terms of decision variables which enable a partial improvement in the corporation's welfare. The research team might seek to discover a policy which is better than the current one but not necessarily the best. Instead of attempting to achieve the optimal solution it is more often possible to forecast the costs and returns associated with minor adjustments in a corporation's policy decisions.

## FURTHER READING

The Harvard Management Simulation Game is discussed by McKenney (1967) and the Carnegie Tech Management Game by Cohen *et al.* (1964) and Dill and Doppelt (1963). Rivet (1971) is useful on concepts in corporate modelling. Naylor and Vernon (1969) is the most complete text on mathematical and computer models of the firm and contains detailed reading lists. On practical aspects of corporate planning the reader is referred to Gershefski (1969). Luce and Raiffa (1967) includes discussion of an experiment performed at the RAND corporation. On strategy planning the reader is referred to Willis (1987).

# References


Alfred, A.M. and Evans, J.B. (1965) *Discounted Cash Flow: Principles and Some Short-Cut Techniques* (Chapman & Hall, London).

Allan, C.M. (1981) 'The demand for herring: a single-equation model', contained in Wagner, L. (ed.) (1981).

Allen, R.G.D. (1983) *Macroeconomic Theory: A Mathematical Treatment* (Macmillan, London).

Attfield, C.L.F., Demery, D. and Duck, N.W. (1985) *Rational Expectations in Macroeconomics* (Blackwell, Oxford).

American Economic Association (1968) *Surveys of Economic Theory, Volume 3* (Macmillan, London).

Anderson, L.G. (1977) *The Economics of Fisheries Management*, (Johns Hopkins University Press, Baltimore, Maryland).

Axelrod, R. (1984) *The Evolution of Cooperation* (Basic Books, New York).

Bacharach, M. (1976) *Economics and the Theory of Games* (Macmillan, London).

Ball, R.J., Burns, T. and Warburton, P.J. (1979) 'The London Business School model of the UK economy: an exercise in international monetarism', contained in Ormerod, P. (ed.) (1979).

Baumol, W.J. (1977) *Economic Theory and Operations Analysis* (Prentice-Hall, Englewood Cliffs, New Jersey).

Begg, D.K.H. (1982) *The Rational Expectations Revolution in Macroeconomics: Theories and Evidence* (Philip Allan, Oxford).

Begg, D.K.H., Fisher, R. and Dornbusch, R. (1987) *Economics* (McGraw-Hill, London and New York).

Bell, D.E., Keeney, R.L. and Raiffa, H. (ed.) (1978) *Conflicting Objectives in Decisions* (Wiley, New York).

Bennett, A. (1986) 'Expenditure, wealth and the rate of interest' *Economic Modelling*, January.

Binks, M. and Jennings, A. (1986) *Chancellors I and II and Macroeconomics in Focus* (McGraw-Hill, London and New York).

Bosworth, D.L. (1976) *Production Functions: A Theoretical and Empirical Study* (Saxon House, Farnborough, Hants).

Box, G.E.P. and Jenkins, G.M. (1976) *Time Series Analysis, Forecasting and Control* (Holden Day, New York).

Bresnahan, T. (1981) 'Duopoly models with consistent conjectures', *American Economic Review* **71**, December.

British Broadcasting Corporation (1986) *Horizon: Nice Guys Finish First* (BBC, London).

Brown, J.A. and Deaton, A.S. (1972) 'Surveys in applied economics: models of consumer behaviour' *Economic Journal* **82**, December.

Brown, R.H. (1963) 'Theory of combat: the probability of winning', *Operations Research* **11**, May–June.

Brownless, C., Hurd, S. and Randall, K. (1985) *BASIC economics* (Butterworths, London).

Chrystal, K. (1979) *Controversies in British Macroeconomics* (Philip Allan, Oxford).

Clarke, R. (1985) *Industrial Economics* (Blackwell, Oxford and New York).

Clarke, R. and Davies, S.W. (1982) 'Market structure and price cost margins' *Economica*, N.S., **49**, August.

Cockerill, T.A.J. and Kinloch, H. (1984) 'Managing risk and uncertainty', contained in Pickering, J.F. and Cockerill, T.A.J. (1984).

Cohen, K.J. (1960) *Computer Models of the Shoe, Leather Hide Sequence* (Prentice-Hall, Englewood Cliffs, New Jersey).

Cohen, K.J. *et al.* (1964) *The Carnegie Tech Management Game* (Richard Irwin, Homewood, Illinois)

Cohen, K.J. and Cyert, R.M. (1975) *Theory of the Firm: Resource Allocation in a Market Economy* (Prentice-Hall, Englewood Cliffs, New Jersey)

Cohen, S.S. (1985) *Operational Analysis* (Arnold, London and Baltimore, Maryland).

Cournot, A. (1838) translated by N.T. Bacon (1927) *Researches into the Mathematical Principles of the Theory of Wealth* (Macmillan, London).

Cowling, K. and Waterson, M. (1976) 'Price cost margins and market structure', *Economica*, N.S., **43**, August

CSO (1986) *Economic Trends* (HMSO London), January.

Cuthbertson, K. (1979) *Macroeconomic Policy: The New Cambridge Keynesian and Monetarist Controversies* (Macmillan, London)

Cyert, R.M. and March, J.G. (1963) *A Behavioural Theory of the Firm* (Prentice-Hall, Englewood Cliffs, New Jersey).

Dennis, L.B. and Dennis, T.L. (1986) *Microcomputer Models for Management Decision-Making* (West Publishing Company, New York).

Dewey, D. (1965) *Modern Capital Theory* (Columbia University Press, New York and London).

Dill, W.R. and Dopple, N. (1963) 'The acquisition of experience in a complex management game', *Management Science* **10** October.

Dorfman R. (1968) 'Operational research', contained in American Economic Association (1968).

Dorfman R., Samuelson, P.A. and Solow, R. (1958) *Linear Programming and Economic Analysis* (McGraw-Hill, London and New York).

Elton, E.J. and Gruber, M.J. (ed.) (1979) *Portfolio Theory, 25 Years After* (North Holland, Amsterdam).

Fair, R.C. (1984) *Specification, Estimation and Analysis of Macroeconometric Models* (Harvard University Press, Cambridge Massachusetts and London).

Firth, M. (1977) *Forecasting Methods in Business and Management* (Edward Arnold, London and Baltimore, Maryland).

Frank, J. (1986) *The New Keynesian Economics—Unemployment, Search and Contracting* (Wheatsheaf Books, Sussex).

Friedman, S. (1983) *Oligopoly Theory* (Cambridge University Press).

Fromm, G. and Taubmann, P.J. (1968) *Policy Simulations with an Econometric Model* (North Holland, Amsterdam).

Gershefski, G. (1969) 'Building a corporate financial model', *Harvard Business Review*, July.

Godley W. and Cripps, F. (1983) *Macroeconomics* (Oxford University Press).

Gujarati, D. (1978) *Basic Econometrics* (McGraw-Hill, London and New York).

Harvey, A.C. (1981a) *The Econometric Analysis of Time Series* (Philip Allan, Oxford).

Harvey, A.C. (1981b) *Time Series Models* (Philip Allan, Oxford).

Hawkins, C.J. and Pearce, D.W. (1971) *Capital Investment Appraisal* (Macmillan, London).

Heady, E.O. (1957) 'An econometric investigation of the technology of agricultural production functions', *Econometrica* **5**, April.

Heathfield, D. (1971) *Production Functions* (Macmillan, London).

Henderson, J. and Quandt, R.E. (1980) *Microeconomic Theory: A Mathematical Approach* (McGraw-Hill, London and New York).

Higgins, J.C. (1980) *Strategic and Operational Planning Systems* (Prentice-Hall, Englewood Cliffs, New Jersey).

HM Treasury (1979) 'Some problems in the development of the Treasury Model', contained in Ormerod, P. (ed.) 1979.

Holden, K., Peel, D.A. and Thompson, J.L. (1982) *Modelling the UK Economy: An Introduction* (Martin Robertson, Oxford).

Holt, C.C.(1955) *Forecasting Seasonals and Trends by Exponentially Weighted Moving Averages* (Carnegie Institute of Technology).

Horowitz, I. (1970) *Decision Making and the Theory of the Firm* (Holt, Rinehart and Winston, New York).

Hussey, D.E. (1985) *Introductory Corporate Planning* (Pergamon, Oxford).

Intriligator, M.D. (1978) *Econometric Models, Techniques and Applications* (North Holland, Amsterdam).

Jackson, D. (1982) *Introduction to Economics, Theory and Data* (Macmillan, London).

Johansen, L. (1972) *Production Functions—an Integration of Micro and Macro, Short Run and Long Run Aspects* (North Holland, Amsterdam).

Keating, G. (1985) *The Production and Use of Economic Forecasts* (Methuen, London).

Keynes, J.M. (1936) *The General Theory of Employment Interest and Money*, (Macmillan, London).

Kelejian, H.H. and Oats, W.E. (1981) *Introduction to Econometrics, Principles and Applications* (Harper and Row, New York).

Koutsoyiannis, A. (1982) *Non Price Decisions: The Firm in a Modern Context* (Macmillan, London)

Laidler, D. (1981) *Microeconomics* (Philip Allan, Oxford).

Lancaster, K. (1966) 'Change and innovation in the technology of consumption', *American Economic Review* **56**, May.

Lancaster, K. (1979) *Variety, Equity and Efficiency* (Columbia University Press)

Lanchester, F.W. (1916) *Aircraft in Modern Warfare. The Dawn of the Fourth Arm* (Constable and Co., London)

Laury, J. Lew, G. and Ormerod, P. (1978) 'Properties of macroeconomic models of the UK economy: a comparative study' *National Institute Economic Review*, **83**, February.

Lawler, K.A.L. and Seddighi, H. (1987) *Economic Theory and Modelling: An Integrated Approach* (Peter Andrew, Droitwich).
Levacic, R. and Rebmann (1982) *Macroeconomics: An Introduction to Keynesian—Neoclassical Controversies* (Macmillan, London and New York).
Levy, H. and Sarnat, M. (1982) *Capital Investment and Financial Decisions* (Prentice-Hall, London).
Lewis, C.D. (1981) *Scientific Inventory Control* (Butterworths, London).
Lilien, D. (1986) *Micro TSP Version 5.0* (McGraw-Hill, London and New York).
Luce, R.D. and Raiffa, H. (1967) *Games and Decisions: Introduction and Critical Survey* (Wiley, New York).
McKenney, J.L. (1967) *Simulation Gaming for Management Development* (Harvard University Press, Boston).
McLaughlin, F.S. and Pickhard, E.P.C. (1979) *Quantitative Techniques for Management Decision* (Houghton Mifflin, Boston).
Markowitz, H. (1952) 'Portfolio selection', *Journal of Finance*, **7**, March.
Markowitz, H. (1959) *Portfolio selection* (Wiley, New York).
Morris D. (1985) *The Economic System in the UK* (Oxford University Press, Oxford).
Napoleoni, C. (1972) *Economic Thought of the Twentieth Century* (Martin Robertson, London)
Nash, J.F. (1950) 'The bargaining problem'. *Econometrica*, **18**, April.
Nash, J.F. (1953) 'Two-person co-operative games', *Econometrica*, **21**, January.
Naylor, T.H. and Vernon, J.M. (1969) *Microeconomics and decision Models of the Firm*, (Harcourt, Brace & World, New York).
Neumann, J. Von and Morgenstern, O. (1944) *Theory of Games and Economic Behaviour* (Princeton University Press, Princeton).
Open University, Maths/Science/Technology, MST 204 (1981a) *Mathematical Models and Methods Unit 3* (Open University, Milton Keynes).
Open University, Maths/Science/Technology, MST 204 (1981b) *Mathematical Models and Methods Unit 10* (Open University, Milton Keynes).
Open University, Probability and Statistics, M245, (1984) *Random Processes*, Unit 8 (Open University, Milton Keynes).
Ormerod, P. (ed.) (1979) *Economic Modelling* (Heinemann, London).

Phillips, L. (1974) *Applied Consumption Analysis* (North Holland, Amsterdam).

Pickering, J.F. and Cockerill, T.A.J. (1984) *The Economic Management of the Firm* (Philip Allan, Oxford).

Pindyck, R.S. and Rubinfeld (1981) *Econometric Models and Economic Forecasts* (McGraw-Hill, New York).

Price Commission (1978) 'Prices, costs and margins in the production and distribution of compound feeding stuff for cattle, pigs and poultry', *Price Commission* (HMSO, London).

Ramsey, J. (1977) *Economic Forecasting—Models or Markets* (Institute of Economic Affairs, London).

Rapoport, A. (ed.) (1974) *Game Theory as a Theory of Conflict Resolution* (D. Reidel Publishing Company, Dordrech–Holland/Boston–USA).

Rivet, P. (1971) *Principles of Model Building* (Wiley, New York).

Robinson, G. (1986) *Making Sense of Marketing* (Macmillan, London)

Savage, D. (1978) 'The channels of monetary influence—a survey of empirical evidence', *National Institute Economic Review*, **83**, February.

Shaw, G.K. (1984) *Rational Expectations, an Elementary Approach* (Wheatsheaf Books, Brighton).

Shepherd, J.R., Evans, H.P. and Riley, C.J. (1974) *The Treasury Short-term Forecasting Model* (HMSO, London).

Stackelberg, H. (1934) translated by A.T. Peacock (1952) *The Theory of the Market Economy* (William Hodge, London).

Stewart, J. (1985) *ECOS: An Econometric Estimation Package* (McGraw-Hill, London and New York).

Surrey, M.J.C. (1985) 'Assessing the Economy', contained in Morris, D. (1985).

Theil, H. (1975) *The Theory and Measurement of Consumer Demand. Volume 1* (North Holland, Amsterdam).

Thomas, J. (1985) *Introductory Econometrics—Theory and Applications* (Harlow and New York).

Thompson A. Jr. (1985) *Economics of the Firm; Theory and Practice*, (Prentice-Hall, Englewood Cliffs, New Jersey).

University Software (1985) *Unimax* (University Software–Unisoft, London).

Wagner, L. (ed.) (1981) *Readings in Applied Microeconomics* (Oxford University Press, Oxford).

Wallis, K.F. (1979) *Topics in Applied Econometrics* (Blackwell, Oxford).

Wallis, K.F. (ed.) (1985) *Models of the UK Economy: A Review by the ESRC Macroeconomic Modelling Bureau* (Oxford University Press, Oxford.

Walters, A.A. (1963) 'Production and cost functions', *Econometrica*, **31**, January–April.

Wheelwright, S. and Makridakis, S. (1980) *Forecasting Methods for Management* (Wiley, New York).

Willis, R.E. (1987) *A Guide to Forecasting for Planners and Managers* (Prentice-Hall, Englewood Cliffs, New Jersey).

Winters, P.R. (1960) 'Forecasting sales by exponentially moving weights'. *Management Science*, **6**.

Younger, M.S. (1985) *A First Course in Linear Regression* (Duxbury Press, Boston).

# Index